# NOSHER

## NOSHER POWELL
## WITH WILLIAM HALL

BLAKE

Published by Blake Publishing Ltd,
3 Bramber Court, 2 Bramber Road,
London W14 9PB, England

First published in 1999

ISBN 1 85782 3710

British Library Cataloguing-in-Publication Data:
A catalogue record for this book is available
from the British Library.

Typeset by BCP

Printed by Creative Print and Design (Wales), Ebbw Vale, Gwent

1 3 5 7 9 10 8 6 4 2

For the good, the bad and the ugly, because without their existence this book could never have been written.

*ROUGH DIAMOND:*
*An essentially coarse, but basically decent and likeable person.*

Dictionary definition

When I hit you, you stay bloody hit.

Nosher Powell, 1999

# CONTENTS

*"Is there a 'k' in Ecu, Mr Powell?"*

Cartoon that appeared in the *Evening Standard* when Pauline and me started running the Prince of Wales in 1990.

# FOREWORD

I would like to thank my old pal William Hall, who shared my adventures on many of my films around the world, for his help in writing this book. Bill worked on more than thirty hours of taped interviews, and we spent many weeks putting the material together.

It didn't help that I've been a bit deaf in one ear for the past ten years, ever since the phone rang at my home one evening. When I answered, a voice I knew said, 'This is for you, c--tface!'

And he fired a shooter down the phone. It turned me totally deaf for a year.

The voice belonged to a South London gangster I'd offended. But I took my time, and finally went round and did the bastard, so that's all right. Now I hold the phone well away when it rings.

But sorry, Bill, if I spoke a bit loud at times.

Licence No 51610ko

Renewal Fee Due

24. 8. 50

Sig.

My British Boxing Board of Control licence,
which was issued in 1949

# PROLOGUE: WHO GIVES A VAN DAMME?

Scene: Casablanca, Morocco, 1998.

The movie is *Legionnaire*, which as you might have sussed is a remake of the 1939 classic *Beau Geste*. For Gary Cooper, read Jean-Claude Van Damme, otherwise known as the Muscles from Brussels.

I'm here to teach the Muscles how to box. Not fight — because the guy's a martial arts champion. But he doesn't know how to throw a real punch, whereas I do.

We meet in the rooftop Panorama Bar of the Riff Hotel, with its spectacular view of the Grand Mosque and the sparkling Mediterranean, and I'm immediately impressed with what I see. Tough, agile, Van Damme has the air of a caged cougar, walking lightly on the balls of his feet, hands dangling at his side with the palms turned backwards the way every professional fighter or bodyguard stands.

I look into steel-grey eyes and my first thought is: *Any man who takes this guy on in a bar or the street would want his head examined.*

"So, Nosher, are you going to teach me something?"

The voice is friendly enough, but I sense a hidden challenge.

"That's what I'm here for."

In the script, our hero joins the Foreign Legion, and becomes the Legion's light-heavyweight champion. Which is where I came in, hired as referee as well as to teach him a few moves. But his movements — no offence meant, Jean-Claude — are more like a ballet dancer's than a boxer's.

I've got two weeks to get him into shape. We're using an old mosque in the Arab quarter for training, and although it's not my religion I send up a mental prayer when I realise what I'm in for.

First thing Jean-Claude does when we get into the ring together is to whirl round and lash out with a backward high kick, which isn't going to earn him any Brownie points though it might go down a bundle at Sadler's Wells. I think he might have been showing off, but I couldn't afford to take chances. "*Oi, watch it!*" was my first professional exchange with the great man.

Hired as his "personal technical adviser", my job is to see that the Muscles is nifty with his gloves as well as his trainers, and looks good in the ring.

He's barrel-chested, slim-wasted, and looks what he is — supremely fit and capable of taking on the world. Problem. He punches like a martial-arts expert, not like a proper boxer.

He had also found out that I had once sparred with his namesake, though no relation, Luc Van Damme, European middleweight champion, and that got us on to a good footing from the first bell.

Jean-Claude's idea of how to hit someone is more of a flick than a solid *whack*. I couldn't blame him. He'd studied martial arts from the age of eleven like a religion, and he was European middleweight karate champion before he was twenty. Then he made his fortune with wham-bang movies like *Bloodsport*, *Kickboxer* and the international box-office hit *Universal Soldier*. So he was brainwashed.

But, I have to tell him: "All that prancing and dancing is not boxing, my son!" For two solid weeks I work on him to get the message through, dawn till dusk. "No, don't do that! Do it this way." Martial arts and boxing are like rugby and soccer. It's still football but utterly different.

For a start, you don't turn your back on your opponent in the boxing ring. But it's hard to break the habits of a lifetime, and once he instinctively aimed a forward high kick — which I caught in my gloves. I tucked his size-nine trainer under my arm and had him hopping around on one leg as I waved a warning hand at him. "Watch it, sunshine, or you'll find my knee in your bollocks!"

I was joking, of course. Wasn't I? Jean-Claude responded with a grin and a wink. "Sorry, Nosher. Force of habit!"

But he listened to me and, the complete professional, he made the moves come good. In the end, I couldn't fault him.

We had mutual respect for each other, but I sensed unfinished business. I'd put on the growl. "Just remember: in my game, I only have to hit someone once and they stay fucking hit. There's none of this prancing about and smacking someone thirty times, plus half a dozen kicks — and at the end the guy's still standing. Okay, sport?"

"Sure, Nosher, okay."

On our last day together, Jean-Claude is as good as he'd ever be. He looks at me with that direct stare and its glint of humour.

"Okay, Nosher, now it's you and me!" He slings me a pair of sixteen-ounce gloves.

"What you on about?"

"You and me," he says firmly. "This is personal. I just want to know."

I wasn't sure that it was a good idea to get physical. I mean, you damage the star and you're in big trouble. But it's the end of another baking hot day in Casablanca, and a few of the crowd are still standing around talking. So why not have a bit of malarkey?

I'm reminded of that scene in one of the *Rocky* films when ex-champ Carl Weathers challenges Sly Stallone to a grudge match in an empty gym. So I put on the gloves, and we square up to each other, shuffling and weaving.

The Muscles is as lithe as a leopard, and moves just as fast. He comes at me like a pro, ducking and dodging, popping out his left hand the way I'd taught him — and hitting air. I slide under, avoiding him easily. Then, momentarily, he leaves himself open — and *pop!* I nail him on the chin with my own trusty left jab.

Just one punch is all it takes. But Van Damme's eyes water, and he pulls up short. Then he laughs.

"Heh, Nosher, *mon ami*! You are not so bad, after all!" He claps me on the shoulder, keeping his smile intact, and looks at me with a certain added respect. And I gather that's the end of our brief encounter.

That night the director Peter MacDonald approached me about wearing my referee's hat. I hadn't seen the script, because I didn't have too many lines. Peter said: "Nosher, we're shooting tomorrow. All you've got to say are a few words, like '*Break!*' or '*Stop holding!*' Are you okay for it?"

I thought: Cor, even I can manage that. It won't strain the memory cells too much, and it'll mean a few more days in the sun. So I said, "Sure I'm okay", and went for it.

The boxing scenes were actually filmed in an old brothel close to the Foreign Legion headquarters they'd built in the desert. Van Damme's opponent was a Dutchman, who shaped very well. The place was packed, and the heat was almost unbearable. There was no air conditioning, nothing to cool us down except a flapping towel.

The sweat was pouring off us, and every few minutes they handed up bottles of saline water into the ring to put the liquid back into us. I must have drunk gallons — but all I can tell you is that I weighed seventeen stone when I went out to Morocco, and fifteen when I came back a month later. Say hello to the Incredible Shrinking Man!

But it was all worthwhile. The film worked out brilliantly, and Van Damme looked the dog's bollocks. After it was all over, he shook my hand. "I have just seen the rushes. You were right. It looks better than I could ever have done it."

That was handsome of him, and I guess it made us friends. But he never did invite me to mix it with him again.

The fact that I could still hold my own in a ring with a European black-belt karate champion shows that the years must have taught me something.

So where does it all start?

In a pram, that's where.

## 1: EARLY DAYS

My first memory was being pushed around in a pram with my future wife lying beside me, gurgling happily away. I wasn't to know it then because I was only a year old, and Pauline, a little bundle tucked in beside me, was just twelve months older.

Her mum Ada Wellman and my mum Lil were good friends, you see. So I can rightly say that I bedded my wife very, very early on.

South London. I'd been born at home in Camberwell on 15 August 1928, in a poky two-room flat where we lived in John Ruskin Street down by the Avenue School. I was a bouncing nine-pound, fair-haired baby with a powerful set of lungs who caused no trouble at all with the birth, nice and easy, when he came into the world.

Trouble would come later.

I was christened Frederick Bernard, after my dad, but from my first teat it was always Nosher. As Mum, full name Mabel Lilian, said: "You had an appetite like a horse before you could even stand up." So Nosher it was, and Nosher it has stayed to this day.

We weren't rich, but we weren't on the breadline. Dad was a cart man, loading his four-wheeler and two horses for cash, and he would bring home four quid a week. Which was a lot of money considering the average weekly manual wage was £2 10s, with dole queues stretching round the block. The country was building up to the Great Depression, with everything in the doldrums, prices forced down, labour dirt cheap.

But Dad was a good thief, by which I don't mean he went creeping, but he knew how to make a shilling out of any opportunity.

He was called Nosher by everybody, so it would seem that gluttony ran in the family. He was Big Nosher, all five foot nine of him, and I was Little Nosher — even when I overtook him and went up to six foot four. Dad was working for a firm called Prescott's in the Tower Bridge Road. His job was to go over to King's Cross station in the middle of the night with his cart and horses, Darby and Joan, to pick up fish from the trains where they'd come down from Lowestoft.

Dad filled me in later on how bad those times really were. Three million unemployed, around 20 per cent of the country's workers. The Jarrow shipbuilders marching on London. New houses going up at the rate of a thousand a day, and selling for £350 each, with a down-payment of just a fiver to clinch the deal.

My own childhood memories are of grimy houses nestling together in narrow streets, chimneys belching grey smoke, dark doorways, lamp-posts like skeletons with bare lightbulbs shining through a misty drizzle. South London.

None of this touched us, because Dad wouldn't let it. He was the breadwinner, and a fiercely proud man. We weren't going to starve — even when there was another addition to the family with the arrival of my brother Dinny (Dennis on his birth certificate) four years after me, on 27 July 1932, weighing in at a similar nine pounds and with an equally voracious appetite.

Dad would pick up two ton of fish from King's Cross, around midnight. Darby and Joan knew the journey to Billingsgate by heart, so Dad would doze off on the dicky seat, and just let them walk their way through the ill-lit streets. At the Thames market, the cart-minder would be there waiting, with a friendly bellow of "Oi, Nosher!" to get Dad jumping awake as if someone had stuck a pitchfork up his arse.

The routine was always the same. At King's Cross he'd back the horses into the loading bay, shove the boxes of fish on, and head for home. This was where the thieving came in. Dad had a jemmy iron he'd lever under the slats of the boxes. Then he'd take out a nice plaice, or a cod, or a couple of eels, and pop them into his rush bag.

Wicked or what? Dad operated on the Yiddisher system, the way they work it on the kibbutz. You do something for me, I do something for you. Oi-vay! You clean my carpet, I'll do your electrics. Dad was supplying the people with fish, they gave him bread. So we lived extremely well. We even managed two weeks' holiday every year in a boarding house at Margate.

Dad was a superb horseman — not in the saddle, I'm talking about the original horse whisperer. Darby and Joan were two huge strawberry roans, the Suffolk Punch breed similar to a Clydesdale but without any of the thick "feather" hairs on the legs. The Punch was bred to go through heavy quagmires of Suffolk mud without getting itself encrusted and weighed down. They're beautiful beasts, as old as time itself, and reputed to be the forerunners of the steeds used by the knights of the Middle Ages.

I can believe it. The movies you see with guys in chainmail galloping around on Arab stallions just don't ring true. A man in armour can weigh seventeen stone — five of them the armour. Then add the big saddle. You don't need to be Einstein to work out that the poor bloody horse would be carrying more than eighteen stone. So the animals have to be a lot bigger than they're portrayed by Hollywood.

The big 'uns were slower — but they had the power. Moreover, they could sustain themselves all day long. Yon knight of old would use his trusty steed to flatten people, on the premise that if you get a horse weighing near enough a ton to go over the top of someone, that someone isn't going to be a lot of good afterwards.

Dad's true passion, in fact, was trotting horses, the Hackney high-steppers, and he produced the best you ever came across. I'm telling you, Dad's idea of heaven was to see a horse in its stable with its head stuck into a feed bag eating its guts off. What's more, he was a really genuine horse whisperer, and I could only marvel when I saw him at work.

He taught me how you can tell a horse's age by the teeth. "It's like tree trunks, lad. You get milk teeth that fall out around the age of two. Then they mature with new molars." And the tricks of the trade: "Going on eight or nine, the pikeys [gypsies] would file the teeth down and overnight turn an eight-year-old into a three-year-old."

It's the same way you turn a car's milometer back to zero when it's done a hundred thousand miles and you want to sell the old banger. The oldest trick in the game, but my dad knew how to spot it, and now so did I.

Dad would go over to the Elephant and Castle Horse Repository down by the Regal Cinema, a huge cobblestoned area fenced in like a vast paddock. Every Monday they had the largest sale of horses in the whole country — a couple of hundred every week.

The pikeys used to run the horses up and down the road under the railway arches to try them out. One day — Christ, how could I forget it? — the old man invested in a racehorse that wasn't that brilliant. He called it Blazer. It looked okay to me, a grey thoroughbred, chomping away at the hay in its stall. But me, at eight years old, what did I know?

Dad had forked out a fiver for it — just five quid. Leaning over the fence and eyeing it with a thoughtful air, he suddenly looked round at me, and said quietly: "What we've got to do now, son, is break it to harness. It ain't going to win no races, so I'll sell it on as a trap horse, and make a profit."

Dad waited until the following Sunday morning when there would be no traffic about. Then we took a walk down to the stables he rented behind the Walworth Road, right beneath those railway arches. He got out the four-wheeler, attached the rig to the harness — then slung the harness over the horse and quickly made it fast. The animal must have been taken by surprise, because for an instant it stood stock still. Then all hell broke loose.

Eyes rolling, Blazer started leaping and bucking and jumping with all four feet off the ground as if the cobbles had turned into red hot coals. I never saw anything like it.

It turned out that the horse had never been strung with a pair of blinkers or a collar in its life. My old man's sidekick was Sonny Tobart, a perky little guy in a flat cap and battered jacket who had been around horses all his life. But even he had his work cut out.

Sonny managed to grab Blazer's head, and hung on like a limpet. "Quick," Dad hissed at me. "Get on!"

He was up on the dicky in a trice, slamming himself down into the seat with me rolling into the back as he grabbed the reins, while Sonny pointed the horse's flaring nostrils in the direction of Walworth Road and let go. At which point, a train roars over the railway arches above us, making the whole place shake like an earthquake.

We're right smack underneath it, and the effect is even more dramatic than before. Blazer rears up, so does the trap — and then he's off like the three-thirty at Cheltenham. Out into Walworth Road — and now a tram comes rattling round the corner, all noise and clanging bells, and, of course, our horse has never seen a tram before. I'm thinking: This is not our day.

"Fuck me!" I heard Dad's shout above the clatter of hoofs and the thunder of wheels over the cobbles as our panic-stricken steed took off.

I tell you, we gallop the entire length of the Walworth Road, close to a mile, with the old man hanging on for dear life and me shitting myself in the back. "*Dad! Dad!*" I'd never been so scared in my life.

"Hang on, son!" Somehow Dad steers the trap round into Albany Road, and we gallop the length of it, too, before he turns us into the Old

Kent Road. How, I'll never know. Now we're in the New Kent Road, still at full stretch. And when we finally get to the Elephant and Castle, that racehorse is one mass of white lather.

Years later, when I was testing a chariot for the famous race in *Ben Hur*, I would remember this cavalry charge through the streets of South London. I always said I started young.

But poor old Blazer was fucked. He had galloped two miles flat out. When we got back to the yard Sonny Taber was sitting in the doorway of Baldwin's the Herbalist, and he'd actually pissed himself — with laughter.

All through the week the old man took that horse out, blinkered him up, talked to him as only a horse whisperer can, and two weeks later he'd sold Blazer for twelve quid. So we finally showed a profit — and later his business grew until Dad had ten horses tucked away in there.

Somehow, in the middle of the gigantic depression between the wars, Dad grafted us a good living. On the mean streets of South London I saw lines of men in mufflers and cloth caps, grey faces hunched into thin coats against the rain, queuing on the dole line. They were part of the "irreducible million", which was how the Home Office explained away the fact that unemployment never fell below the million mark.

Dad never allowed that to happen to us. His game was to buy horses that other people couldn't manage. People used to come from near and far, bringing their horses for Dad to cure. He had these old pikey tricks, see.

Dad would wink at me, and say: "Come on, son!"

And off we'd go in the cart down to some farm or stables in Kent, and as we got through the gates we could hear this awful squealing and raging and kicking ... and the farmer would be standing by the barn, relief flooding his face, saying: "Thank Gawd you got here, Nosh — 'e's in there!"

And my dad would walk over to the stable where all the ruckus was coming from, and peer over the top half of the door into the interior, careful to keep the lower part bolted. "Stay where you are!" he'd order me, without even looking round.

Then he would slowly open the bottom half of the door and go in.

And gradually, as the farmer and I stood in the yard outside holding our breath, the terrifying sounds from inside would die away.

It could take half an hour — or two hours. But suddenly the door would swing open, and out would walk Dad with a jaunty stride, and the horse following behind him, its nose almost resting on his shoulder. No reins, no halter, no rope, nothing. Just one man and a horse. Then he'd say to me: "Right, young Nosh, do your job."

That's how I learned about horses.

My job was to start walking round that animal, slowly and at a distance. After a few minutes, I'd hear Dad's voice, low and calm. "Closer ... closer ... closer ... Keep it slow." That was the signal for me to move in, still walking casually round and round the animal, with my hand finally laid gently on his body. If he jumped I'd move away, then go in again.

And eventually I'd stop right in front of him, look him straight in the eye, and put the back of my hand out to him. That horse would either try to bite me — in which case I'd simply walk away, and come back a few minutes later — or he'd nuzzle my hand.

I never got kicked, not once. If Dad ever got a horseshoe in the wrong place, no one ever saw it or knew about it. He taught me everything I know about horse flesh, including how to recognise when something was going to happen — which more than once helped me avoid a kicking. "You'll feel the body tense a split second before it lashes out" — and that's the way it was.

One day I had a row with the old man after asking the wrong question. The yard in Walworth was all rutted and sloping, so it seemed sensible for an inquisitive young shaver to ask: "Dad, why don't you get this levelled?"

He turned on me as if he'd been stung. "That shows how much brains you've got! If I had that yard all lovely and flat, laid out in cement, and a would-be buyer comes up to a lame horse — he'd see that horse was hobbling, wouldn't he?"

Well, yes, Dad.

"So that's why we keep the ruts. On the cobbles he can't see he's lame. Okay?"

Okay, Dad.

The war started. Dad must have had a spark of lightning go through his skull, because amid all the chaos and the air raids he spotted a winner — in fish! A fishmonger's stall at the Elephant was doing good business, owned by a geezer called Fatty Plancard. Except that his real name was Plancardi, and he was Italian. When Italy came out against us in the war, Fatty was interned. So his stall came up for grabs.

Fatty had been leaving his stall outside our home at nights, out of the way, and Dad somehow got himself a permit that allowed him an allocation of fish from Billingsgate market. Next thing, he's opened up as a fishmonger, using Fatty's old site in Draper Street market. Crate of plaice here, a few kippers there. He'd sell his own haddock, stained by Mum at home, using yellow dye to make them look as if they were smoked. Naughty — but it worked a treat. Nobody ever sussed it, and the housewives always came back for more.

Dad expanded the business. He even had a shop at Epsom racecourse called Tattenham Corner Fisheries. At which point he moved us into a house at the back of East Street, close to the fish bringing in the business from Fatty's old stall. And that's what saved our lives.

Mum would be on the stall at nine in the morning, haranguing the customers like a circus barker. "Roll up! Roll up! Get yer fresh fish 'ere!" Or words to that effect. She had a good pair of lungs, and made full use of them.

Dad would come trotting along with his cases of fish to find a queue waiting patiently on the pavement. By noon we'd pack up, wash out, and be on the horse and cart heading for home. It was only a half-mile trot, but on the way we'd stop off for a well-earned bite at Vince's Café on the Walworth Road. On this particular day we loaded the gear, had our lunch at Vinnie's, trotted on home — and found the place a smouldering ruin.

Christ, what a mess. A direct hit. The bomb had struck our house at two o'clock, around the time Dad was washing down his meat pie with a cup of coffee half a mile up the road. We'd heard the siren, but ignored it as usual. I suppppose you could say we were lucky, though we had lost everything. At least we were alive.

The one horse that had been there was dead. I saw bits of poor old Darby lying around the yard. Mum cried her eyes out. All we had to our name were the clothes we were standing up in, Joan, our last horse, the cart, and a stall down the road smelling of fish. Mum wandered through the debris picking up bits of cloth, and throwing them down again. They were filthy and soaked from the firemen's hoses anyway, and everything had gone.

But we survived. Dad found a place for us down near the public baths, and as bombed-out victims we got clothes and bits and pieces of furniture from the Government to keep us out of the gutter.

Even at that young age, I found myself thinking: What's all this about? I've got no argument with Fritz in Berlin, though I couldn't say the same for Adolf Hitler. And I don't suppose Fritz had heard of Nosher Powell. Yet here he was not only blowing my house up and killing our pet horse, but trying to fucking kill me at the same time.

I think that's taking a liberty. Don't you?

## 2: GROWING PAINS

Funny thing. As a kid I always knew I was going to be something special. If that sounds arrogant, sorry — but it's still a fact. I wasn't a brilliant scholar, I couldn't tell my calculus from my past participle. I wasn't a particularly good athlete either, even though I ran for my school in the hundred yards and used to win more races than lose them.

But I always felt I was destined for something out of the ordinary, don't ask me what or why.

I had an overactive imagination, maybe that was it. I was brilliant at making up stories to get off school. I could come up with fantastic yarns. Sample: I'd limp in after two days' playing truant and say: "Sorry, teacher. But me dad's horse trampled on me foot in the stable. Ooh — ow!" And I'd hobble off to my desk amid sympathetic noises all round. Another time, holding my stomach and grimacing with pain: "Sorry, teacher, I've been in bed with food poisoning. But it's okay now ... at least I think it is." And I'd sit down bravely and open my exercise book.

But finally I came a cropper when I stayed away for a week. Over-confidence.

They sent one of the teachers over to our house, and when I got home that evening Mum was waiting for me with an expression that spelled trouble. I was right. She gave me a belting I never forgot. That's the day when I thought: *This ain't fucking worth it!*

The Elephant in those days was surrounded by cinemas, and my brother Dinny and I knew every back door to get in. There was the ABC, and right opposite stood the Gaumont. Just round the corner was the Rialto, and up the road was the Gate. Then there was the Trocette and the Globe in the Old Kent Road — they were all over the shop.

We couldn't afford threepence to go in, so the trick was to wait for someone to come out of the exit door, listen to the sound of the bar going up — and then we were in. Once inside we had to be on the lookout for the "hostiles" — the attendants with flashing torches — because if they caught you, the penalty was a thick ear and you were slung out on the street with a well-aimed kick to see you on your way.

But Dinny and I used to box clever. There was always a thick red curtain over the door. The pair of us would slip in and hide behind it, not moving a muscle until we heard the film start with the usual ta-ra fanfare and the music. Then we'd drop on to our stomachs and wriggle in like small soldiers, sliding across into the seats.

When the attendant came along we'd be sitting calmly eating a packet of crisps — and as often as not we got away with it. The secret was not to look guilty.

The cinema became our second home. Those "formative years" would affect my whole life, cocooned in the safe darkness of fantasy. We were just kids, Dinny and I — but the films we watched, entranced, broadened our outlook, showed us new horizons, and took us into a wonderful world of make-believe. I never lost it.

But occasionally reality insisted on spoiling the show. The worst walloping that came my way was when the Gate screened the original *Frankenstein*, with Boris Karloff. It had first come out in 1931, with an H certificate, but you still had to be sixteen to get in.

Now it was 1938, I was ten and Dinny was six. We were thoroughly enjoying the lightning flashes and the nuts and bolts through the neck and the rest of it, when suddenly this big lug in a green uniform loomed up and demanded: "What are you two doing here?"

He grabbed me by the ear, and it was really fucking hurting, so I turned round to let one go at him. But then he whacked me, and I saw all sorts of coloured lights that didn't belong to what was happening up there on a black and white screen.

Then Dinny jumped him, hanging on to his back. Next thing we were into a right ruck, rolling around the aisle and shouting and swearing fit to bust. Yes, even us kids knew the rude words.

Eventually they had to put the lights up, and we were escorted off the premises, as they say in polite language — with a boot up our trousers again to speed our departure. I never did get to see the end of *Frankenstein* until eventually I caught up with it on TV.

Years later, when I was working in Covent Garden market, I actually got to meet Boris Karloff. They were filming on the corner of Southampton Street, and I saw the crowd with the cameras and the lights, and wandered over for a look.

I was astounded when I caught sight of him. Without that droopy eyelid and the club-footed limp he was a really handsome man, with a head of thick grey hair and piercing dark eyes. I summoned up the bottle to approach him, though I was absolutely awed by his sheer presence. He turned out to be a lovely man, no side on him whatsoever, and we chatted for several minutes before I asked him for his autograph. His name was actually William Pratt, can you believe that? But he signed my bit of paper with one word: *Karloff!* To me, he would always remain the epitome of the English gentleman.

Being Nosher, I had to tell him: "I never did see the end of your *Frankenstein*, because I was being thrown out of the cinema!" I regaled him with what had happened all those years ago, and he threw back that great head of his and roared with laughter.

Dinny and I were both right little devils, but the one person we did respect was our mum. I always say that the reason why my brother and I were such good fighters was because Lil had the best left hook in the business! I kid you not. If you could slip my mother's left hook, you could slip any geezer's!

I don't believe in abusing children, of course not. But if a child does wrong, I tell him once: "Don't do it again!" And if he does it again, I give him a clip. That's how we were brought up, and it didn't do us any harm that I'm aware of. I still say to this day that the so-called judges who punish people for dispensing instant justice are wrong. Believe me, I know — I've been there!

Why do you think there's so much crime on the streets today? You get a kid who mugs an old bird for a couple of quid, and they send the little bastard for a fortnight's fucking holiday to Portugal. So how can the tearaways ever learn the meaning of the words "discipline" and "respect"?

Once, when I was about nine, I did something wrong. I can't remember exactly what it was, but it must have been bad because Mum went into the screaming heebie-jeebies. We had an open coal fire then, and she picked up this metal shovel from the grate and actually flung it at me! I must have wound her up because I'd never seen her so mad.

The shovel came whizzing at me across the kitchen, I ducked — and it went straight through the scullery window. What a noise! *"Now look what you've done!"* Mum raged. Me! All I'd done was get out of the way sharpish, but there's women for you.

Mum was flaxen-haired and blue-eyed, with a great figure. She only weighed nine stone, but could she pack a wallop! Still, I loved that woman. She never actually marked me — any punishment was always on the arse or the legs, or the side of my head, never my face. Like all good working-class mothers she protected her brood with the ferocity of a lioness.

Lil stood no nonsense from anyone, and she could be wicked. There was a neighbour who lived at the top of our turning, a Mrs Taylor, who had five kids. They were a right noisy scruff of a family, and made all our lives a misery.

One day they made off with Dinny's little tricycle. He was only four, but he went round himself to get it back. The old bag came to the door — and kicked him. Dinny came home crying, rubbing his backside. I was in the kitchen having my tea, and I did my best to comfort him.

"They've got my bike!" he sobbed. "And that woman kicked me!"

I remember Mum's face, suddenly set in stone. She took off her apron, opened the door and marched purposefully up the road with me and Dinny following at a safe distance. She went up there, banged on the door, and when Mrs Taylor answered it — wallop! You've guessed it. The famous matriarchal left hook.

Mum not only took the woman out, and left her sprawled in the doorway — she took out two of the smart-arse sons as well, and I'm talking about husky young teenagers. Punched them out! Flattened them!

You'll gather from this that Mum could be a right virago when roused, and her language matched her temper. "You touch my fucking kids again and I'll kill the lot of you!" were her parting words as she stormed off the battlefield of the front porch.

After that we had a bit of peace and quiet in the neighbourhood.

Diamond Lil, as she was known to all and sundry, did the same thing with a teacher who gave me two strokes of the cane on my hand. It wasn't for anything major, just being caught throwing a few books around, and normally I could take it without flinching. But this time my left hand was cut badly, right across the palm, and it hurt like mad. Mrs Canton, she was — you never forget the names of teachers who do you a mischief.

"What happened, son?" Mum saw the bloodstained handkerchief wrapped round my hand when I got home for tea.

"Nothing, Mum."

"Don't you hold out on me, Nosher! I asked you a question."

Well, I was more frightened of her than of that Mrs Canton, so I told her. That same look came into her eye. Next day I was sitting at my desk when the door crashed open and Mum just burst into the classroom. She grabbed the teacher by the hair, and pulled her over the table in front of everyone. Christ, what a ruckus! She was about to thump the living daylights out of her struggling victim when Mr Tonkin, the senior master, appeared. He tried to restrain her. "Please, Mrs Powell —"

But Mum shook him off, and bellowed to the hapless Mrs Canton: "If you ever hit my children again, I'll fucking *bunnock* you."

*Bunnock*? I never did find out what that word meant, except I knew it was the worst word in her vocabulary. Maybe she was trying to say "bollock".

The whole class sat gob-smacked around me, and I didn't know where to look. I think Mum went a bit over the top that day.

For all that, I enjoyed my schooldays. Rockingham Street School was for kids up to age eleven. There were gangs, as there always are, and the worst crew was led by a kid with one arm. He had a stump for the other, with his shirtsleeve tied in a knot below the elbow, and his bodyguard was a tall, ginger-haired bloke called Wally Simmons. Both of them were right young villains, and I sensed it was wise to steer well clear. To put it more bluntly, I was scared of tangling with them, like just about everybody else.

I was coming up eleven years old, in my last term, and I'd kept out of trouble with that mob — until the day I saw Stumpy and Wally, with two or three of their cronies in tow, barge deliberately into my kid brother outside the school gates and send him flying. Dinny was only six, and they knocked him half across the street. In that moment I saw red.

I tore into Wally, who was a size bigger than me, and we had a right go in the street, while the kid with one arm used his stump as a weapon, shoving it at me like a cattle prod. At least it didn't reach where the sun doesn't shine — but it really hurt, though by then I was beyond caring anyway.

The fight surged over the pavement and down to the United Dairies depot, with the other kids yelling me on. I spotted a milk crate, heaved it up, and smashed it over Wally's skull. Then I whacked Stumpy, and he went rolling into the gutter. I turned on the others — but without their two leaders they'd had enough and ran for it.

I heard myself shouting: "You touch my brother again and I'll fucking kill the lot of you!" I must have picked up the lingo from my mum. Or maybe it just ran in the family, having a way with words.

But from that moment the Stumpy gang walked around me very carefully, never coming near me again.

After I did that crew, I realised something: I was good at beating people up if I had to! I'd never given it a thought before, and never thought of myself as a fighter.

But I learned something that day. When I did my nut, I turned into a fucking handful.

## 3: THE FIST OF NUMBNESS

The war temporarily ended my education in London. The first wail of an air-raid siren echoed down our street. A couple of mornings later Mum got Dinny and me out of bed early, and told us we had to go away for a bit. "I don't know how long, but I'll keep in touch," she promised. Her face was pale, and she looked more strained than I'd ever seen her.

An hour later we were in a queue of children, scores of us lining the cold platforms at London Bridge station to be evacuated, like so many others, to all corners of the country. The poorer ones like us had all our clothes stuffed into a pillow-case. The kids from richer families carried suitcases.

Dinny and I ended up at Seaford, on the Sussex coast, in a neat little boarding-house run by a Mrs Jessop. I never did know her first name, and after what happened on the third night I didn't have time to find out.

Mrs Jessop was a plumpish, motherly woman with dark hair, a bright smile and wandering hands. She could only have been around forty, but to me that made her a grandmother. The first night she put us into two small iron beds in a room on the first floor, a cosy bedroom with flowered wallpaper, pictures of seagulls, and the sounds of the sea through the half-open window lulling us to sleep.

Or they would have done if other sounds hadn't intruded through the wall from Mrs J's bedroom next door.

There were two coppers boarding there along with us. The first hint I had that all was not quite kosher was the sound of heavy feet marching past our bedroom with measured tread, followed by a door opening and closing. Then silence — before the most almighty thumps and thuds resounded like a steam hammer, followed by a wail that rivalled the air-raid sirens we'd heard in London.

"What's that, Nosh?" little Dinny asked fearfully from beneath his blanket.

"I think it's the all clear!" I told him. Even at that age, I could manage a witty line.

For the first two nights Mrs Jessop contented herself with planting a kiss on our foreheads, and bidding us "Goodnight, dears!" as she switched out the light. But on the third night she came back to my bed in the darkness, sat down quietly, slid a hand under my pyjamas, and ran it lightly over my bollocks. I froze. No one had ever done that, except maybe me. Then she gave me a gentle squeeze in the same place. I was rigid — my whole body, top to bottom and everywhere in between, if you get my meaning.

Then she kissed me again, this time on the cheek, and tiptoed out.

Young Nosher wasn't happy with that at all, though if he'd been a few years older it might have been a different story. Next day I was on the phone home. "We don't like it down here, Mum. Please come and take us away!"

I didn't tell her the real reason, or Lil would have killed that woman. Bless her, she came the next day and took us back to the Elephant. No questions asked.

We stuck out the Blitz for a few weeks, until there seemed to be more buildings flattened around us than were left standing. At which time Mum and Dad held a crisis meeting, and next thing Dinny and I were on another train crowded with kids, bound for what seemed like the end of the earth: Dorset.

On Wareham platform, grown-ups were pointing at us, and beckoning. "I'll take that one ... That little girl, she can come with us ... Hey, young lad, over here ..." It was like a cattle auction, and for the first time in our lives Dinny and me were separated because nobody wanted to take more than one kid under one roof. Fair enough, but my heart felt like a lump of lead as I watched my small brother being led to a car and driven off — though it turned out later that he was only half a mile away.

I ended up with a family called Dugdale, above a butcher's shop on the edge of town. Nothing fancy, but warm and homely. Straight up, they were, and no malarkey. Percy Dugdale was the local butcher, in North Street. He was bald and jovial, and he had an old black pedal bike for deliveries. "You can run a few for me, young Nosh, and earn yourself a bit of pocket money." He beamed — and off I went into the country roads, pedalling like mad.

I was still in short trousers then, even though I was coming up twelve, until Mum saved my blushes by sending me down one of Dad's suits — which more or less fitted. By now I was springing up like a tree in a rainforest, only faster. On Thursdays I'd go down to the market place to watch "Mr Percy" buying chickens and lumps of meat and the rest for his customers. I went to a local school, and joined the Army Cadets. All in all, I was having a whale of a time.

They'd enrolled me at Swanage Grammar School, in an old Henry VIII hunting lodge, very posh for a London townie. They kitted me out in a blue blazer with white stripes, blue cap, grey trousers, the works. Okay, I felt like a rusty hub cap on a Rolls-Royce, and the other boys took the piss out of me from day one, but by now I was getting handy with my fists, and I wasn't scared of anyone. So soon enough I earned a bit of respect and made a few friends.

But one day something happened that gave me nightmares for weeks. Did I say weeks? Make that the rest of my life. I can still see the bodies floating there.

I was a day pupil, which meant I had to catch the train every day from Wareham to Swanage, and back. On this particular day in April 1944 we finished at 3.30 p.m., and had the usual mad scamper for Swanage station. But a whisper went round that something was going on in the sea — and I could smell smoke in the air, a nasty oily vapour that made our eyes sting.

Instead of taking the train, me and a few mates headed for the seafront, with its masses of curling barbed wire and warning notices about mines. A kid named Trevor ran on ahead, and peered out over the Channel. When he turned back to us, his face was as chalk white as the cliffs of Dover. "Look, Nosher!" He pointed out over the promenade.

And there, along the whole length of the sea front and beyond the cliffs, were bodies. Figures in soggy uniforms, some still wearing helmets, lying face down in the sand. Others were washing around in the swell, like shop-window dummies. Except that these were — or had been — real people.

Out on the horizon, the Channel was ablaze. A thick pall of black smoke darkened the sky, drifting towards the coast. We could see flames flickering spasmodically underneath, as if someone was striking matches then blowing them out again.

Us lads stood by the railings open-mouthed — then ducked as two huge transport planes roared low overhead, lumbering out to sea to spray the waves with some kind of detergent. Two-engined fighter bombers were firing tracer bullets into the sea, and we saw the whole Channel exploding in the distance.

"Over there!" Another boy was staring west along the sands. I saw the twisted iron skeletons of landing barges washed up on the rocks, and more bodies impaled on the spiralling barbed wire as far as the eye could see. Most of the corpses were charred, and almost unrecognisable as human beings. Others lay sprawled on the slimy green rocks, covered in seaweed.

"What is it? Are they Germans?" But that day there was no answer. We trudged back to the railway station in silence.

Next day, after school, some of us couldn't resist the lure of the seafront. Rooted to the spot, I watched groups of Sappers making their way gingerly along the sands with metal detectors to carve a path through the mines.

When they reached the bodies, they dragged them back and slung them bodily into DUKWs, which were like landing-craft on wheels.

German invasion? I believed it at the time. It seemed the obvious answer. But much later I found I had witnessed one of the truly horrific blunders of the war.

The bodies had been US servicemen taking part in a D-Day rehearsal that had gone tragically wrong. A mock battle turned into a slaughterhouse as thirty thousand men carried out an amphibious landing on Slapton Sands, ten miles down the coast, only to have scores of them shot by their fellow GIs playing the roles of Nazis defending the beaches.

That same night, hours later on, real German E-boats located another American convoy, and wreaked havoc on two ammunition ships. In all, more than nine hundred GIs died in forty-eight hours of carnage — and for days their bodies were washed up along the coast.

I'll never forget that sight. Even now, thinking about it makes me feel sick.

But life went on, and the nightmare faded. School was okay, and the townie boy was even accepted into the local Young Farmers Club, though I hardly knew which end of a cow mooed and which broke wind. More importantly, that's where I started boxing.

The Young Farmers had use of the Market Hall, an echoing red-brick building with a lot of space inside. Part of it was turned into a makeshift gym in the evenings. They dragged an old punch-bag and skipping ropes out of a cupboard, and came up with a few gloves with the horsehair sprouting out of them. I started sparring around with some of the lads, and found I took to it like the proverbial duck.

I got thumped a few times, but it didn't worry me. I just tried to make sure it didn't happen too often. After a week I borrowed a book by Bombardier Billy Wells, full of pictures of "How to do a straight left" — *pop! pop! pop!* — and applied myself to the game as if I'd stumbled on the burning bush. Which, in a way, I had.

After six weeks of belting the bag and sweating it out on the skipping-rope, which isn't as easy as it looks if you're doing it properly, I felt ready to go into the ring. My first ever public fight (not counting Stumpy and Co) took place in the Market Hall. I hate to admit it, but I got beat rotten! On points, over three rounds, by a pink-cheeked young farmer, who was built like a side of Aberdeen Angus beef.

Everyone was shouting conflicting instructions, that's my excuse, but the end result was the same. I got clobbered. Was I downcast? As Fred Flintstone once memorably put it: Is the earth flat?

On the contrary, I was mad as hell! It made me even more determined. Night after night I sat up with Bombardier Billy, pouring over the pages, getting to know the moves.

Then, one day, it all went pear-shaped.

I was sixteen now, a lively lad sky-larking about in the market with his pals. A chase was on, with me being hunted. *"There he goes. Get him, someone!"*

I ran full pelt through the stalls, laughing and shouting: "Come on, you can't catch me!" Out of the market entrance I raced — and slam-bang-smack into the side of a car!

I was running so hard, really flying, that I hurtled right through the side window, which unfortunately happened to be closed. After which all I remember is people screaming, the windscreen smeared crimson, hands pulling me free, gently laying me down on the pavement, then blood everywhere. My claret! That was when I passed out. If that was the first stunt I ever pulled, it was almost my last.

The ambulance took me to hospital in Poole. When I came round, they'd operated on me. They told me later that my hand had been out one way, my arm another. It looked like I'd be a semi-cripple for life. But the surgeon performed miracles.

Okay, my right arm was in plaster, my face looked like Mr Dugdale's butcher's block, all beaten and livid, and I'd been cut to pieces. To this day I've still got the scars around my ribs to remind me not to run into the road without looking. But I'd come through.

I lay in that hospital for more than three months. All the tendons on my right hand had been severed, and I never did get the muscle tone fully back. The good news about this excerpt from *Casualty* is that I never felt any pain in my fist when I hit someone, not from that day to this. My whole hand had gone numb, and it has stayed numb all my life.

It meant I could use my fist like a club, and not feel a thing. Believe me, that helped me settle a few scores, and would surprise a few of the ungodly in years to come.

I called it my "Fist of Numbness".

Eventually they let me out of hospital, and Mum took me back to the dubious safety of south London. The bombing was still ferocious. Hitler cranked the war up a notch with the buzz-bombs, the V1s, and the terrible V2s.

But Mum got it into her head that her young lads would be safer at home — and the way I looked, she had a point. Talk about the walking wounded! I was pasty white, unhealthily fat, and the bruises took an age to fade. One day I looked in the mirror, and didn't like what I saw staring back at me.

It was time to do something drastic.

## 4: OF MACE AND MEN

The sullen *crump* of exploding bombs from the docks became a nightly background chorus as Dinny and I lay in our beds watching the sky light up through the chinks in the blackout curtains. At that time it was more like a grand adventure, and we had no real sense that the flickering orange glow spelled doom, gloom or danger.

When the siren sounded from the ARP station down the road, Mum would hurry in and lean a thick mattress against the bedroom wall to create a makeshift tent. Then the three of us would huddle under it, sometimes clutching each other when there was a particularly loud explosion nearby that made the walls shake and brought bits of plaster floating down from the ceiling. In the dark we would make up stories and tell them in turns, keeping our spirits up until the reassuring wail of the all-clear.

The V2s were the worst. Sometimes, when I went off to school next morning, there would be just an awful yawning gap where there had once been a house, with smoke rising from the rubble and firemen and ARP wardens in their blue uniforms and white helmets picking through the ruins.

Meantime I joined the Air Training Corps — with an ulterior motive. It gave me entry into their boxing club, which was based in a famous gym in Southwark called the Fitzroy-Lynn.

A guy called Charlie Bunnett ran it. He was little, and he was fat — but you learned very quickly to treat him with respect, and not mention his height or his waistline within his hearing. When I walked in and announced myself, he sized me up with a shrewd gaze, said, "Okay, let's see what you can do," and threw me a set of gloves. I changed into shorts and singlet, and ducked into the ring.

Like I say, Charlie was short and fat, but he was a will-o'-the-wisp in the ring. Like many stout men, he could move deceptively fast. I kept hitting air, and if I wasn't hitting air I was missing Charlie's shadow by what seemed a mile. After a couple of minutes, I started to feel depressed, and it must have showed.

Charlie held up a hand. "Okay, big feller, now listen to me. You're tall, and you've got a long left hand. Your fist in a straight line can hit anybody else before they can hit you. But don't push it out — *throw* it out, and then recoil it like a gun!"

That was the first bit of serious advice I ever had, and because of it I would survive against first-class fighters for my whole ring career.

If any man had anything to do with keeping me alive in the ring, it was that little geezer. So thanks, Charlie! Here's to you, mate.

Better still, the muscle tone came back into my right hand. I started using it with more confidence. But always the left hand to save me from punishment, moving around, throwing it out then whipping it back just as fast.

The band of the ATC [Air Training Corps] used to practise in the club's main hall. After a couple of weeks watching them, I got chatting to the officer in charge, a bloke with a pleasant manner and a moustache that stretched from one ear to the other. "We're short of a drum major," he said. "You're big enough. Do you think you could do it?"

It meant four stripes upside down on my sleeve, with a silver drum embossed above them. I would also be expected to twirl a heavy silver mace. Fuck my old boots, I thought. That'll make me Jack the Lad. Course I can do it.

Aloud I said: "I'll certainly give it a try, sir!"

Sure enough, I found that I could.

First day, they stuck me in front of the band, and taught me what to shout. "Band of the ATC, three-man line! By the left, quick *march!*"

And rat-a-tat-a-tat, the kettle drums would roll, and strutting out there in front I felt as proud as a peacock — and probably looked like one with all that blue-and-grey plumage.

I also had the silver mace. Believe me, that thing weighed a ton. I started to experiment, going off by myself into dark corners to practise. Twirling it above my head, balancing it, finally daring to throw it up and catch it. And since you're wondering — no, I never did drop it. Never, ever, not even in private. You wouldn't find a single dent on it, or in my pride either. And slinging it around did wonders for my right arm, building up the muscles.

You have to be careful throwing a mace. Apart from the fact it would break all five of your toes if you dropped it, it was weighted at one end, and there was also a chain round the top where you caught it. That chain could rip the flesh off your finger before you knew it.

Dad, equally proud of his son, bought me a pair of leather gauntlets, and added some stitching inside the thumb. Then I painted the gauntlets white — and I could throw the thing up without any fear.

One day I was heading for Kennington Park for a practice turn-out, just a walk from home. I was carrying my mace — *my mace*, please note — in a long cloth cover for protection. Though I say it myself, I was immaculate in my uniform, boots polished like a mirror, and looking forward to a nice afternoon's marching around with the lads.

Then the siren went.

By that time I was so used to the sound that, like many Londoners, I never paid much attention. I was just coming up by the clock-tower when from overhead there was a tremendous roar that battered my eardrums like a clap of thunder. I looked up to see this peculiar-looking plane flying across the sky less than a thousand feet up, with a flame burning from its rear like a pencil torch. My first thought was: *What the fuck's that?* My second was: *Shit, it's a doodle-bug!* And that was when the engine cut out. It sounded like a motor-bike on its last legs — then, suddenly, nothing ... except an eerie silence.

This was the V1, of course, the notorious "buzz-bomb" that was okay while you could hear it — and not-at-all-okay when you couldn't. I stood frozen in my tracks, following its ominous grey shape all the way as it went into a steep dive, then thumped into the ground four hundred yards down the road.

Then everything blew sky high. Smoke, flames and shrapnel, showering everywhere in lethal steel shards.

I raced over to the carnage, coughing my way through swirling smoke. The bomb had struck Rowton House, the dossers' hang-out, and the devastation all around was unbelievable. The street had become a row of rotting teeth that needed fillings.

A grey pall hung in the sky. I could hear screams coming from everywhere and nowhere. Without thinking of what the ATC would say, I grabbed my mace from its cloth and used it to lever bricks and plaster aside to try to get to people trapped under the rubble.

The ARP boys came racing up. A voice said: "That's all right, son. Well done. We'll take over now."

I looked at my poor old mace — and oh dear! It was bent at the end like a huge silver boomerang. What would the regiment say? I was shitting dust.

I made it to the park, and reported for duty, apologising for being late on parade and also for being covered in dirt. The commanding officer was very understanding. "Just get up to the front, Drum Major!"

"But my mace?" Gingerly, and with some difficulty, I slid the battered symbol from its cloth.

He clapped me on the shoulder. "Don't worry, Nosher. We'll get you a new one." Someone must have passed the word on what had happened. A week later, he presented me with a new mace in front of the whole outfit. Good guy, the CO.

Now you've seen those wartime photographs of people huddled together on tube platforms during air-raids, spending the night far below the ground to escape the bombs. What they don't show is the choking dust that filled the air, especially after a bad raid.

A station like the Borough where Mum, Dinny and I took refuge was particularly bad for the lungs. We only went once, on a night when the V2s were raining down from nowhere and the first you knew of it was after a whole street went up. You got to this safe haven through a church crypt, and descended what seemed like hundreds of stairs to the platforms.

But the walls were all fresh cement, and the dust and heat were intolerable. There was no such thing as air-conditioning, and people were stretched out on blankets, sweating and roasting.

It was foolhardy to be outside, but I had to get away from there. So did Mum and Dinny. That night we came up into the park gasping and choking, clutching on to each other. "I can't stay in there," I gasped, gulping in blessed fresh night air.

"We can't either, son."

I looked around. The whole of London seemed to be alight. From horizon to horizon the sky was one ball of red flames. But we didn't go back. And somehow we survived the last days and nights of the war, and all the shit that Hitler threw at London before the final curtain.

Our personal legacy was that Mum and Dinny both suffered from claustrophobia ever after, stemming from that one night underground. I'm sure they were not alone.

# 5: DAD'S ROUND

I must have inherited some of my boxing prowess from my father. Dad used to fight in the ring at Blackfriars, though he was never what I'd call a good 'un. To add to our income, he was fighting to put breakfast on the table, getting money wherever he could.

When most people went to church of a Sunday, Dad went out to get his head knocked off. "Sunday at the Ring" was a weekly ritual — a boxing arena set up in a derelict chapel opposite the old Ring pub on Blackfriars Road, run by Bella Burge, the widow of Dick Burge who had set up the place back in 1910. The word spread. It became a Mecca for every fighter who thought something of himself, and for visiting boxers from overseas who always made sure they paid a call. Bella took it over when Dick died and, now I think of it, that made her Britain's first woman boxing promoter.

World-famous fighters went in there to train or to give themselves a workout in the ring. Punters would pay 1s 6d for the privilege of seeing them in action, laying on bets, and watching the bouts from seats that sloped up so steeply that you almost fell over the bloke in front when you stood up.

As a nipper I saw the god-like figure of Primo Carnera box in there once, and I'll never forget his massive frame, six foot five of him and nineteen stone. How anyone ever knocked him over I'll never know, but several fighters managed it during his career.

Sunday lunchtimes were special. As a treat, Dad would succumb to my pleadings and take me along to watch him fight — and, I have to say, usually get pasted. That tiny place was packed to the rafters, and the atmosphere was incredible.

"Half a quid, first loser" was what they called the first fights, open to all comers, and to anyone fit enough or drunk enough to climb in the ring and have the gloves strapped on. They never knew who they'd find glowering at them from the opposite corner — but they did know that there was half a quid in it for them, even if they lost. Winners would get more, because if they put on a good show the audience would chuck coins into the ring, and the winner was allowed to pocket the lot.

Dad would go in for it, though I never actually saw him win. But fighting so regularly, he got to know a few moves, and he passed these on to me when I was a nipper. He was getting beaten up regularly too, and as often as not I took him home nursing a sore head with a lump of meat pressed to a black eye.

But for half a quid he figured it was worth the pain and the strain, and though Mum muttered a bit in disapproval, she never tried to stop him. Half a quid? The rent for our place was twelve and six a week, so that was our lodgings just about paid for.

Mum worked out the housekeeping. On Mondays she used to send me out to the butcher's — "but don't spend no more than half a crown". A loaf of bread was fourpence, a newspaper was a penny. A pair of shoes set you back three and six. So half a quid was gold-dust. And if Dad walked out a winner, which he sometimes did, that was a nicker, a whole pound, plus the nobbins from the audience if he'd given them a good smash-up fight.

At home, Dad had an even temper, though he and Mum could have a ruck together. He never laid a hand on her, ever — in fact, it was the other way round, and I saw her thump him more than once. "Have you been drinking? Who are you laughing at?" *Whack!*

I used to watch people like Jock McAvoy, Jack Peterson, Len Harvey, Dave Crowley, Dave Finn and look at their moves. Slowly I absorbed some of the things they did.

And I learned one thing: you're either born with a punch, or you're not. No matter how much training you do, you'll never learn a punch. You've got to have it there, inside you, ready to unleash.

Dad taught me something else: Don't punch *at* the target, punch *through* it. You get more impact. If you punch the target, you slow up as you're getting to it, even if you don't realise it. I've seen guys hitting the heavy bag, doing the weights — and at the end they haven't punched one ounce heavier than when they started.

Me, I've got a punch.

My father finally popped his clogs in 1985 at the ripe old age of eighty. He collapsed on the floor at home, and was rushed to Guy's Hospital in the ambulance. Dad actually died in my arms as I sat with my brother at his bedside. Both Dinny and I were gutted.

But we saw the old man out proud. "Let's make it special," I said. "Give him a send-off everyone will remember. " And we did.

I got hold of one of his horsy mates, and the geezer brought down the flashest black stallion you ever saw to lead the cortège. We walked to Tooting cemetery, Mum, Dinny and I, leading the procession with that great black horse pulling the hearse, and a fleet of cars following.

People came from near and far to pay their own homage, and afterwards we all went back to the Prince of Wales in Wimbledon to have a drink. I raised a few glasses with some stunt men friends, and one said: "That's the way to see your dad off!"

I like to think Dad would have agreed.

Strangely, the same thing happened with our mum — me being there at her death, I mean. Poor Lil had cancer, and fought it bravely for months before finally going into hospital.

Dinny and I were sitting there beside her, when all of a sudden she perked up and said: "Do you know what I really fancy, boys?"

"No, Mum, what?" we said together.

"I'd really like some fish and chips."

I looked at the tired face on the pillow, worn down with fighting the pain. "If that's what you want, Mum, that's what you'll get." And I raced out of the hospital, and down to the nearest fish shop and bought a piece of plaice and some chips.

Mum nibbled a little bit of it, said, "That was lovely," then lay back with a smile and shut her eyes. She never opened them again.

I looked across the bed at my brother. "Dinny. She's gone."

He said: "I know."

Her death devastated us. Dinny must have cried in his own time, not in front of anybody because that's not his way.

And, like him, I cried alone too.

# 6: THE BROWN BOMBER

I left school without too much regret on either side. There was a whole world waiting out there, and I couldn't see myself in a mortar board and gown heading for the gleaming spires of Oxford or taking up punting at Cambridge.

Through Dad's friends, I got my first job at Covent Garden, unloading flowers from the Channel Islands, shifting crates of fruit and veg, and getting acquainted with such exotic delicacies as bananas, oranges, grapes and pineapples, the like of which we had never seen in the war years. Humping those crates around kept me fighting fit, and fit to fight.

I had three years of it, working with a firm called David Ingamells, and enjoyed every minute of it. Mind you, I did have my moments. One early morning, around 5 a.m. when we started our shift, the boss told me to load up a hand-cart with sacks of potatoes and vegetables, and take them down to Berwick Street market in Soho.

I spent half an hour heaving the sacks on, and it took me another thirty minutes to trundle the cart down Long Acre and through Soho to the bustling market.

There was a lorry unloading other goods on to a stall, and I stuck my cart behind it, whistling away happily as I shifted my sacks. A thought had occurred to me.

As the driver cleared his final load, I approached him casually. "Where you going back to, mate?"

He looked at me, and said shortly: "Across the river — Waterloo. Why?"

"Oh ... just wondered."

But I'd done more than wonder. I was knackered after that hike across the West End, and a bright idea had sparked into my head. I seized the handles of the cart, and shoved them into two rings on either side by the tailboard, jamming them firm. All at once  the lorry revved up. I hopped on to one of the handles with my legs swinging over the side, sat back comfortably — then grabbed for the tailboard in sudden panic as the lorry took off at a rate of knots down the street.

"Hey!" My hoarse shout was whipped away in the wind. "Hey — slow down!" But the driver couldn't see me in his mirror, and I had no way of attracting his attention as we roared through the empty streets. Down Regent Street, on to Piccadilly Circus and then away to the wide open spaces of Trafalgar Square. It isn't often you see a hand-cart travelling at thirty miles an hour, with its owner hanging on for grim life and shouting fit to bust. A few early-risers let their jaws sag as I went past like one of those early silent-movie chases, but making a lot of noise.

Over Waterloo Bridge ... and finally he swung into a yard and pulled up under the railway arches. I heard a door open and shut. Then the driver's face was staring in disbelief at my own dirt-streaked features from a few inches away. "What the — ?"

"I got caught up," I said weakly, disengaging the handles as discreetly as possible. "Thanks for the ride." Now I had the long walk back. I trudged off with my cart, back over the river to Covent Garden. I could hardly stand up when I got there, and my backside was black and blue.

The boss demanded: "Where the fucking hell have you been?"

I said: "If I told you, guv'nor, you'd never believe it!"

At least the boys got a laugh out of it. But I never tried that trick again.

At which point something happened to this lowly Covent Garden porter that was like finding the pot of gold at the end of the rainbow. I got to spar with Joe Louis. I'll say that again, because I can still scarcely believe it happened. I got to spar with Joe Louis, and not just once but for a whole month. Heavyweight champion of the world. The legendary Brown Bomber, undefeated over twelve incredible years and a record twenty-five title defences.

And there was Nosher, aged all of seventeen, in the ring squaring up to the most fearsome fighting machine on God's earth!

It began in Jack Solomons' gymnasium off Shaftesbury Avenue. I'd been given the green light to train in the gym whenever I wanted, thanks to my mentor, Charlie Bunnett. I would work out most nights, and somehow the promoter took a shine to the eager young ginger-headed kid thumping the big bag as if it was his worst enemy.

"Nosher, my son, how would you like to earn a few quid for yourself — by sparring with Joe Louis?" Jack Solomons' rasping tones reverberated in my ear as I paused for a breather.

"Come again?" I thought I hadn't heard correctly.

"Joe's over here doing a series of exhibition bouts for the troops. You're the right size and the right weight. I think you'd be ideal."

Two days later I met the big man in Jack's gym, and I honestly don't think I got a wink of sleep in between. But what a gent! Louis was courtesy itself, quietly spoken, with a friendly grin and a Ronald Colman moustache, extending a hand the size of a baseball glove for me to shake. And saying: "Good to meet you, kid. Let's give the boys a show."

The show took us all round the country. We started off at High Wycombe in Buckinghamshire, staying for three days at a pub which had a gym next door, getting to know each other in the ring. Altogether I would spar twelve times a week with the world champ, two US bases a day, all the way from Dorset right up to Scarborough Flow. I didn't know there were that many Yanks in the country.

I have to say that fine gentleman taught me things about the noble art that I didn't know existed. "Get *behind* the jab, kid!" And I'd shift my weight so that my whole body went into my left jab, making it even more telling.

He worked on my left hook. "You've got natural ability. Remember the left hook is a punch worth waiting to land. It *has* to be thrown with precision." The king of the ring shifted and shuffled, demonstrating. "If it misses, you're thrown off balance and you become an immediate target for a counter-punch."

He was impressed with my reach. "That's a long left hand you've got, kid. Make use of it. Stab your opponent's face with a straight left, then follow up with another left, turning your wrist and making the jaw your target. Got it?"

Got it! He showed me how to be in the right place at the right time, making the most of "ring space", and even how to turn a man with a mere touch on his elbow.

Joe was the guv'nor, but he never let any of his "big bombs" go. Oh, except once ... That's when he caught me on the button with a right cross — and, believe me, I felt like I'd been hit by a truck! My knees went, and I was actually going down, but the big feller grabbed me before I sank to my knees. He said urgently: "Move your feet, Nosher! Stamp them, hard!" That's how to make the paralysis go. I obeyed him automatically, stamping on the canvas as if I'd found a nest of scorpions.

And it worked. Slowly my head cleared and life came back into my body. Joe got me moving. "Sorry about that, young Nosher!"

There are times when you know you're out of your league, and this was one of them. But through the sound of bells I managed a smile. "That's all right, Joe."

Well, what else could I say? I was getting a free lesson every day from the best teacher in the world — and on top of that, getting paid for it. Fifteen quid a day. We travelled the country by coach, with a small entourage of hangers-on, and in every camp we visited Joe was given the five-star treatment by five-star generals. But he still had time to chat away on the bus or over a meal, when he wasn't being mobbed. We talked boxing, and other things too, and I learned to respect not only that man's attitude to the game but to life itself.

Someone once remarked that Joe Louis was a credit to his race — adding hastily: "I mean the human race." That same guy, a New York boxing writer named Jimmy Cannon, also said: "Joe's observations were made profoundly witty by his candour. I never knew him to seek the sanctuary of a lie."

Well, I'll drink to that. We would go for long strolls together around the camps, with Joe in a casual wool cardigan that seemed to be his security blanket — he was never without it — talking fights. Once I pressed him to tell me the greatest night of his life.

There was a long pause. Then: "Guess what, Nosher. It wasn't the night I knocked out James Braddock to take the championship. Neither was it the time I destroyed Max Schmeling inside two minutes.

"No, it was when I fought Max Baer in 1935. I KO'd him in the fourth — but on that night I felt I could go on fighting for two days!"

At the time, Joe Louis was in dead hock to the US Internal Revenue Service with over a million dollars owed in back taxes. It was a burden he would take to his grave.

Two years after I spent that momentous month with him, while I was slogging — or slugging — my guts out by the sands of the Nile, Joe Louis retired as undefeated world champion. Three years after that he made the mistake of trying a comeback.

He fought eight times in the first ten months of 1951, and the last of those eight was the one where he was counted out — at the hands of the virtually indestructible Rocky Marciano.

The last time I saw the Brown Bomber was in 1980, a year before his death. I've wished ever since that I hadn't. It was in Las Vegas, at Caesar's Palace, where Joe was the celebrity "meeter and greeter", standing around in the foyer to shake hands with the folks as they arrived to see the show. I went up to him, shook the big paw that was extended automatically in my direction, and said: "Joe! Remember me? It's Nosher."

The eyes remained blank. He stared back as if he hadn't understood a word. He didn't even recognise me. Was this the man I'd once idolised, the world champion I'd sparred one hundred and thirty rounds with, now potless and brain scrambled? I turned away, feeling sick and close to tears. Ask me if this is what being punch-drunk is all about and, sadly, the answer to that is yes.

But back to my youth. Joe Louis went home, and I went back to Covent Garden. I was having a ripe old time, which I suppose is what you do among the fruit and veg, until one day it all came to a grinding halt with a brown envelope through the door and an invitation I couldn't refuse — to serve King and country. In short, I was called up for National Service.

A lot of geezers tried to duck it, some successfully — if they were articled clerks in accountancy or trying for a legal career. Conscientious objectors, the "conchies", were summoned before a board, and asked questions like: "What would you do if a Nazi burst into your kitchen and threatened your mother with a gun? Would you shoot him?"

If they said yes, they were into the front line, which could have been India where there was unrest over the Partition, or the Middle East, equally volatile with Jews and Arabs at each other's throats over Palestine. If they said no, because "I don't believe in violence", they were into the front line anyway, in the Ambulance Brigade. Either way, they couldn't win.

Personally, I wanted to get in and do my bit. The real reason was that I hoped to see a spot of action and a lot of the world, and the Army could provide both — as well as feed, clothe and give me a few quid into the bargain. That seemed like a reasonable deal.

I could have got out of it if I'd exaggerated my slightly mangled hand. Instead I duly reported to the Queen's Regiment Barracks in Canterbury.

The first morning I was out of my bunk at 4.30 a.m., purely through force of habit, because that's the time I'd always started out for the Garden.

The colour sergeant came crashing noisily into the barracks at 6 a.m. expecting to see forty snoring bodies tucked up in their warm beds, only to find Private Nosher showered and dressed and standing smartly to attention, ready for parade.

He stared in disbelief. "Where the bloody hell have you been?" he bellowed. Colour sergeants tend to speak in a loud voice. "Just crept in after a night out, have you?"

"Nowhere, Sarge," I replied. "Honest. I always get up early. I used to work in Covent Garden."

"Oh, did you?" He eyed me shrewdly. "Well, in that case you can go down to the quartermaster's store and get yourself a stripe. From now on it's your job to get these lazy buggers out of bed at six o'clock every morning. It will save me time — and give me a lie-in!"

That made me a lance-corporal on my first day. At this rate I could see myself being full colonel inside a month. Instead I just about made it through six weeks of basic training, arduous ten-mile, full-pack marches, cross-country runs, and a spoonful of malt every morning to keep our bowels open. I was so fit I felt like Popeye, with bulging muscles and an inclination to walk through doors without opening them.

Which is when the Army, in its infinite wisdom, decided I could do more for the Empire in the Royal Army Medical Corps. Okay, I could handle a syringe as well as the next man. But a week later, before I had a chance to practise my first appendix operation, I found myself on a ship bound for Egypt, heading for the desert with no idea what lay ahead. No reason given, and I knew better than to ask questions.

The day before I packed my bags and left home, Dad sat me down in the front room and gave me some words of advice.

"Don't do no boxing in the Army, boy. They'll fucking *ruin* you," he said.

## 7: FOR KING AND COUNTRY

I ignored Dad's words of wisdom from the outset. You've got to remember I'd been in one of the best clubs in Britain, and sparring with some of the top lights, welters and middles that this country could produce. So Nosher fancied himself a bit.

Meantime, more serious matters were at hand. The year was 1947. Word went round the barracks that we were to be sent overseas to the Middle East, which had erupted in violence with the post-war partition of Palestine from Israel. Our lot were in the middle trying to keep order, but Jewish terror groups like the Stern Gang and the Irgun mob, led by Menachem Begin — "top of the most wanted list" — were causing us all sorts of grief.

Eight of our boys had been killed in one day in a wave of bombings and shootings in Jerusalem. British families were being evacuated. Two British sergeants who had been kidnapped in Haifa were found hanging from a eucalyptus tree with a note pinned to their shirts saying they had been executed as spies.

The word became fact. Into this hotbed of conflict we sailed from Liverpool, two hundred likely lads bound first for Egypt, then wherever the top brass decided. Ours not to reason why.

The vessel was the SS *Orduna*, an old cruise liner which the MoD had salvaged from somewhere and converted into a troop ship. The crew wound us youngsters up something rotten as we came up the gangplank, spinning us yarns about how she'd "turned turtle, with the funnels under the water", referring to her as the *Mary Celeste*, and generally frightening the life out of us.

At least we were heading for the sun, leaving behind one of the worst winters on record. That year, 1947, recorded "non-stop blizzards and a serious fuel shortage combining to bring Britain to its economic knees". Over four million workers were made idle by power-cuts, thousands of homes throughout the country were without heat or light, and even Buckingham Palace was candle-lit.

In that kind of weather, it was no wonder everybody on board was seasick. All bar one, that is — yours truly, who else? Battling down to the Bay of Biscay, the poor old *Orduna* was plunging from peak to trough on the high seas like a yo-yo.

When it came to grub on the first day, long tables had been laid out in the main saloon below deck, with a huge tureen of soup for starters and roast beef piled a foot high on a big dish to follow, waiting for us to queue up and help ourselves.

But the dining room was empty, and stayed empty! Only Nosher arrived, and nothing would ever spoil his appetite. So there was just me sitting there aboard my personal *Mary Celeste*, never one to look a gift horse in the mouth, chomping away while the rest were spewing their guts up in the bogs below decks. Well, I had to live up to my name, didn't I?

"Anyone for greasy pork chops?" I would call out heartily to any soul putting a tentative foot through the lurching doorway. That usually put paid to any company, and I was left alone to enjoy my meal in peace.

It was like that all the way to Gibraltar. As the Rock came into sight out of the mist I spotted a giant tanker going the other way. It was behaving like a submarine, wallowing around with more of the hull under the water than over it, the sea was that rough. No wonder the other poor guys felt green.

In Gibraltar I got my first taste of what it was like to be in trouble in the Army. A corporal from the King's African Rifles came aboard to join us for the rest of the trip to Suez, a tough-looking bastard with mean eyes and an attitude to match. He was as tall as me, and as hard-faced as Steven Seagal on a bad day.

The whisper went round that he had been broken down from sergeant-major — for brutality. *Brutality?* Shit! Worse, he was put in charge of my deck.

"Trust us to get Corporal Punishment," I muttered, half in jest, to one of my mates. But he did his best to fit the bill, and from then on the name stuck.

Our first meeting was not encouraging. CP cornered me on deck, gripped me by the shoulders, and peered into my face. "You," he said loudly, from a few inches away. "You're supposed to be at cookhouse duties. What are you doing up here?"

My one stripe didn't stand up against his two. "Sorry, sir." I resisted the temptation to nut him and end up in the brig, but it was a close call. I swallowed my temper, just. "I didn't realise —"

But being the typical bully, he had to go all the way. He put me on a fizzer, which meant being hauled up before the commanding officer to explain, eyeball to eyeball, why I hadn't reported for duty. In this case it was making a mountain out of a fucking molehill, but I had to go through the charade. They removed my belt, presumably in case I tried to top myself, and marched me into the officers' quarters. The Colonel sat behind his desk, a Blimp-like figure with a small moustache who wanted to get the whole thing over as quickly as I did.

I snapped a smart salute, hoping my trousers wouldn't descend to my ankles.

"Yes? What's the charge?"

"Well, sir, if —"

"No ifs, no buts. Are you guilty or not? I'm not looking for extenuating circumstances. How do you plead?"

Behind me Corporal Punishment hissed: "Keep quiet!"

So I kept quiet. And I was given twenty-eight days in the brig anyway. Gritting my teeth, I took up residence below the water-line.

The brig consisted of four small cells in the bowels of the ship. Mine was dark and dank and smelt of urine. But light was at hand. I've always said that wherever I go on this planet, someone is going to recognise me. Why should I think that being flung into a tiny cell in the bowels of a creaking old troop ship on the way to Egypt should be any different?

Sure enough, it was a military policeman. Roughest of the rough, toughest of the tough. Those uniforms may look smart, but the red band round the cap is a giveaway — red for danger, okay? So, sailor, beware. Above all, don't take the piss, or they'll have you.

But this time a voice said: "Hello, Nosher. What are you doing here?" It was Dick, an old mate and fellow porter, last seen toting bags of the green stuff around Covent Garden. "Sorry about this, Nosh. It's too bad!"

I said: "Dick, for Gawd's sake! Listen, don't lock the cell door. Give me a chance to get out if the fucking boat sinks!"

Dick was sympathetic. But he said: "Can't do that, Nosh. But she's not going to sink. Just keep your head down, and stay quiet."

The next couple of days added up to one of the worst fucking experiences of my life. Locked away in semi-darkness in that tiny damp cell in the bottom of the ship, I felt like one of those galley slaves in *Ben Hur.* None of the other cells was occupied, so it was like being in solitary.

We were so far down in the bilge I kept looking around for the rats, which at least would give me someone to talk to. But I never saw any, and somehow I managed to keep my nerve.

After two days that seemed like two months, the sound of the engines changed. I couldn't see anything out of the grimy porthole, but it turned out we were pulling in to Malta, and the big naval harbour at Valletta. This was where the ships copped it during the war and earned the island its George Cross for valour. I could hear the lads whooping it up as they went off for shore leave, and I sank back on my bunk, put my head in my hands, and thought: What the fuck have I done to deserve this?

We set sail next day. Then word came down that the CO wanted to see me. By that time, I'd had it up to my armpits. Despite the strong stomach I've boasted about, I had finally given way to nature and been violently seasick. Not just once but for hours on end. The stench of the bilges and the rocking of the ship combined to make Nosher's stomach finally mutiny.

The light was too poor to read by, so I spent hours lying on my bunk inventing word games in my head. To this day, I'm a wow at Scrabble and brain-teasers!

Suddenly I heard a rattle of keys, and the figure of my mate the MP loomed large. "This way, son," said Dick. "The CO wants you. Look smart!"

What now? I made myself as presentable as I could, seeing there were no mirrors around, and clattered upstairs after my escort. As I was waved through, the Colonel rose and eyed me as if a bad smell had come into the room, which it probably had.

I snapped a crisp salute. "Sah!"

"All right, Powell, relax." He looked up at me, weighing his words. "I've been hearing about you. They tell me you're a bit of a boxer."

I remembered my dad's advice. "No — *sah!*" Then I thought: Wait a minute! He must have heard something. "Well, that is ... I've done a bit — "

"So I gather. Well ... It happens that we have the heavyweight champion of the Palestine police force on board. Chap called Ahmed. He joined us at Malta. We're planning a boxing tournament to relieve the monotony before we get to Port Said." Port Said was four days away. "So," he added, almost as an afterthought, "you're going to box him."

I replied with all the zeal that has made the British a true fighting nation. "*Oh, no, I'm not!*" Those were my actual words, I promise you.

"Oh, yes, you are!"

The last time I'd heard that kind of dialogue was in pantomime. "But, sir," I said desperately, "this guy must be much heavier than me. He has to be in training and in tip-top condition. How on earth can I fight him when I'm stuck in a cell all day with no decent food and no exercise?"

The Colonel sat down again, and considered this for a moment. He tugged thoughtfully at his moustache. Then, reluctantly: "You have a point. I'll tell you what we'll do. If you box this man, I'll release you from your cell, as of this minute.

"Moreover, if you give a good account of yourself you will walk ashore at Port Said a free man. All charges dropped. Not a blemish on your record."

He had me. That's what they call an offer you can't refuse, because I still had twenty-six days to serve. The wily old bastard was holding a gun to my head, and all I could do was smile down the barrel.

"You've got a deal," I said. "Sir!"

"One more thing," said the Colonel. "This Ahmed chappie — I hear he takes his boxing rather seriously. Everything with him is, er, personal. If you see what I mean."

I saw what he meant. But I took my gear back to its rightful place beside my bunk, a free man for the moment, and started back into training. Mostly it was shadow-boxing on deck, breathing in good fresh sea air, keeping myself to myself.

Then I caught sight of the heavyweight champion of the Palestine police force, and I nearly shit myself.

He was fifteen stone four, as we found out later at the weigh-in, and all of it looked like muscle. Me, I was twelve nine. Ahmed had curly black hair, a permanent five o'clock shadow, and a scowl and a growl to match.

He was aged around thirty-five, in peak condition, and I watched him limbering up on the for'ard deck, heaving iron weights around as if they were ping-pong balls. His savage grunts reminded me of a camel in labour, and it was obvious he was working up a pathological dislike for me.

*Christ, what am I in for?*

# 8: RING CRAFT

I found out what I was in for the evening before we docked at Port Said. They had a ring laid out ready on the big deck astern, the sea was calm, the sun was setting and there was a nice breeze to keep us cool. Any other time it would have been idyllic. But I had a gorilla about to clamber into the opposite corner, bent on tearing me to shreds, and it wasn't a moment to admire the scenery. First there would be a couple of warm-up preliminaries, then the heavy guns would be wheeled out. Ahmed versus Nosher.

In the fight game, I've always said you need to be scared, just a little. You wouldn't be human if you didn't sweat before a match, however hard you try to disguise it — especially from your opponent. In fact, a little fear helps get the adrenalin up and pumping.

In all, I would eventually have seventy-eight fights, and get beaten nine times — though never KO'd. But on this night, with the stars coming out overhead and the decks packed, it was my first big contest and the one I'd never forget.

I had an old towelling robe round my shoulders, nothing fancy, and a natty pair of blue shorts. My boxing boots were size twelve, and the gloves were eight ounces. All of it basic, but good enough for the business at hand.

Everywhere I looked as I emerged on deck, men were hanging over the rails. They'd cheered themselves hoarse at the preliminary bouts. It was almost surreal, setting sun, shimmering gun-metal sea, like something out of a Hollywood musical — except that the only dancing would be going on in a ring sixteen foot square with two guys about to hammer the daylights out of one another.

My turn. There's only one thing for you to do, my son — and that's *move*! Otherwise the big bastard will have you. As the bell went for round one I cheered myself up with a thought: How many useful heavyweights are there in the Palestine police force, anyway? There can't be that many.

Ahmed came out like Guy the Gorilla, only uglier, oozing menace, three stone heavier than me. For a second I felt like David facing Goliath and finding the stone had dropped out of his sling.

The moment of panic passed. I was on the move, and suddenly I knew I was going to be all right. Ahmed was slow, almost cumbersome, and I started prodding the left hand out, just as I'd been taught by Fat Charlie and Joe Louis himself. *Pop! Pop!* And an explosive *POP!* All the time moving away from haymakers that swirled past my ear like windmills. *Pop!* again. And slowly his face began to take on the shade and texture of a lump of raw steak.

It stayed that way into the third round: Ahmed lumbering about, Nosher ducking and weaving.

Suddenly I saw an opening — and it was the moment to unload my famous Fist of Numbness, smack on to his chin. Ahmed stopped absolutely still in his tracks, and I swear he was out on his feet before he began to topple. I managed to wallop him four more times before he hit the deck.

I'll give him this — he had the guts to try to get up, which was when the referee stepped in to stop it.

As my hand went up you'd think I'd won the championship of the world. A cheer rose that rattled the funnels, and for the first time I knew what it felt like to be a sporting hero. The whole boat was behind me — minus one, of course. Corporal Punishment scowled briefly, and disappeared below decks. I happened to glance up, and caught the eye of Colonel Blimp watching from the officers' deck. He gave me a brief nod before turning on his heel, but it was enough.

Years later, I found myself at a boxing dinner at the Royal Lancaster Hotel in London. As I got into the lift, a voice said: "Hello, Nosh!" There was Frankie Vaughan in his black tie and penguin suit, grinning at me. "It's been a long time!"

Now I knew Frankie had been a bit useful in the ring himself, fighting welter for the Enniskillen Fusiliers in Ireland before settling for a song and dance to earn a crust. I still say his rendering of 'Green Door' has never been bettered. But I'd never actually had the pleasure.

He saw my face, and chuckled. "You don't know this," he said, "but I was on the old *Orduna* when you took that big ape to pieces. I won a nice few quid on you, bet my shirt — but I lost my bloody hat. When they stopped it, I threw my hat in the air, and it sailed over the side! I was put on a charge for not having one ..."

It turned out Frankie had been a squaddie on that ship doing his National Service same as me. But it took thirty years for our paths to cross again.

Heat, sun, sand and more sand. The sun blazing down through a haze of dust, searing your eyeballs until they watered. Palm trees towering by the banks of the Suez Canal like spiky sentinels, providing pools of shade for the camels and mules standing patiently nearby.

I'm not rewriting *The Desert Song*. This is Port Said, which the guidebooks will tell you is at the top end of the canal, and was founded in 1859 for its "geographical importance". As far as I'm concerned, it was a shithole full of flies, fleas, and fellers in robes trying to extract filthy lucre from the unwary.

We were there, the two hundred recruits and myself, to do a job. But whatever the job was, no one ever told us and I never did find out. If there was an overall master plan to keep us kicking our heels in the desert, it eluded me — just as it apparently eluded all the other squaddies I met who felt they were wasting two years of their lives staring at sand dunes.

We were stationed just off the canal. I'd made a lot of new mates through that fight on the ship, won some respect, and was looking forward to a few months of getting a nice sun-tan without too much exertion.

"What do you think, lads?" We were bouncing around in the back of an Army six-wheeler taking us from the dock to our new quarters. "Three square meals a day, all found. A bit of guard duty. Keep our heads down and out of trouble. Can't be bad."

"Can't be bad, Nosh!" came the chorus of assent.

The camp was the usual collection of wooden huts, set out in long lines behind a barbed wire perimeter fence to keep the ungodly out and us conscripts in.

But as I unloaded my kit in Hut D, fourth along on the left by the square, I realised my reputation with the gloves had gone ahead of me

like a bush telegraph. A large figure in khaki shirt and shorts loomed up.
The shirt had three stripes on the sleeve.

"Lance Corporal Powell?"

"That's me, Sarge!"

"You're about to see some action, sonny boy. Come with me!"

"Action? Why? Is there a war on?" The joke fell on stony ground.

At the end of the block, another office. Knock on the door. Different
colonel. Same dialogue. "Ah, Powell. Useful with your fists, so we hear?"

"Well, sir —"

"Good. We're putting you up against the Royal Australian Air
Force." Colonel Peters was his name. He consulted a sheet of paper on
his desk. "Lance Corporal Stewart. Heavyweight, so you'll be on last.
We'll give you time off to train."

Hostilities took place a week later at the Royal El Balaam Military
Hospital, which provided some comfort in the knowledge that rapid
mouth-to-mouth was available if anything went wrong. Open air again, in
the warm desert night. I stopped the Aussie in two rounds, and became
the hero of the hour and the camp.

After that they brought blokes in against me like an Aunt Sally stall
at a fairground. They put 'em up, I knocked 'em down. Simple.

Life was good, and all I did was keep fit in the end hut, which had
been turned into a gym, and put on a show for the Colonel with the heavy
bag and the skipping-rope when he poked his nose round the door to see
how his boy was doing.

But one morning it all came to an abrupt end. A new bloke in
sergeant's uniform appeared by my bunk as I was relaxing with a dog-
eared issue of *Razzle*, and thrust a bit of paper at me. "Pack your bag, son.
You're on your way."

I hadn't requested a transfer, but it seemed I was being moved to the
Para Field Ambulance Unit in 61 Camp at Pardess Hannan. In Palestine.
As usual, mine not to reason why. I just went where I was told.

This wasn't such good news. Now I find myself under canvas, in a
camp stuck in a wilderness of scrub and stones, without even a decent
sand dune in sight to relieve the skyline. The tents are set up around a
square of bare hard earth which served as the parade-ground, stamped flat
by scores of boots.

Worse, I'm wasting my time patrolling the perimeter wire, thinking
of my mates back home in Blighty and the new friends I'd left behind in
Suez. There had obviously been a breakdown in communication, and
none of the top brass realised they had a star in their midst.

For our own protection, we weren't allowed to step out of the camp.

Protection from what? Snakes? Nasty rough men with guns? Randy camels? This, I eventually figured out, must be the front line. I kept my eyes open, and my finger on the trigger of my .303 rifle, constantly spooked by shadows in the desert night as I patrolled the wire.

Nothing. No one took a pot shot at me. Not even the local youths high on arrack, out to prove they were John Wayne. Arrack, incidentally, is the local firewater made from molasses that can send you blind in a way your dad never warned you about.

To save myself from going berserk with boredom, I took up serious sport. Jogging clockwise round the camp took fifteen minutes, but under the broiling sun it was a marathon. I was watched by a few incurious camels chewing the cud and occasionally giving vent to a disdainful belch outside the wire as I passed. Back beside my tent, fifty press-ups, with the sweat streaming off my back like Niagara. Then another jog, anti-clockwise to change the view. This time it was the camels' backsides, even less inspiring. What a dump!

During my second week I heard the sound of scuffing feet behind the tents. I peered round the flap. There, all by himself, was a swarthy, muscular fellow about the same build as me, shadow-boxing all on his own. Ducking, weaving, fists flailing at thin air, he'd marked out a primitive ring on the ground with stones. The strange sight reminded me of a monk going through a daily ritual in his private temple. I left him to it. But that evening in the mess hall I approached our sergeant, an Irishman named O'Reilly with whom I was quite pally. "Who's that geezer doing the shadow-boxing, Sarge?" I nodded over to a far table, where the swarthy one was wolfing down a huge plate of stew.

"That, lad? He's our regimental heavyweight. He also happens to be the Palestine Army champion."

First their police, now their army. "Why is he training all by himself? Is he any good?"

"He's good, all right. He can't get himself any sparring partners, that's why."

I took a closer look. "He's got one now. What's in it for me if I mix it with him?"

"You get extra grub for a start. Like he's getting."

"Say no more." Sergeant O'Reilly eyed me with some doubt. He hadn't seen me in the ring, and looks can be deceptive. I never did look like a bruiser, there wasn't a mark on me, and some people in need of a white stick and a tin cup actually suggested I had the appearance of a college professor.

O'Reilly took me over, and made the introductions. The champ's name was Bellamy.

"Okay if I have a go with you tomorrow?"

He nodded happily. He was Welsh, and he was pleased to find a sparring partner. As for me, it got me off guard duty and increased my calorie intake at the same time.

For a week we threw punches at each other in the area behind the tents, wearing sixteen-ounce gloves and without doing too much damage. He left himself open a lot, but I just contented myself with riding his jabs and making him look good.

We were now under the watchful eye of the Army physical training instructor, a hard man named Steve whose job, I learned, was to keep Bellamy in peak condition, along with the rest of the regimental team — seven of them, all the way down to flyweight.

After a week of pussyfooting around, I took the PT instructor to one side. "Sarge," I said quietly, "what would happen if somebody knocked this bloke out?"

Sergeant Steve looked surprised. "Whoever did that would take his place in the team — and get all the benefits that go with it."

Benefits? My ears pricked up. Like what? "Like no guard duties, extra food, special leave to holiday camps in Cyprus, that kind of thing. Oh, and an extra stripe."

Next session I knocked Bellamy out inside a minute.

The instructor looked puzzled. "Where did that one come from?" he asked, as they splashed water on the champ's face to bring him round.

"Lucky punch, Sarge, I guess."

Next day I did it again, this time in thirty seconds.

"Lucky punch, eh?" growled the instructor, as they helped Palestine's finest away and filled in the dent in the ground. "All right, you're in the team — Corporal!"

I was on my way.

# 9: GIVING THEM GYP!

The commanding officer called me in. "Powell?" he said briskly. "Ah, yes. You're that boxer feller, aren't you?"

This was Colonel mark three, I thought, snapping into a smart salute and eyeing the languid figure across the desk. But all from the same mould. Same look as the others. Same uniform. Same dialogue. Same drill. Same sperm bank, probably.

"Sir!"

"Glad to have you on the team. You look in good shape. Must make sure we keep you that way. Meantime, float around the camp and get yourself something to do!"

*Float around the camp!* If this was the new model army, I was happy to be a part of it. No one since the unlovable Corporal Punishment on the ship had shouted an order at me. No one had even raised their voice, though I'd heard an occasional bellow from the parade ground and the sound of marching feet to show that someone knew the drill.

So I floated. I floated to the sergeants' mess, where I volunteered to work behind the bar, serving drinks. During the day I floated all the way to the swimming pool, and sometimes in it. It was Olympic size, located at the far end of the compound. There I became a lifeguard.

Well, I felt I had to do something to justify my time, and it was a healthy open-air life. The pool was hidden from prying eyes by a high fence covered with vines so no one could peer through the gaps or, more important, poke a rifle through.

I sat high up in my lifeguard's seat in my swimming trunks, reading magazines, getting a nice tan, and occasionally taking a dive into the water to cool off. But I also kept in training with the jogging and press-ups, though I couldn't help noticing that Bellamy had gone back to shadow-boxing on his own.

The Army put a few fights my way, and I won them all. I figured it was a bit ironic for me to be with the Medical Corps, seeing that I was causing more injuries than patching them up, but at least I kept the first-aid tent in business. In no time I had become United Services and Imperial Services heavyweight champion, flattening all comers. I was a bit of a celebrity round the camp, and all in all life was a bowl of cherries.

It lasted that way for two months. Until one morning a hard, nut-brown face peered into my tent at six a.m. without so much as an "Excuse me", and a voice bellowed into my ear from about three inches away: "Right, you! *Out!*" And from that moment life became more like a bowl of cherry stones.

"What is it? Where's the fire?"

The face didn't appreciate my witty riposte. "Fuck that! You're going to a holiday camp, sonny Jim. Get your gear packed. Fifteen minutes!"

"Hi-di-hi!" I said. Only quietish.

The holiday camp turned out to be Timsah Lakes, hidden away in the parched brown hills and miles from anywhere. As our lorry bounced over unmade roads and civilisation faded  away into the heat-hazy distance, I took a closer look at the others in the back. And suddenly realised the company I was keeping.

I recognised Lance Corporal Eric McQuade, who would become British middleweight champion, Private Tommy O'Sullivan, later a flyweight champ, Private Jock Porter, who boxed with Bruce Woodcock and Freddie Mills to become Scotland's light-heavyweight golden boy, Sid Band, from Worcester, later an ABA champion, featherweight Jock Noon, one of the best I've known, and a couple of other likely-looking lads I couldn't place.

Christ! This was the A-team, the United Services champions, and it didn't take a crystal ball to tell us we were about to be groomed for something special.

Just as they prepared the gladiators of old for their date with destiny — you've seen *Spartacus*, I imagine? — so they kept us fed, watered and happy. "We who are about to die", and all that ... On second thoughts, forget "happy" ... That's unless there was a masochist in our midst.

The big show was nothing less than a match against the Egyptian Olympic team, to take place in the open-air Moascar Stadium in a month's time, with King Farouk and Queen Farida attending in person. This was the seal of royal approval — but not for Nosher and his pals.

The world's press would be there. Even if the punishment wasn't actually beheading, the local boys knew their lives wouldn't be worth a camel's fart if they lost.

The contest would go all the way from flyweight to heavyweight, and guess who was top of the bill? Corporal Powell, you've got it in one.

And now for the first time in our otherwise carefree young lives we had the countdown to serious training. A Staff Sergeant Gregory of the Royal Physical Training Corps was put in charge of us, and one look at those rock-like, unsmiling features and lantern jaw told me it was no-nonsense time. He probably loved his great-aunt Edith, and kept goldfish, but he had a job to do and he was one tough bastard. But, by God, he made us fucking fit.

We had a hint of the shape of things to come when the lorry drove through the gates of the holiday camp, and pulled up at the furthest end, well away from any of the proper guests.

Staff Sergeant Gregory called a meet in his hut. "Right, you lot," he began, "my job is to lick you into shape. The reputation of the British Army is at stake, and we're not going to let the side down. Are we?"

We shook our heads vigorously. "No, sir. Certainly not ... Leave it to us, Sarge!" And all the rest of it.

Gregory smiled fondly at us. "Good," he said. "Remember, you are the *crème de la crème* — and I'm not having you go sour on me." A sense of humour! "If any single one of you steps out of line, do you know what I'm going to do?"

"No, sir."

"I'm going to sit you round this table, climb on top of it, undo my zip and piss on the lot of you. From a great height. Okay?" Silence to that one. "I said: *okay?*" he repeated, only louder.

"Umm — okay ... sir!" Message received and understood.

From then on, it began.

We were two to a hut. Four huts, plus two more for the instructors. The Army had laid on a full team of minders. First day, six a.m., and the door slammed open. "Right, *outside!*" And in singlets and shorts off we raced, out of the camp and on to the road, with two instructors setting the pace and one in the rear armed with a webbing belt.

Any slackers — and *crack!* A lash across our backsides, and a shout: "Move, you bastards!!" We moved. It was more like a boot camp than a holiday camp — but it worked.

We did five miles before breakfast every morning. What we didn't know was that the guy in front was a cross-country runner — and he could fucking move! The first day, we could hardly stand up after we staggered back to camp. We had a shower, and they allowed us a brief rest before a bell rang for breakfast. And that's when we made up for lost time — shredded wheat, three eggs, bacon, sausages, toast. You name it, we ate it. And washed down by cups of lovely hot, steaming tea. Then, at 11.00 a.m., they weighed us.

Being on the scales meant nothing to me, because as a heavyweight I could soar to any size I wanted. Nobody gave me a limit. I was also aware that if the Egyptians are famous for anything apart from the pyramids, the Sphinx, a few ancient tombs and Cleopatra, it's for their weight-lifters. So I needed a bit of extra padding.

The others had to watch their waistlines. If one was even an ounce over the limit, he was given an extra fifty dip-ups, which in the midday heat was no joke.

In the afternoons, we sparred. The camp had a fully kitted-out gym, which we had to ourselves for two hours every day. More important, there was also a constant flow of soldiers from different outfits passing through the camp to enjoy a few days' leave, and there was always some mug wanting to chance his arm and take us on. We never said no to any of them.

We had no head guards, the gloves were all knobbly with the pads split so that the horsehair came through, and you could feel your knuckles — or the other bloke could, if you played it right. Somehow no one got seriously damaged, though there were a few bloody noses and the occasional bucket of water slung over a bloke to bring him round.

"Another one bites the dust!" And the rest of the team gave a raised thumb as the poor sod was helped back to his hut to have a little lie-down for the rest of the day. But it was all oddly good-humoured, considering that we were building up to the biggest day of our young lives.

Afterwards we'd shower ourselves off, have a big dinner at six, plates heaped high with meat, potatoes and all the veg we could muster, then it was off for a brisk two-mile walk to get it all down before we hit the sack by eight. Knackered! Talk about Spartans! But I never slept so well in my life.

Show time! "All right, you lot. I've done my best with you."

We didn't like Staff Sergeant Gregory much, and would never have voted him the Charm of the Year award. But, by God, we respected him.

That blue-chinned bastard had turned us into Charles Atlases — and if you don't know who *he* was, then you never were a seven-stone weakling getting sand kicked in your face on the beach.

We saw his teeth for the first time, actually bared in a smile. "Good luck, lads! You can do it. We'll give you a special treat afterwards — sheep's eyes! How about that?"

5.00 p.m. The main ferocious heat of the day had gone, but it was still warm as we climbed out of an army bus and took our first look at the scene of combat. The Moascar Stadium was as big as Wembley, and packed so tight that even a bead of sweat wouldn't get through. The Royal Box was about sixty foot long, decked out with baskets of flowers and full of guys in white robes or in khaki uniforms with a lot of medals weighing them down.

We were introduced to the King before being taken to the dressing room below. "Just bow and wait for him to speak first," each of us had been told as we filed up to the rostrum. Farouk was as fat as a pig's bladder, and it would be his extravagant lifestyle that alienated him from his people and finally caused him to quit and make way for a young officer named Abdul Nasser.

But that was in the future, and destined for the history books. Right now he was in his prime, a big oily git with a cheesy grin and a flabby handshake — the kind that makes you count your fingers to make sure they're all there — and eyes that looked just past you, so you never made real contact.

My own quick look round told me that the only woman there seemed to be Queen Farida. All the rest were blokes, including a bunch of our lads from the base, bless 'em, come to cheer us on.

The ring was immediately below the Royal Box, which meant Farouk and his lady got a bird's eye view of the action, whereas from across the arena we must have looked like two fleas hopping about.

First in was the flyweight, our Tommy, who went in like a Spitfire and knocked the Egyptian champ to kingdom come before the referee stepped in and stopped it in the fourth. Same with Jock Noon, likewise a stoppage. And Sid Band. And the rest. Our boys went through the card and left Egypt's finest battered and bewildered, possibly because none of them had been doing five-mile runs for the past month. No one had actually been knocked out, but there was a lot of Middle Eastern pride left on the canvas.

I was number eight on the song sheet, top of the bill, final bout of the evening. There was a slight pause to allow the tension to build, or possibly to let the top brass have a slash.

I'm sitting on the massage table in the visitors' dressing room, getting myself psyched up for the big moment, when the door opens and in walk the seven other members of our team, marching in line like dwarfs without Snow White. Heigh-ho, I think, what's this all about?

They gather round. Jock Porter still has a trickle of blood coming from his nose, which he keeps sniffing back. Eric's eye is swelling up. Otherwise they're in good nick.

"Hello, lads. What can I do for you?"

Tommy O'Sullivan pipes up. "Listen, Nosher. We've beaten those c--ts seven-nil. You're last on. We're just here to wish you luck — and to tell you that if you get beat we're going to kick seven colours of fucking shit out of you! Understand?"

"Oh ... Ah ... Sure, fellers. Thanks for the good wishes."

I think I was more frightened of them than the guy in the far corner. He was a big lug, a weight-lifter topping the scales at more than seventeen stone. But I'd put on enough muscle to touch twelve stone, I was fast on my feet, and when I moved around popping the left he couldn't touch me. After a couple of minutes I saw the opening I wanted. It took one shot from my right, and it was all over. He went down with a crash that shook the ring, clambered groggily to his feet after seven, but the fight was stopped there and then. Technical KO, first round!

The stadium went mad, and I'm not sure we did Anglo–Egyptian relations any favours that night. We queued up to receive our trophies from His Majesty, and this time the smile on Farouk's mug was cheesier than ever. He muttered something I couldn't make out above the din, then turned and left with what struck me as unseemly abruptness. He was not at all happy to see his fighting best humiliated eight–nil, and went off straight away in the convoy.

We were taken back to camp, and all the instructors joined us for a celebration dinner. Staff Sergeant Gregory was there, too, in jocular mood. "Fancy sheep's eyes, anyone?"

Instead, our reward was ... egg, sausage and chips, as much as we could stuff down us. It wasn't the Savoy, but that night it tasted just as sweet.

## 10: FIRST DEFEAT

By now, I'm starting to feel like Superman, Captain Marvel and the Incredible Hulk rolled into one. Unbeatable, that's me. Bring 'em on, I'll knock 'em down.

*Top of the world, Ma!* The blue-eyed boy. The lads treated me with respect, and so did the officers. I was back in floating mode.

As if to confirm this ego trip, the Brigadier General sent for me. Obviously, I'd progressed beyond mere Colonel status, I thought, as I knocked on the door marked "Commanding Officer" and stepped through at the gruff bark, "Come in!"

General Gale looked up from his desk as I saluted, and nodded pleasantly. He was an impressive figure, crackling with energy, with a black patch over one eye that enhanced his buccaneer image. If his spare-time hobby had been plundering the Spanish Main it wouldn't have surprised me. "Sit down, Powell." I sat down.

"Now," he said without preamble, "we are going to have a *fight*!"

"We are, sir?" He wasn't quite my size, and didn't look as if he was about to square up to me. All the same, I didn't like the "we" and I didn't like the emphasis on the word "fight".

It smacked too much of the stories I'd heard about General "Blood and Guts" Patton — "Our blood, his guts" — as the GIs dubbed him. If

General Gale was in my corner, I sensed he'd be staying on the safe side of the ropes.

Unperturbed, he continued, "They have a boxer here in Egypt named Al a-Sayeed. He is their *professional* heavyweight champion. Meaning that he did it for a living.

"And, Powell," the General's one eye fixed me with a steady gaze, "I know that you can beat him."

"But, Sir, I'm an amateur!"

"Not for this one. As from now, you are Leroy Brown from a tanker that's lying out there in Alexandria harbour. I've already booked you to fight this man at the Cairo Sports and Tennis Club on Friday week." General Gale paused to let his next words sink in. "And ... you're getting £30 for the fight.

Well, that settled it. Our take-home pay was 15 shillings a week, and £30 was a small fortune, equivalent to six months for the average squaddie's square-bashing. So for the only time in my life I broke the golden rule of boxing: an amateur and a pro must never be in the ring together.

So on another hot night near the sands of the Nile, Corporal Nosher Powell, alias Leroy Brown, took on the pride of Egypt in the élite surroundings of the Sports and Tennis Club.

I climbed into the ring, waiting for the first voice to shout: "That's Nosher!" But, amazing, not a murmur. And thirty minutes later, Leroy Brown ran out an eight-round points winner, meanest man in the whole dam' town, as the song goes. But I'd kept one thing secret: up to that point I'd never gone beyond three rounds in my life — and, hands up, I was absolutely fucked! My legs were like water, and I could hardly make it back to my stool to hear the verdict.

In the dressing room, General Gale pumped my hand. "Well done, Leroy," he said, his single eye gleaming in triumph. "We did it!"

"Yes, sir," I said. "We did."

It couldn't last, and my comeuppance finally came at the hands of a guy named Andy Gill. I'll never forget that name because he was the only man to beat me in 30 fights I had in Egypt. He was a staff sergeant in the Military Police, and these boys are tough buggers, believe me, as many a drunken soldier has testified when he's woken up in the morning with a hangover and a splitting head from an ungentle baton applied to his cranium.

It took me down a peg, because up to then I didn't think anybody could live with me in the ring.

The truth is, I got cocky. Also, I'd gone a bit soft. Perhaps I hadn't doen as many press-ups as usual, or run the full whack round the fence every day. Familiarity bred contempt, and I paid the price.

For a start, nobody told me that this guy Gill was an ABA man who, in another life, belonged to the Caius Boxing Club back in Blighty. I should have paid due attention when he stepped into the ring and gave me a cold, calculating stare before we went at it.

He was good. That night I saw more stars than were ever in the desert sky as we hammered the living hell out of each other, with the boys cheering their lungs out from all sides. At the end I was still on my feet. But I'd been beaten black and blue, my face was puffed up, and I was no longer looking at Clark Gable when I saw my reflection through swollen eyes in the mirror next morning.

When I heard the verdict it took some time to sink in. What the fuck had happened to me? Where had he come from? I was totally gutted.

Next day I sulked. I'm man enough to admit it. I was rude to everyone, no longer sunny side up, a bear with a very sore head. The CO sent for me, a new officer named Captain Ablanulpe.

"What happened, Powell?"

Without thinking too clearly, I told him. "I got fucking beat, that's what happened." You don't normally speak to your commanding officer like that, but I well and truly had the hump.

He held up a hand. Then pointed — first at my stripes, then at his pips. "Remember these, Nosher!" Point taken. I simmered down. More kindly, he repeated: "What happended?"

"I don't know, sir."

Captain Abbelove was a United Services light-heavyweight champion himself. "Well, I do. I was watching, and I'll tell you why you were beaten. You never trained. You thought your knowledge could get you through. But in the end you just stood there and had to take it. If you had been fit, you would have moved faster."

It was a lesson, and I'd learned it the hard way. I nodded curtly, forced a salute, and strode out. And then, moping on my bunk, I suddenly became mad. My brain went into overdrive. *I'll show them how good Nosher is! I'll get fucking fit!*

From that moment I went back to the drawing-board, and into a new fitness regime like a fanatic. I didn't eat any bread. Instead, I ate all the fruit I could lay my hands on, even climbing the barbed-wire fence on my trot round the compound to sneak into the orange groves and pick the oranges off the trees.

Eventually, they let me out into the forbidden territory beyond the wire, and I was pounding the dirt track alongside the Suez Canal in the early dawn, with only a few braying camels for company. Three miles down the track, turn right into the Sweetwater Canal Road, then run all the way back.

The area was supposed to be a hotbed of Arab terrorist activity, but all that happened was a few scruffy kids called out to me as I plodded past in my singlet and shorts. First, there were insults. Then one day a football they were kicking around came bouncing into my path. I stopped, picked it up and did my party trick, spinning it on my finger! That got them. Next day I took a skipping-rope with me, wound round my shoulder. This time I gave them a demonstration of how to use the rope.

And from that moment I'd made a small army of friends. In the end they were shouting, "Hey, Mr Ginge!" and pleading with me to teach them to skip. Soccer is the world's international calling card, isn't it, where you all speak the same language? I must have been doing something right, because I never got knifed and always made it back to camp in one piece.

Six weeks later I fought Gill again, and by now I was a changed man. My weight, for a start, had dropped from thirteen stone to twelve five, all of it lean, mean and itching for revenge.

The return match took place in a camp at Port Said, and it was a show-stopper. Full house, the gym packed to the rafters. He was fifteen six, which meant that once again I was three stone lighter than the opposition. Now I listened to the captain: *Move! Don't give him a chance to settle for the big punches.*

But I found a fresh problem. They had only put up a small ring. Most people don't realise there are different-sized boxing rings, varying from twelve foot square all the way up to twenty-four feet for the world heavyweight championships. In those days a champion could nominate the size of the ring in which he wanted to defend his title.

If he was a fighter matched against a boxer, he'd ask for a small ring so the other guy couldn't move around too far. If he was a boxer up against a fighter, he'd ask for the biggest fucking ring possible. Mohammad Ali, for instance, always asked for a twenty-four footer.

But, oh dear! When I saw that ring I realised it was the smallest, only twelve tiny feet, with two big blokes making it even smaller and the referee trying to keep out of our way too. I did my best to move around, but the only result was a legacy of burn marks along my back that were there for weeks because I was spinning along the ropes like a dervish trying to get out of the way of his bombs.

After two rounds, Gill was blowing like a beached whale. Now it was my turn, and I stood up to him at last, trading leather, glove for glove. I watched his strength evaporate — that's what happens when your nose is mashed, you're sniffing blood into the back of your throat and suddenly you can't fucking breathe.

Half-way through the third I caught him on the ropes, and whacked him with all my fire-power. I must have put every ounce of the frustration and anger I'd bottled up for so long into that one punch, because he deflated like a pricked balloon and started to slide down the corner post. I was still hitting him when the referee jumped in, grabbed me and hauled me off.

That was it. Fight stopped. Respect earned.

I was king of the jungle again. They even promoted me to acting sergeant.

All too soon my National Service was over. I'd had two great years. The Army invited me to stay on for a commission and I was sorely temped, but I was missing the old country. Before I went, they laid on one last fight for me — and, Christ, they couldn't have picked a tougher one for my farewell to arms.

It started innocently enough, as these things do. "One for the road, Powell," said the CO encouragingly. Another new brass hat on the base — they were going through them like senna pods.

"Who is it this time, sir?"

This time it was the heavyweight champion of the American Pacific Fleet, no less. The aircraft carrier *Valley Forge*, pride of the US Navy, had been diverted through Suez, and was currently moored off Alexandria waiting for the nod to proceed to her next stretch of water, wherever that might be.

The contest actually took place aboard the carrier. The ring had been fixed up on the flight deck with a line of fighter planes at one end and half the American navy, or so it seemed, filling the rest of the space like a scene out of *South Pacific* — even down to the little white hats they all wore with their uniforms. I clambered up the ladder from the tender, to be saluted aboard by the captain himself, a grizzled figure at the head of a line of senior officers waiting to welcome me. It was enough to turn anyone's head.

"Welcome aboard, Sergeant!"

"Why, thank you, Captain." Common courtesies over, exchange of unpleasantries imminent.

"This way." He led me along endless passages and up iron staircases, and I began to feel as if I was inside a skyscraper. Up and up — that ship was a monster. On each floor there was a map on the wall showing the interior design, complete with a little arrow saying: *You are here.*

"Easy to get lost, even when you know your way about," said the captain jovially. "If you go missing, we'll send out the bloodhounds." I couldn't be sure if he was joking or not. He showed me to a cabin to change.

It felt like party time, and I was starting to relax as we finally stepped out on deck into the warm evening air. That's when a torrent of noise from literally thousands of servicemen hit me. A warning bell sounded in my head. This was not a moment to say, "Hello, sailor!" to anyone, or try for a cheap laugh. *You're here to do a job, Nosher. Time for the niceties afterwards.*

The warning bell had been right. Through the crowd, almost disappearing under a flurry of back slaps and cheers, strode a big Italian-looking American sailor, with a grin for his pals and a confident air I didn't altogether like. Big? Close up, as we gave each other the usual eye-balling while the ref exhorted us to play fair, he was huge. I'm a big, strong feller, but I was looking someone bigger and stronger in the face.

Okay, I'll hold my hands up again. He was better than me, too. You can tell these things, mainly when you're sagging on the ropes at a man's mercy, and he holds back from knocking your head off your shoulders. This guy held off two or three times, and I began to wonder if he was in the wrong outfit. The Salvation Army would have taken him on trust that day.

It didn't help the cause that I wasn't fighting one man — I was fighting five thousand and one. The whole mob was rooting for their boy. But I kept my nerve, defending desperately, warding off his attacks as best I could with my trusty left jab — and because he knew I was a goner he started doing a bit of what would become known as the "Muhammad Alis". Dropping his hands. Doing a spot of jitterbug around the ring. Showing off.

Okay, he was a nice guy. But nice guys don't always come first, and that day I proved it. In the fourth round I suddenly glimpsed his chin, and I knew if I could reach it I'd be home in time for dinner. I let go with my choicest right-hander, a punch that went all the way round the flight deck, through the torpedo tube and out again before it connected. And when it did, anyone who got hit with that punch could have got nicked for loitering.

It was a beauty. I saw his face change from confident to blank, then down he went like a falling tree. Somehow he picked himself up at the count of five and got to his feet, how I'll never know. So I clubbed him again with a left hook, then unloaded the big right — and this time he went back through the ropes like a blob of jelly. That's when the ref stopped it.

I must say the Yanks were sporting about it. They didn't like their champ beaten, but after the first stunned silence you wouldn't have known it from the cheers that echoed around the harbour.

And the guy I beat? He was named Tami Moriella. Two years later I saw his name in the papers with a picture of him, flat on his back. He had gone on to fight Joe Louis for the heavyweight championship of the world.

He lost that one, too, though he floored the Brown Bomber early on. But at least I had the satisfaction of actually getting a TKO over a world title contender — and still only twenty-one years old.

Now it was time to hang up my Army boots, and head for home.

# 11: TURNING PRO

I could have gone back to Covent Garden. There was a job waiting for me, and plenty of barrows that needed shifting. Instead, I took the biggest gamble of my life, and turned pro.

I started small. A guy called Joe Jones ran a haulage contractor's in North London, but he was better known as a fight promoter who staged contests at the Prince of Wales baths in Kentish Town. He agreed to be my manager for six months, and I signed a deal to fight every two weeks.

My first foray into the ring under his banner took place at the baths. Joe put me in with a guy named Hugh O'Reilly, a veteran pugilist who hailed from Cork. I knew they made the best Guinness in the world there, but I didn't know they bred prize-fighters too. Hughie had been in with the best — and Joe mentioned he had never been knocked out.

This, for me, became a personal challenge. Four three-minute rounds, no more than a work-out.

Hughie came on like a lovable Irish leprechaun, mischievous grin, nose as flat as a pudding. I peppered him around for a while, left hand, left hand, *jab, jab*.

Joe was in my corner, handling the bucket and towel. "Just keep jabbing."

"Aw, c'mon, Joe," I protested, after the third. "I'm going to knock this geezer out!"

"Don't," he said sharply. "Don't try it. Just keep that left hand all the way."

But I couldn't stand pussyfooting around. Finally I unloaded my big bomber, the right hook, and smacked him flash on the button, just at that point on the jaw where the guidebooks tell you. But Hughie simply stood back with that elfin grin, and actually said: "Good punch, Nosher!"

I couldn't believe it. I'd given him my best shot, and all I had to show for it was a knuckle that was blowing up the size of a football. I couldn't use my right hand for the rest of that last round, and was nursing it like a midwife when the bell went and I headed back to my corner.

Joe was less than sympathetic. "I told you. He's got a jaw like fucking granite. He's famous for it."

Looking back on it now, I felt like that cowboy in *Blazing Saddles* who kicked Iron Balls Cody in the goolies, and hopped around afterwards clutching his toe and yelling in agony. But at least I got the verdict, if only on points.

And I came away with the magnificent sum of five pounds for my first genuine pro fight.

Jack Solomons was the biggest name in the fight game. He had known me from before my National Service, when I did the business with Joe Louis. With my six-month contract about to expire, I requested an interview.

Now the formidable large figure, flamboyant in a bow tie, sat back in its chair in the small office next to the gym off Shaftesbury Avenue, prodded a king-size cigar at me through a cloud of smoke, and said: "If that's what you want, my son, go for it. I'll get you the fights. And I'll back you all the way."

What more could I ask? Mr Solomons was as good as his word, but I had to sweat for it. Just to get me into the swing of things, he entered me into an open heavyweight tournament at Haringey Arena in North London. I had three fights — yes, three — in that one night, scoring two points victories and finishing up with a KO. The first prize was five hundred quid, a small fortune. If I'd stayed with the barrows, it would have taken me three months or more to trouser that much.

The gravy train started to roll. Jack put me into the ring with anyone who would put up a good show, and I saw the inside of every stadium in London and a few outside, too. White City, Streatham Ice Rink, Haringey Arena and the big one — Wembley Stadium.

I tell a lie about Covent Garden. I did occasional shifts for my mates, and also for a bit of extra bread. In a normal day in the market I would personally shift forty tons of produce, sacks of potatoes, carrots, oranges, apples, you name it. I wore an apron and my old working cap — and I tell you, heaving sacks of potatoes all day makes you fucking fit!

One time I entered the London-to-Brighton cart contest, with four-man teams pushing and pulling a costermonger's barrow from Westminster Bridge to the Black Rock. We started at 6 a.m., with the mist still rising from the Thames, four teams from each of the markets — Smithfield, Spitalfields, Billingsgate, Covent Garden — charging through the streets of South London as if our carts were battering rams. The barrows weighed half a ton each, loaded with five bags of potatoes.

Smithfield came in first, in ten hours and forty-five minutes, God knows how. It must be all those sides of beef they were used to toting around. We came second, in eleven hours ten, and I always blame Burgess Hill, which knackered all of us! We took turns to push from the back and pull from the handles. And if I say I was fucked — that's the understatement of the century!

All the time, Jack was building me up, looking for the big one. In return we agreed a deal: I would spar with all the American fighters he brought over, and in return he would find me a spot on the bill. So I got a sparring fee, and money for the contest. "You happy with that, Nosher?"

"Very content, thanks, Jack."

I also put on weight, deliberately. I don't mean muscle, either. If you're hard-man fit like, say, Joe Louis who topped the scales at thirteen nine, and you get whacked with a body punch, it fucking hurts, even for him. So you need protection, natural padding to absorb it. It's called fat! They've learned their lesson today, which is why you see heavyweights of seventeen stone, scaling a minimum of fifteen plus.

But the added weight couldn't save me from the biggest beating I ever took. I don't mean I lost, just got beaten to a pulp. It happened at Wembley, and I forgot all about my golden rule: don't get up just to get knocked down again! I was always a sensible fighter. Like I say, I wanted to look in a mirror after a fight and see Clark Gable smiling back at me.

So I always tried to put them away quick, and take a nice early shower. And I had the punch to do it. My trusty Fist of Numbness, remember? I was never knocked out, meaning hammered senseless, not in all my seventy-eight fights. Okay, I was beaten nine times, but mostly on points.

I did have a spot of bad luck when I came up against Don Scott, the British Empire heavyweight champ, at Streatham. The fight was only two rounds old when he sailed in a left hook to my head. I never used to overdo the bobbing and ducking; a small movement was enough to make them miss — usually. But this time his glove caught me a glancing blow that nicked the tip of my left eyelid, slashing it wide open. You never saw such blood, as if someone had slaughtered a pig. The ref stopped it there and then.

But a couple of times I was stopped — *wallop!* And that's when I prefer to take the count, sitting there on my arse thinking: *Fuck this! I'm not getting up!* It would always happen towards the end of a fight, when I couldn't put the geezer away, I was behind on points and getting hit with the heavy ammunition. You tell yourself: If you do manage to get up, Nosh my son, you're still going to lose, so why take a battering? Let's have an easy night out!

But this night at Wembley something went wrong with my brain cells. Badly wrong. Jack Solomons had put me in for a purse of £300, an absolute fortune in those days, with a guy called Jack Longford. He was one tough mother, that feller, and if I tell you that over eight rounds there were *thirteen* knock-downs, you'll get some idea of the carnage. And we didn't start flattening one another till the fourth, either!

Jack took nine on the deck, I took four. My brother Dinny was in my corner, and his arms became quite tired with flapping the towel to get me off the stool to start the next round.

The scenario went something like this, and I've got a tape of Eamonn Andrews's commentary on BBC Radio to bring the pain flooding back. First I catch him with a left, and down he goes for a count of eight. Now I've gotcha! When you knock a man down, you don't hang around or let him off the hook. I move straight in — and *bam!* Out of nowhere he slugs me on the chin.

When you get hit by a heavyweight, they've got sixteen stone to back it up, and I'm telling you: I don't care who you are, you're going to know it. Just think of Evander Holyfield's face after mixing it with Lennox Lewis if you have any doubts. Well, that night I knew it.

Canvas is rough, because it's supposed to be non-slip with all that water and blood splashing about. It tastes even rougher when you hit it with your face. But I get up at nine, and glare at Jack, temporarily forgetting my manners. "You bastard!" Then I whack him — and down he goes. He gets up, and *bang!*, he's back on the floor. But he's up again, and I go sailing in for the kill, only to walk into a punch that came all the way around Trafalgar Square before it connected. Where did that haymaker come from? Now it's my turn to eat the canvas.

I can hear Eamonn's Irish brogue yelling hoarsely into his mike above the uproar. "He's up ... he's down ... up ... down ...What's going on here?" It was pandemonium, and both of us were black and blue at the end of it.

Somehow the referee saw it my way, and raised my bloodstained glove to prove it. But as Jack and me embraced afterwards I knew it had been a close call. "Let's not do this too often, Jack," I mumbled through swollen lips.

He looked at me through one good eye. The other had puffed up like an egg. "Best idea you've had all night, Nosh," he replied thickly.

That was one night when I was in no hurry to look at myself in the mirror afterwards.

Funny enough, I was so pumped up with adrenalin, despite my battered good looks, that I felt I needed to walk. Dinny and I took the tube from Wembley into town, and found we were walking through Covent Garden. The market, of course, was alive and buzzing. Like the Windmill Theatre, it never closed. There was always something happening somewhere.

Dinny was carrying my training bag, and I could hardly see anyway. But I heard the first shouts as I stepped through the stalls.

"Great fight, Nosh!" ... "Hey, how come you're still walking?" ... "Good on yer, big feller!" They'd heard it on the radio, and Eamonn had made it sound like World War III had started early.

I gave the lads a cheery wave of gratitude, which hurt a bit because I was one walking bruise. But we went on all the way across Waterloo Bridge to the Elephant, which is where I started to stagger a bit as the energy level ebbed away. I felt like Marlon Brando in that last scene from *On the Waterfront*, when he just made it up to the dock.

Back home I lay in a hot bath for an hour. Then I slept like a baby.

Next day I couldn't wait to get back to the gym.

## 12: BUT NO CIGAR

My sparring deal with Jack Solomons meant that I found myself in the ring with the world's best heavyweights, plus a few light-heavies too. Nothing too lethal, you understand, but I had to keep on my toes to avoid getting my brains scrambled, even with a headguard. My job was to keep the big boys honed and razor sharp for their upcoming fight, and meant I traded punches with names that have been written into boxing legend.

And they all taught me something, even if they didn't realise it at the time. So later, when anyone stepped into the ring with me, they weren't just fighting Nosher Powell. They were fighting Sugar Ray Robinson, Archie Moore, Jersey Joe Walcott, Ingmar Johannson, Muhammad Ali, all the way back to Joe Louis ... and the British contingent too, headed by Bruce Woodcock, Joe Bygraves, Freddie Mills, Joe Erskine, and many more. I could even copy Jersey Joe's sudden spin from orthodox stance to southpaw as if it was my own. Talk about plagiarism!

But even sparring you have to be careful. People don't realise that the majority of fighters don't get punch-drunk in the ring, they get it from the gym. For every single round they box in the arena, they've done fifty sparring. If Ali had a fifteen-rounder, you can bet he sparred at least ten rounds a day to prepare for it.

Think about it. Your brain is a very delicate thing, and held in a confined area by fine ligaments. It's allowed to move. But now imagine all the jolting it gets through jumping and skipping, let alone from the punches. Slowly those ligaments lose their tautness, so instead of your brain staying where it should, it's banging around inside your skull. I once had this lesson spelled out by one of the Boxing Board of Control's top doctors. "Even when you're moving your head from side to side quickly to avoid the punches in training, you're stretching those ligaments," he warned.

Joe Louis got invalided that way. Other fighters, too. You see them at boxing dinners all togged up and looking as if they've just stepped out of a tailor's shop window. It's when they start to speak that they give the game away. Voice slurred. Eyes doing their best to look at you, but you wonder what they're seeing.

The one exception is Muhammad Ali. People think he's punch-drunk, but he's not. His brain is still active, and if you sit down with him he'll listen intently, then come out with intelligent replies. It's just that he was hit by something against which he had no defence: parkinsonism, a form of Parkinson's disease, where muscle and speech co-ordination have gone. Sad? It's a tragedy.

Ali always defended his corner when people asked the obvious question: was boxing responsible? The symptoms of parkinsonism include tremor, muscle rigidity and slowness of movement — and he suffers from all three. But he would point out that twenty million people in the US alone suffer from it, and most of them have never been near a boxing ring, let alone inside one. Moreover, plenty of his opponents took more blows to the head than he ever did in twenty-one years of heavyweight professional fights.

In his search for a cure, Ali had even undertaken a course of "blood cleansing" to wash out antibodies from his bloodstream that he believed had come from pesticides. None of it worked.

I'd sparred with the Greatest when he was in his prime, more for movement and speed than to swap blows. Afterwards we'd chat and joke in the dressing room, and wish each other luck for the next fight. When I heard he was in London recently and guest of honour at a boxing night at the Royal Lancaster Hotel, I wasn't going to miss the chance of catching up on old times.

His book was on sale, and I bought a copy and joined the queue round his table to get him to sign it. Finally there was just me left. He looked up, and a light of recognition came into his eyes. But the words, when they came, were barely audible. "Nosh? Is that you?"

"It's me, Al," I said as cheerfully as I could. "Will you sign this for me?" Inside, I was choked to see that wonderful athlete reduced to a shambling hulk. I pushed the book in front of him. His hand shaking, he wrote something in the fly-leaf, the tip of the pen crawling unsteadily over the paper.

"That all right, Nosh?"

It was an illegible scrawl. I put a hand on his shoulder, and squeezed it gently. "That's fine, Al. Just fine."

Afterwards I read a report from the Parkinson's Disease Society which stated:

> *Ali showed all the symptoms of parkinsonism at a recent opening ceremony in Atlanta. When he held the torch in his right hand, his left hand shook. But when he held it in both hands, the shaking stopped. That's what we describe as "resting tremor".*
>
> *His movements were very slow, and although some people criticised him for not smiling much, it may have been his muscles preventing him from doing that.*

Knowing that great guy, I believe he was smiling inside.

At that time they put you into ratings: one-star heavyweight, then two-star, up into three-star. It sounds like the forecourt of a petrol station, but we took it very seriously, and there were big bucks at stake.

When you got a four-star rating you were a ten-round fighter, big league. And I finally made it.

I boxed a draw with Joe Bygraves, then British Empire champion, and made two hundred pounds. Since you could buy a house for five hundred quid, you're talking good money.

Now I was a blue-eyed boy with the Jack Solomons stable. Jack was the biggest promoter in Europe, and he made me a fighter with money burning holes in my pocket. It took me a year of blood and sweat to get up to that four-star level, and the highest I ever made it was to number three in the British ratings. Top was Bruce Woodcock, then came Johnny Williams, then me. But that made me number five in Europe, which can't be bad. So I kept my pride, and my self-respect.

And I always put on a show. I would come dancing down the aisle in my plum-coloured shorts with the cream edging, tailor made for me by Cyril Wright who had a sports shop in the Elephant and Castle, long before today's boxers made their entry like something out of *Hooray for Hollywood*. I was in there first, way ahead of them all. I wore Yankee boots half-way up the calf, made out of kangaroo skin, dyed black and light as a feather. Great for prancing around in and, let's face it, I covered more mileage than most in the ring, if only to get out of the way.

I like to think I was one of the best-dressed fighters in the ring, and it always annoyed me if any blood went over my shorts, even if it came from my opponent. I was also very vain about my hair. It was fine, auburn, and if it was mussed up at the end of a round when I got back to my corner, the first thing I'd say was: "Look after Nosher's hair, fellers!" Talk about a prima donna!

But I started getting the big accolades where it counted — in print. Peter Wilson, the doyen of boxing writers with his handlebar moustache and biting wit, came to watch Archie Moore training to defend his title, with me doing the hopping about and occasional clowning to lighten the atmosphere in the gym. Next day Wilson wrote in the *Daily Mirror*: "Anybody would think it was Nosher Powell who was the champion of the world!" Nice one, that.

While another big noise in the media, the legendary commentator W. Barrington Dalby, a guy with a voice like rich treacle, paid me an even greater compliment in his book *Come In, Barry*.

> *In all the years I have been watching boxing, and despite the many disappointments of recent years when so many prospective swans have turned out to be geese, I have never lost my enthusiasm.*
>
> *Quite suddenly, up will come someone to pull out all those lovely crisp punches that you thought you would never see again, and you think:* Ah, now this makes it all worthwhile!
>
> *It happened to me quite recently when a big, smiling, red-headed heavyweight named Nosher Powell came into the ring at short notice to oppose a promising youngster with a terrific right hand.*
>
> *Nosher gave his opponent a beautiful boxing lesson. It was a joy to watch the way he moved and blocked and slipped punches, while*

*his opponent got more and more frustrated.
The faster and more furious the right hand
punches were delivered, the more confident
Nosher became in picking them off in mid-air.*

*It was the sort of exhibition by a real
craftsman that restores one's faith in boxing.*

Pardon my blushes. But thanks, Barry — with a tribute like that, you can
come in as often as you want.

Mention of Archie Moore reminds me of the extraordinary sight I
witnessed after one of our workouts. Archie always put on a skull cap
before taking a shower after training. Since he had his hair permed flat, I
assumed he didn't want it to go all frizzy.

But one day we had been going at it hammer and tongs in the ring,
and we were both sweating like pigs. Archie disappeared into the shower,
without his cap. Maybe he was over-tired, maybe it was just a memory
lapse, because when he came out, his hair was snow white!

As Archie went back to his locker to towel himself down, I
muttered to his trainer Harry Wiley: "Look at his hair! What's happened
to it?"

"Nothing," said Harry quietly. "That's its real colour. He just dyes
it, that's all — and no one's supposed to know."

"Know what?"

"That he lies about his age. He always has — ever since he first
became a serious contender for the world title. He's actually five years
older than he says he is."

Now, five years is a long time in the fight game. A very long time.
But Archie Moore got away with it — and with another secret he kept
close to his chest: how he lost weight as a light-heavy to make the scales
at twelve seven. He revealed all to me one evening: "Nosher, I gotta tell
you. Maybe it's sneaky, but when I ate those T-bone steaks, I'd have a
bucket under the table, and after chewing all the nourishment I'd spit out
the leftovers."

It didn't make Archie the best dinner guest you could invite round,
but it worked a treat on his weight and his performance. He simply
starved himself of bulk in the last days before the big fight.

I watched him weigh in at the Solomons gym, and the needle
trembled at twelve seven. But when he climbed in the ring eight hours
later, I'll lay odds he was closer to thirteen seven!

All he had to do was dive round the corner to the nearest steak
house and get a couple of T-bones and a lot of carbohydrates down him.

And presto! The champ was a whole stone heavier, while his poor bloody opponent languished at twelve and a half!

So who was the greatest fighter of all time? I've been asked that question a thousand times, and the answer is always the same: it's like asking how long is a plank of wood. The styles from flyweight to heavyweight are so different, you can never compare them.

But for sheer ferocity of punching power, one man stands out above all others. We called him El Nino. But this El Nino wasn't a warm Pacific current destroying continents. This Nino destroyed opponents.

His name was Nino Valdes. He was a huge Cuban who in his day I swear would have taken out Mike Tyson before the third. In my book he was the most frightening figure I would ever face in the ring.

In February 1957 Jack Solomons flew Valdes over for a match with our own great white hope, Joe Erskine, a guy I'd sparred with so many times that I knew his every move and could virtually read his mind, too.

"Will you spar with this Cuban bloke for me, Nosher?" Solomons was affability itself, and I had no suspicion that he was about to let a maverick loose in the gym.

"Sure, Jack. Usual rates?"

"You've got a deal, son. Hundred quid for a week's work. And I'll put you on the bill with Basil Kew for another two fifty." That was good money, and it would be a good fight. Basil was a former ABA champion, who had recently knocked out Henry Cooper.

"Fine, Jack. Let's have a look at him."

I went into the gym and found two other sparring mates, Ansell Adams and 'Baby' Fenwick Ward, both from Jamaica, standing inside the door with apprehension written all over their shining black faces. They were watching a big guy working out on the speed ball — and when I joined them, what I saw boded no good for all three of us.

Nino Valdes stood six foot four, weighed close to fifteen stone, had shoulders like a barn door and a waist like a middleweight. The ball was a blur on its chain, and the sounds were like the rattle of a machine-gun. "Jesus," said Ansell. "We're going to earn our pay today, man."

"Get ready now, fellers," said Jack. "Nino will be finished with the solo stuff in ten minutes, and wants to spar right away while he's still warm."

Ten minutes later we put our heads round the door. Valdes was getting gloved up with the sparring mitts, and his trainer Pablo was adjusting a headguard. The place had filled up with spectators, many of them boxing writers, all of them keen to see the unknown from an equally little-known island. Our boy Erskine was a popular figure in Britain, and the contest was attracting a lot of pre-fight attention.

The trainer beckoned us over. "Who is first, please?"

Before anyone else could answer, I pointed at Fenwick. "He is!" I wasn't a mug, and I wanted to see the opposition.

Baby climbed into the ring, taking his time. He weighed all of nineteen stone, and was no slouch with the gloves. The bell went *ding* — and a cyclone hit him. Valdes was across the ring like a torpedo, clipped Baby with two sharp left-handers to his face, then a heavy right hand and then a double left hook. But Fenwick was as tough as teak, and although I could see he was shaken, none of us expected what happened next. Nino showed no mercy. He moved in with a barrage of punches that had the big Jamaican on his knees, dazed and waving him away. "No more ... no more!"

They actually dragged Nino away, which was not a sight to inspire the two of us left gawping at the ringside. The writers scribbled in notebooks. Baby was given the cold-sponge treatment, and slouched off, shaking his head.

The trainer again. "Who is next?"

"Ansell!" I yelled.

My one-time buddy glared at me as he climbed up on the ring apron to duck under the ropes. "You cunning bastard!" But he was a good fighter, who had boxed the best in Europe, and could surely take care of himself.

Wrong. He was slugged from pillar to post. How he stayed on his feet for the three scheduled rounds I'll never know, but only his experience and toughness saved him for the final bell. As he clambered painfully out of the ring I heard him say to Pablo: "That's it for me. I ain't gonna be no punch-bag for that ornery son-of-a-bitch." And he was gone, too.

More scribbling from the scribes. I got into the ring, but I headed straight for the Cuban's corner.

"Listen to me," I said urgently. "There's only me left. So you better tell Homicide here to go easy, or he'll wind up with no sparring partner for the rest of the week. *Comprende?*"

The trainer thought a moment, then bent to mutter something in the big Cuban's ear as he sat on his stool. Valdes nodded. The bell went for round one, and we were on.

Well, I never moved so fast in my life. He came at me like a tiger looking for his pound of meat at feeding time, and I backed away ducking and diving, popping my left hand out as if it was on elastic. But Nino kept his big punches under wraps, and when I got whacked — which was more often than I would have liked — there was no real venom in them. For which I was duly grateful.

But just to confirm our relationship, next morning I went bright and early to the market, got hold of a three-foot wooden basket, and filled it with pineapples, oranges, strawberries, bananas and other tasty-looking fruit. Then I wrapped a sheet of cellophane round it, tied a nice blue ribbon in a bow, and took it with me to the gym.

I knocked on the door of Valdes' dressing room. Inside he was sitting on a bench, having his hands taped, and looking distinctly morose.

His English wasn't brilliant, so I spoke slowly and distinctly. "*Buenos dias*, Nino."

He looked up. "*Si?*" His voice, like his expression, deadpan.

I said: "I know you must be homesick, so I've brought you a nice basket of fruit from Cuba." Maybe I should have stuck a cigar in it.

But he was smiling, genuinely touched. "Oh, *muchas gracias*. Thank you, Señor Nosher!"

After that, every time he came at me in the ring I muttered: "Pineapple ... oranges ..." Just to let him know to hold back.

But the last day came, and none of those wiles was going to work. I could have shouted "Fruit salad!" from the rooftops, and it wouldn't save me. Valdes, fed up to the teeth after pussyfooting around for five days, was going to have my guts for garters. The gym was packed, with House Full notices outside. Word had got round that Cuba was exporting more than cigars. Somebody rather special was in our midst, preparing to blitz the daylights out of our boy on Saturday night at Wembley.

Meantime, I still had three rounds to survive. I'm not that stupid and, now I wasn't wanted any more, I knew Nino might just forget the niceties and play rough. I was right. In the first round he started putting together combination punches that I hadn't seen all week, and they were raining into me like a hailstorm.

He hit me so hard I thought my ribs had gone. In the second round, the only thing I could do was hang on, grabbing him in a bear-hug clinch and not letting go until the trainer prised us apart. But I had to get out alive, and I knew that Señor Valdes was going to put me away in the third and make me pay for those five easy days. Round three was one date I didn't intend to keep.

Crunch time in round two was coming up. On the far wall was a huge clock, ticking away the seconds. Every time we went into a clinch I peered over his shoulder, anxiously watching the big hand. It seemed to be moving awfully slowly.

Twenty seconds to go. Now was the time to call up my secret weapon, the Fist of Numbness, to get me home safe and dry. In all those five days I hadn't really thrown it, mainly because I kept it nestling up against my chin for protection. Maybe Nino got careless, or maybe he'd forgotten I had a right hand. Now I unleashed it like a guided missile — smack on his nose! The Cuban staggered back in surprise and pain, blood spurting out in a crimson stream. I thought maybe I'd broken it.

At the same time I yelped like a puppy, waved my hand in the air, and started hopping around the ring. "Yikes! I've broken it! Help me, someone —"

Voices rose from all sides. Nino's trainer was in the ring, tugging at my elbow. He knew his boy wanted revenge. "Hey, *amigo*! You've only got one more round! Hey —"

"Hey, nothing," I moaned, making it as realistic as I could. "Can't you see I've broken my bloody hand?"

It was an Oscar-winning performance, and Valdes knew it. He let out a low animal growl, turned, and lashed out at the corner post, which was held up by double steel wires down to the floor. There was a twang and a crash as the stay snapped — and then the whole ring collapsed!

I caught Jack Solomons eyeing me, and I couldn't help it — I gave him a wink. He mouthed back at me: "Bastard!" But he was smiling. He knew the publicity that little incident would generate, and he was right. Later, in his office as he counted out the money, I said: "One more round, guv'nor, and that would have been me!"

Later still, twenty-four hours to be exact, Nino Valdes demolished Joe Erskine in one round, after which every top heavyweight in the world gave him a wide berth. Eventually he would be beaten, and more than once. But usually because he hadn't trained properly and was nowhere near fit.

In my opinion, the dangerman from Cuba remained the uncrowned heavyweight champion of the world. I'm just glad I walked away intact.

And for the record, I beat Basil Kew. In the third, technical KO. Nino must have wondered how my hand had been so miraculously cured.

But word went round, and he found it hard to get fights, not even a match for the world championship.

I don't know what they had against him, but he went back to Cuba, then found his way to the States. The last I heard of him, he was shining shoes outside Los Angeles railway station.

## 13: THE CLOCKWORK MOUSE

The last fight of my career was against Menzies Johnson, a guy they said was unbeatable. He was a big lump of muscle from Jamaica, who had been brought over to England by John Huston, the film director, with one aim in mind: to win the heavyweight championship of the world.

By now I was thinking seriously about chucking it in before I lost my good looks. I'd reached thirty, and I was looking for one last really good shot before I hung up my gloves. But Jack Solomons sent for me, and asked me to "look after" Menzies. "He's just a kid. Show him the kind of moves that only come with years of experience," he said persuasively.

I fell for it. Every day for two months I put Menzies into the ring at Jack's gym, and gave him a thorough workout. He was a nice enough young guy, big, black, strong and eager. I'd been like that once — well, big, strong and eager anyway. *Come on, kid. Left hand! Left hand! Now parry with your right.* I worked that boy as if I was a choreographer plotting a complicated dance routine, and he followed my instructions like a clockwork mouse.

And you know what? Menzies Johnson knocked out all the

opposition they put into the ring with him. Every man jack of them. Finally John Huston and his cohorts ran out of opponents, even while they were still trying to work a deal on the big one — setting up the world championship.

But they wanted to keep the boy busy, didn't they? It's no good having a prize heavyweight if he's sitting around all day contemplating his navel.

One Saturday lunchtime I'm at home when the phone rings, and it's Jack Solomons on the line.

Jack says: "Would you fight Menzies Johnson for me, Nosher? He's run out of opponents."

"Run out?" Like I say, I was at the tail end of my ring career, but I wanted to light one last sparkler. I thought for a moment. I hadn't seen Menzies for some time.

Yeah, why not? "When?" I asked.

"Tuesday night," Jack said.

This was Saturday, right? It suddenly dawned on me: *This is a stitch-up to get me knocked out.* They were making a lot of money betting on their boy, and they wanted a patsy. I thought some more. I reckoned I could hang in for a few rounds and give the punters a show.

"How much is Menzies getting?"

Jack said: "Two hundred pounds." In 1959 that was a big wad.

I said: "Look, if Menzies is getting two hundred quid for knocking me out, I want a bit more for getting knocked out!"

Jack sighed heavily down the phone, trying to make me feel guilty. "All right, you'll get £225."

"It's a deal."

It was no use me doing any training. All I got in was a couple of long walks before the big night at Earl's Court. Normally in my fights I used to go on last, even if there was more than one heavyweight bout — I'm proud to say that I was the last man ever to step *out* of the ring at Haringey Arena before they closed it for keeps.

They always put me on last because I gave them value for money from the moment I stepped into the spotlight. Those were the days before the flash motor-bikes and somersaults into the ring, so my showing-off was a bit of a novelty. No one would move from their seats until Nosher Powell had been on, I promise you. Nobody ever left early.

By now I had started to clown around a bit, being the ring jester, good for a laugh and a giggle as well as throwing the punches, even talking back to the customers when I was wrapped up in a clinch, egging on the opposition before I put their lights out with my trusty right hook.

Sometimes this could go on a bit late, like after midnight. And now, unknown to me on my last public appearance, Johnson's manager had lodged an official protest on the lines of "I'm not having my fighter going on that late." Seems it would be way past young Johnson's bedtime.

But I get there in plenty of time, as usual, before any of the fights begin. And make myself comfortable with a nice mug of tea, a packet of crisps and a good book.

I know I'm not going on till midnight, and there's three or four hours ahead to get through.

That's when the door opens, and in comes Danny the Whip, the guy who makes sure all the fighters are ready. He's a sparky little feller with a bright-coloured waistcoat and a fob watch, which he uses like a symbol of authority to get us up and out.

"You're on early, Nosh," he announces.

"What!" I'm gob-smacked. "No one told me nothing about that! I've just had a cup of tea."

"You're going on second!"

I said: "Leave off."

"*Second*," he said. "I'm telling you."

"That's fucking nice," I said. But what could I do? I went and had a slash, in hopes, but not a lot happened. I could feel the tea swishing about inside me.

Two minutes later Danny poked his head round the door again. "You're on!" he said. The first fight had been over in one round. Christ! I went and had another slash, with even less luck, then headed out for the ring.

Now Earl's Court was normally packed whenever I fought, always a full house. But as I strode out into the glare for the last time, prancing and dancing — oh, dear! I could see the great arena was only half full, with people still arriving, searching for their seats.

But I swallowed my pride, thought of the pay packet, and climbed into the ring. Menzies Johnson swung up after me, and we did a spot of shadow-boxing in our corners, skipping around while the announcements were made.

I could still feel the tea washing around inside me, and I could probably have heard it too if the place had been quieter, like you hear waves in a sea-shell. I had never been worse prepared for a fight in my life.

But we got started. I put out my right, and over came his left — *pop!* I did it again, and out came the left hand again. *Pop!* I feinted with my left, and up comes his right to block it. Then I sussed it out. We'd been down this road before — every day for two bleeding months! Menzies was responding to everything I threw at him precisely the way I had taught him.

The boy was brainwashed!

So I had him. Barrington Dalby's book again. "If I didn't know better," he wrote, "I'd have said Nosher knew the punches were coming before they were even thrown!"

And Barry was right. I beat that big bugger, the would-be world champ, out of sight. On points, over eight rounds.

Well, I couldn't miss, could I? I even forgot about the tea.

After the referee raised my arm, and I could make myself heard above the cheering, I grabbed the mike. And there and then, from the centre of the ring that had become like a second home to me, I announced my retirement.

"I've had a great innings, and I've met some wonderful people," I told them. My voice was hoarse and a bit choked, so I kept it short. "But now I'm hanging up my gloves. God bless you all!"

They cheered me all the way back to the dressing room, and it was a sound I can still hear to this day. A few well-wishers came and went, after which I sat there alone thinking about my future. It wasn't a bad one to bow out on, that fight. And my innings *had* been great. I'd had seventy-eight fights, lost only nine, and never been knocked out. I was still as pretty as the day I first climbed through the ropes. More important, I had all my marbles, and my brain wasn't scrambled.

Then there was a knock on the door. In walked Jack Isow, and my life took another leap into the unknown.

If you can imagine a Jewish answer to Alfred Hitchcock, with a Polish accent, that was Jack Isow. Short on height, large on waistline.

Who he? you may ask. His parents came from Krakow, where they had run a food chain in the old Polish capital, which is the clue to his success and status in London.

Everyone knew Isow's restaurant in Soho, and the Jack of Clubs in the basement underneath it. Both were located on the corner of Brewer Street and Walker's Court, an alley leading up to Raymond's Revue Bar in the heart of the red-light district. Jack was also a fight fan, and I'd met him at many a tournament.

He plonked himself down on the bench opposite ne, and said without preamble: "So what you doing now, Nosh?"

I said: "I dunno, Jack. You heard — I'm hanging up my gloves. I'll find something." In fact I'd been trying my hand in the film business, nothing special yet, as a stunt man and film extra. But it was casual work, and you never knew where the next job was coming from.

He said: "Want to come and work for me?"

At that time Jack also owned a big chunk of Soho. The Revue Bar for starters, which he rented out to Paul Raymond — who later became a property king in his own right. Jack's game was to rent out clubs to geezers for a year — payment in advance, naturally.

The SP (Starting Price) was always the same. The mugs would go skint after a few weeks, Jack would pocket a year's rent, then lease the premises out to the next cowboy who rode into town. Personally I had never put a foot inside the Jack of Clubs or Isow's restaurant because they were both too pricey.

But now Jack said: "Be my cloakroom man!"

I was stung. "*What!*"

Christ, here I am, top-of-the-world fighter, being offered a job as a cloakroom monkey. I mean, I've got nothing against cloakroom attendants, they're the salt of the earth, I'm sure. But the thought was enough to make me go pink in the face with indignation.

Jack raised both hands. "Calm down, Nosher. Think about it. What I really want is a minder. I'll throw in the cloakroom — any money comes in, you go home with it." Then the clincher: "I'll give you twenty-five pound a week."

"I can earn twice that in Covent Garden," I told him. But then I had a thought. "What hours are you talking?"

Jack said: "Six in the evening until three in the morning. And I want you there in an evening suit."

"For a pony a week?" I told him. "No way."

He said: "Don't argue with me, son. Come Monday, just turn up and work for a week. If you don't like it, you can sling it."

At the end of that first week I had two hundred and sixty pounds in my pocket from the cloakroom, and along with the pony I was close on three hundred quid a week.

So I took the job.

## 14: ENTER THE MINDER

Soho was a glorious decadent square mile with a split personality. Like a scarlet lady who was both duchess and tart, she was everything to all men. And women, too, of course. A village by day, bustling with activity, complete with its own dairy, bakery, fruit-and-veg market, laundry and newsagent's — and something else by night.

My route to Isow's took me through a jumble of narrow streets and back alleys, past shabby open doorways with a tantalising glimpse of threadbare carpets and creaking stairs leading to God-knows-what pleasures on the upper landing.

That, of course, was if you answered the summons from the bottle-blonde leaning casually in the doorway, a lady in fishnet tights and stilettos, eyes ringed with mascara, murmuring: "Fancy a quick one, darlin'?"

Soho! The streets were paved with gold-diggers, along with bums, layabouts, pimps, poets, Bohemians and whores. All human life was there — and I loved the place.

Who could ever guess how that crazy square mile got its name from "So-ho", the huntsmen's cry when they were chasing hares around the open fields to provide the "finest coursing in England" at the time of Charles II? But apparently it did.

You could learn trivia like that from the eccentric "characters" who were proud to call Soho their real home, even while they were falling off the nearest bar stool in the Coach and Horses or the French House to prove it. The literati and glitterati gathered around personalities like Muriel Belcher, the self-styled "Queen of Soho", along with adoring cohorts such as Brendan Behan, Dylan Thomas, Jeffrey Bernard, Daniel Farson and an unknown painter named Francis Bacon.

Muriel owned the Colony Room, an intimate but ultimately tacky watering-hole, painted a sober dark green, where the famous and the notorious would rub shoulders and drink the afternoon away, and where complete strangers who wandered in would be addressed as "Hitler" if she didn't like their face. Today her handbag still hangs over the bar.

Soho was the centre of the thriving British film industry when it had style, and money to burn, though few of the tourists who took a walk up Wardour Street knew of the dozen private cinemas in basements below the buildings showing the new movies to executives and critics.

Other cinemas were less salubrious, with names like the Paradise, Taboo, Cin Cinema, and the Keyhole, with its warning sign displayed in the tiny foyer: "Anyone masturbating in the cinema will be thrown out." How short-sighted, I always thought, striding past on my way to work.

By day, respectable enough, but when Soho became the lady of the night her identity changed like Jekyll and Hyde, although her veneer was outwardly innocent, too.

Kids came "up West" looking for fun, and found it in candle-lit coffee bars which were sprouting like hothouse plants. Espresso was the buzz word, and along the length of Old Compton Street you'd hear Lonnie Donegan's skiffle being belted out in the Two i's — where Tommy Steele was discovered — while the youngsters did weird "hand jive" at the tables, which as often as not would knock the cups flying.

Overseas tourists flocked in too, looking for a spot of depravity and naughtiness, and if they looked hard enough they found it. I'm not just talking about the rip-off porn cinemas, the sex shops or the strip joints like the Gypsy Lee, the Blue City or Carrie's, where you paid twenty quid for a watered-down glass of "champagne", and a hundred quid for an hour with a tired-looking "hostess". Or those notices in the red phone boxes advertising "Miss Whiplash", "Big Chest for Sale" and "Rare Butterfly Needs Mounting", obligatory reading for the out-of-towners to take home as a memory of their day out in our decadent capital.

Vice was rampant, and you could find any fantasy you wanted if you looked hard enough and had the money to match it.

But it was the villainy around it — the "violent subculture" — that

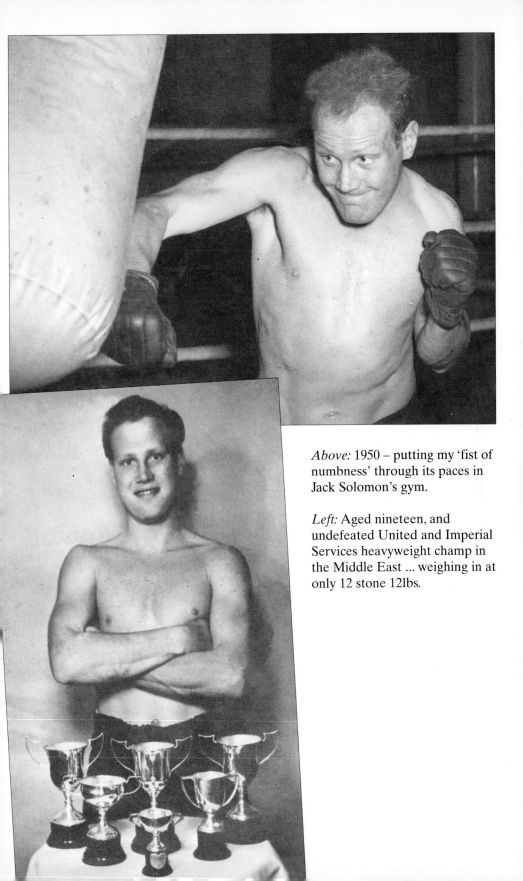

*Above:* 1950 – putting my 'fist of numbness' through its paces in Jack Solomon's gym.

*Left:* Aged nineteen, and undefeated United and Imperial Services heavyweight champ in the Middle East ... weighing in at only 12 stone 12lbs.

*Inset:* On holiday in Jersey. Charles Atlas eat your heart out!

Top American heavyweight Terry O'Connor takes it on the jaw in a bout at the Manor Place Baths, Walworth, where we topped the bill. I walked out a winner after the fight was stopped in the sixth.

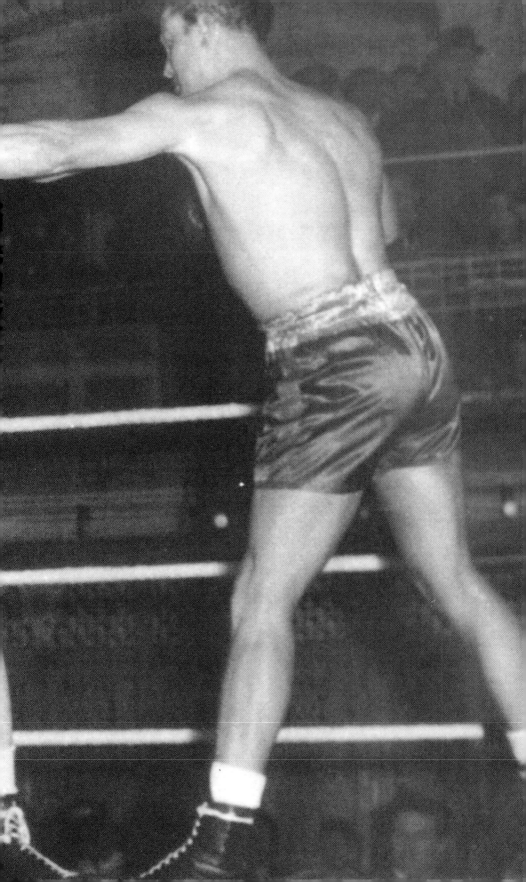

*Top:* Me and son Greg in our well-known horse and trap, pictured in Trafalgar Square. Trindy was a pure bred Hackney gelding, and we were a familiar sight around the streets of London.

*Bottom:* Dinny and I heave crates of fruit and veg at Covent Garden.

*Top:* Dinny and me in a sparring session at Jack Solomon's gym, as I train for another big fight.

*Bottom:* Freddie Mills and me trading punches in a fight scene from *Emergency Call.*

*Top:* What am I doing hanging upside-down above the English Channel? Don't ask! But it's a scene from the riotous comedy *Those Magnificent Men in their Flying Machines*.

*Inset:* I'm the big guy in the centre, back row, with my fellow squaddies starting out on our National Service at Canterbury.

*Top:* Family gathering: Dad, Mum, Pauline and me.

*Bottom:* What's yours? Me and Pauline, mine hosts at the Prince of Wales pub in Wimbledon.

Proud father – with son Greg at the annual Stuntman's Ball, 1998.

was truly frightening, and that's why Jack Isow hired me to watch his back for him. Because I knew the game, you see.

I always trod carefully in clubland. I'd meet the faces every night, either at the Jack of Clubs or when I did the rounds later — in the Astor in Berkeley Square, or the Colony or the Blue Angel.

For some I had respect. Others could crawl back under their stones, and good riddance. Sometimes rival mobs found themselves in the same gaff, and then you could cut the atmosphere with a razor.

For instance, I'd walk into the Astor, and see familiar faces there. Someone would say, "Hello, Nosh," and there'd be introductions — "You know Bill, don'cha?" And it would be a guy I'd chinned three nights before.

I'd say: "'Ello, Bill." And he'd reply in the same monotone: "'Ello, Nosher!" Hating my guts, but because they were with their own godfathers, they'd think twice about starting a ruck. You would certainly never cause a row in front of the Krays or the Nashes or any of the big families. That would be right out of order, and you'd pay dearly for it.

Today everything is much worse. I would like to take the Home Secretary or a local MP round to clubs and pubs and tell them: "Let me see you on the door using your tact and diplomacy, and see how you're going to fucking wind up!"

You have to have a punishment to fit the crime. And I don't mean sending some poor kid to Tenerife for two weeks' holiday because he comes from a maladjusted home, and he hasn't got a very good mum and dad.

That's all bollocks. I mean giving him a hard time in a detention centre so that he won't ever want to stick his nose in there again. And teaching him a bit of respect.

Someone once described a "subtle equation" for successful gangsters: "A delicate balance between fear and respectability, between discreet violence and sound business sense, the elegance of cruelty and the wit to consolidate power."

Me, I put it more simply: if you can scare them shitless, you rule the roost.

I knew all about scaring people because I had grown up with it, not just in the ring but away from the controlled violence of the arena. I developed a gutter instinct for trouble, the kind you don't find in any rule books simply because there *are* no rules except to get in the first punch, and survive.

I knew the villains, and I knew their methods. Ronnie and Reggie Kray had trained alongside me when they were young and making a name for themselves as promising welterweights, long before they started terrifying half of London. Same with Charlie and Eddie Richardson, the Nashes, the Regans and, of course, Frankie Fraser, who came from my manor down in South London. As well as the rest.

At that time a lot of people were running scared in Soho. When I took up my post inside the bulletproof glass doors of Isow's, I was quite pleased to learn you couldn't break them with a brick. Because the "infamous square mile" could get rough, erupting in violence and bloodshed at the drop of a hat or an insult.

Ninety per cent of the vice was, in fact, controlled by Greeks, Maltese and Cypriots, nasty oily yobs who liked to be known as "the Brothers".

Being a lady of the night wasn't a lot of fun, either. Three prostitutes — Russian Dora, Black Rita and Ginger Raye — were all murdered within a year, either by a client or their ponce, we never knew who.

Other gangs took care of other business. Protection and drugs were the two big earners, and when they had a gangland popping it was usually due to those or a squabble over territory.

The territory I had to defend was the carpeted foyer of Isow's restaurant and the Jack of Clubs in the basement below it. Immaculate, though I say it myself, in black tie and dinner jacket, I was the gentleman who discouraged unwanted intruders and unseemly behaviour on the premises. In other words, the club bouncer.

To be honest, I thought I might be embarrassed, particularly at the beginning. What would my mates in showbusiness think? But it worked the other way. Isow's was a magnet to the top celebrities, and any night you'd find a name in there somewhere. Home-grown actors and visiting movie stars were attracted to it like flies to fly-paper, along with entertainers, politicians and sportsmen.

But ... so were the ungodly, I have to say, villains who traditionally liked to rub padded shoulders with the celebs. I knew them all, and if I didn't I could sense a seasoned rogue when I saw one.

So I'd find faces coming through, and see the eyebrows go up in surprise when they found me standing there, larger than life, hands folded below my waistcoat in typical bouncer pose. These guys knew me as a fighter and stunt man, and one thing for sure, whatever Jack said, they weren't going to find me in the cloakroom. I paid a woman a pony a week to do the job for me.

In they came, and from day one the names that signed in on the counter were like a roll call for the *Royal Variety Show* or a cast list for Pinewood, Elstree, Shepperton and Teddington studios in the days when we still had a film industry to be proud of.

Names? Peter O'Toole, Stewart Granger, Jack Hawkins, Orson Welles, Kenneth More, Peter Finch, plus visiting firemen like Kirk Douglas, William Holden and Burt Lancaster, topped with glamour supplied by the likes of Liz Taylor, Brigitte Bardot, Diana Dors and Anita Ekberg. And that's just naming a few. They all walked in, and they all knew me. And if they didn't, I made sure the omission was rectified by the time they left.

Jack, crafty old codger, had a celebrity name engraved on every chair in the restaurant — "My personal friends," he'd say. Sportsmen like Muhammad Ali, "live" entertainers like Bruce Forsyth, Bob Monkhouse and Jimmy Tarbuck, I saw all of them preen with pleasure as the waiter ushered them to their "own" seat. It certainly impressed the rest of the party.

The truth was that Jack kept a lot of extra chairs in the cellar. When some celeb rang to make a booking, he ensured their own seat was ready and waiting at the table. He figured it was good for business, and he was right. Sometimes the celeb would mutter, "Make sure my chair's there" to show off.

If someone turned up unexpectedly, my job was to steer them into the bar for a pre-dinner drink — "on the house, Mr Isow's invitation" — while a couple of waiters frantically scrabbled through the furniture downstairs for the right chair.

Crafty or not, Jack was like a father to me. Each night he'd ask solicitously: "Fancy a salt beef sandwich with cucumber, and a nice cup of coffee, do you, Nosher?"

Yeah, Jack. Just fine. I grew to like salt beef.

But it was the other faces who made their way through those doors, faces more familiar to West End Central Police Station than to Joe Public, where I had to tread carefully. No one in the restaurant wanted a ruck when they were paying big money for a classy night out. And the image of his bouncer rolling around on the carpet locked in combat with the clientele was not one that Jack Isow wanted to encourage. "Take 'em round the corner and do them there, out of sight," were my orders.

Mainly I knew these faces — and, more importantly, they knew me. Like I say, I'd grown up with them, knew their history, and knew their families. I'd been inside most of their homes, and they'd been inside mine.

I'm talking big-time now. Organised crime, protection, and the guys behind the rackets that went with it. London was now divided into gangland territories, with the Regans running the north, the Krays in the north-east, the Nashes in the north-west, and the Brindles and Richardsons in charge south of the river. There were other lesser players, but these were the main men.

My problem was that there could always be a loose cannon in a party when they came in a team, the young Turks out to make an impression with their boss — the impression usually being left on me.

So whenever I could I kept it low-key. If there was trouble, I would invite the offending party to continue the discussion outside, away from the club.

Trouble came the very first night — the shape of things to come. One punter, with a lot of drink inside him and a lot of verbals to go with it, lurched through the door and headed for the Club downstairs. He had to pass me to get there.

"Sorry, sir. Members only."

"Fuck you! I'll join, then."

"Sorry, sir. There's a waiting-list."

He was big, florid and overweight. Most of the overweight was fat rather than muscle. He was also a silly boy, because he took a swing at me.

I kept smiling, because you must always look as if you're enjoying your work. But I caught his arm, twisted it behind his back almost up to his shoulder, and frogmarched him out into the street. Round the corner, just as Mr Isow wanted it, out of sight of the customers. Then my smile disappeared. "Listen, you fat c--t! Try that again and I'll flatten you!"

I said he was a silly boy. He tried it again — so I flattened him. A crisp right hook, no need to move it too far before contact, and next thing he's lying on his back amid the dustbins and cardboard boxes in the alley.

Night night, sleep tight!

I didn't even look back, and he didn't come after me. Round One to Nosher!

In that first month, I chalked up an average of a fight every other night, it was as lively as that. I put them all away, because basically I knew how to punch, and they didn't. As I may have mentioned, once I hit people, they stay hit.

That little area down the alley became Nosher's personal sorting-out spot, his private arena, with bodies rolling into dustbins, and sometimes, if it was bad, with blood and teeth and fillings on the pavement. Nosher's golden rule applied: when you've reached the point of no return, hit 'em first, ask the questions later.

After the first six weeks, things calmed down. So much so that Jack beckoned me into his office for a chat.

"Son," he said. "You've really done the business here. I've been watching you. You've stopped all the fucking ragamuffins coming in and causing trouble. When you belt them, you do it with tact. No slinging right-handers in sight of the restaurant — that way I could get a bad name. I like the way you handle it."

I couldn't see what he was getting at. Now there's a pause while he looks at me for a long moment. Then he's saying: "But ... well ... there's always the possibility of trouble, and you've got enough on your plate. So I'm going to give you some help."

"Help? What sort of help, Jack?"

He says: "I've been on to a top security firm. Every night at ten o'clock they're going to send round a guard with an Alsatian dog to keep you company."

"Well," I tell him doubtfully, "if that's what you want ..."

"You've got enough on your plate," he repeats firmly. "I'm getting you a dog."

Prompt at ten that night in walks this geezer with a white snowdrop helmet and Rin Tin Tin at his heels, the biggest Alsatian I'd ever seen. The dog gives me a nasty look, and growls threateningly.

"Take a seat over there, and make yourself comfortable," I tell the helmet. "And keep your dog on a short chain so we don't frighten any customers we don't need to."

It was a huge beast, and the handler says to me: "Be careful, Mr Powell. Brutus here's a bit vicious."

"I can see that," I tell him. "What I want to know is whose friend he is when the trouble starts!"

Well, we were lucky. For a month there was no trouble. Not an argument. Not a voice or a fist lifted in anger, or even in jest. I raised the order to two salt beef sandwiches, and gave the helmet one, which he shared with Brutus. I didn't think dogs liked salty things, but this one wolfed down anything that came its way.

Over the month, the pair of them just sat in a corner doing fuck-all and getting fat and lazy on my salt-beef sandwiches. Every hour or so the handler would take the dog round the corner for a shit or a piss, then he'd be back again.

Then, one night, it happens.

They came in team-handed — and I'm talking about a very heavy mob indeed. The Regans, from Smithfield. The Regans covered the drinking-clubs in the Clerkenwell area: they were really strong guys and extremely dangerous to tangle with.

Physically, they were big, too — Mickey Regan was an intimidating six foot four and weighed twenty stone, while his brothers weren't much smaller. Three brick shithouses, with a lot of back-up muscle.

On this night they came in, and they were all over the shop. They weren't dressed properly for starters. You had to have a jacket and tie to get into the club, but some of them were in shirtsleeves and not a tie in sight.

I barred their way. "Sorry, fellers," I said. "Not tonight."

"Who you fucking talking to?" asked the first one, a younger Regan brother, with commendable directness.

"Not tonight!" I said, more loudly.

"Where's the guv'nor?"

Jack Isow was not on the premises right then — he was off down the road at another club — but Norman, his son, was there, looking out from his desk behind the window. Even from where I stood, his face looked a bit green.

Mickey led the way, pushing into the office while his team gathered round the desk in a bunch.

I signalled him: *Don't let them in.* But instead, he called out in a somewhat strangulated voice: "It's okay, Nosh, let them downstairs."

Well, it wasn't okay, not by me. To rub it in, as they passed a couple of the flash bastards showed me the finger. That was enough. I marched into the cloakroom, took my hat and coat off the peg and made to walk out — straight into Jack Isow.

He looked baffled. "Where you going, Nosh?"

"Home," I said. "For keeps."

"*What*? Why?"

I gave it to him straight. "If I let anyone in, I put 'em out. If your son lets 'em in, *he* can put 'em out."

"What's the little shit done now?" Jack turned on his unfortunate son, and gave him a tongue-lashing, ending with: "When I'm not here, Nosher's in charge of who comes in, not you. Just you look after the fucking restaurant."

I hung my hat and coat back in the cloakroom, and checked the club downstairs. Everything seemed quiet. But I could smell trouble in the wind, and I was a bit jangly.

The Regan boys had got themselves a big table in the far corner. They were ten-handed I saw, counting them, and going through the booze list like they'd just discovered the keys to the cellar. Bottles of gin, vodka, plus the tonics went down, and they had steak and chips all round to go with it.

They were quite well behaved, I'll give them that. But suddenly one got up and left. He just walked past me out into the street, and disappeared. Then, a few minutes later, two more followed him.

Eventually I put a call down to Pino the manager, who was in charge downstairs. "Here, Pino, has that bill been paid for the party of ten?"

"No, Mr Nosher, it hasn't."

"How much is it?"

"Er ... a hundred and twenty-four pounds."

"How many you got left down there?"

"Seven."

That's when I put the bolt on the door, locked it, and put the key in my pocket. No one was going to break through that bullet-proof double-glass door, either to get in ... or, on this occasion, out.

Up the stairs came another two Regan faces. I said: "Sorry, gents, the bill's got to be paid."

One jerked his thumb downstairs. "They'll look after it."

"Nah," I said. "You will *all* look after it." They stared at me with a nasty glint. After a few seconds of hard eyeballing they turned and went back downstairs, not looking happy. Three minutes later the whole bunch was back, led by twenty-stone Mickey.

He waved a piece of paper in my face. "This fucking bill's a liberty, Nosher. A hundred and twenty-four quid —"

I said: "You've had a lot to eat and drink. It's all on there."

He didn't waste words. "Open the fucking door, Nosher!"

I held my ground. "The bill has not been paid. Pay it, and the door will open."

That's when they started pushing and shoving a bit, always the prelude to a fight. You could see some of the likely lads wanted to throw one, but they weren't quite sure what the outcome would be — even though they were seven-handed against one.

I said loudly: "Keep your fucking hands to yourself!" But it started getting worse, and was moments away from an explosion.

At which point I turned to the white helmet, and shouted: "Fetch that dog over here."

But he just stared and mumbled: "What?"

I repeated it, only more urgently. "Fetch the fucking dog over here."

Snowdrop came half-way across the foyer, and stopped. "Okay," I said to the Regans. "Pay the bill or he'll turn that fucking dog loose."

Maybe it was one vodka too many, but three of them chorused: "All right, turn the fucking dog loose!"

"I will," I said. "And he'll rip your bollocks off."

I turned to the helmet, and bellowed: "*Turn the dog loose!*" Which he did.

And who did Brutus go for? Got it in one. Joe Muggins here!

Well, I done the dog with a right-hander, smack under the jaw.

There's another way to immobilise an animal, and that's to pull its legs apart. But I don't recommend it, especially if he's going for your bollocks. Besides which, it ain't that easy.

One punch did it, and the dog was out cold on the carpet. I had to, or it would have fucking killed me. *Et tu, Brutus*? Then, I had to chin the security guard, because Snowdrop came at me with a bellow of rage for laying out his pet. So there's two of them on the rug, spark out.

I turned to take on the seven of them, fists clenched, all pumped up and ready to kill every one of the bastards. Instead Mickey Regan held up a hand. "Hold it, Nosher! Hold it, fellers. How much was the bill?"

"A hun-hun-hundred and twenty-four quid." I was gasping like a stranded fish.

Mickey counted out a hundred and fifty in oncers, taking his time. He stuck two fivers in my top pocket, and patted my lapel.

"Nosher," he said, "that's the funniest fucking cabaret we've seen this year. Come on, boys!"

I unbolted the door, and watched seven large backs recede in the direction of Piccadilly. Then I went back to try to make my peace with man's best friend and his minder.

I couldn't, of course. They took off that same night. They came in many times afterwards, and always showed me the greatest respect, as I did them.

Thinking of that incident always reminds me of the time I went over to Ireland to work on *The Mackintosh Man*, a thriller with Paul Newman as a government agent sent into a prison to infiltrate a gang of criminals. The director was John Huston, and a cast of Britain's top actors was led by James Mason, Nigel Patrick and Harry Andrews.

Paul, Huston and I sat for hours talking boxing. They were both addicts, and knew their history like nobody's business. We shot the film in Galway — where Huston had an estate and was, in fact, Master of the Galway Blazers. He loved his huntin', shootin' and fishin'.

One scene called for Terry Plummer and me to chase Newman across a bog, along with a third guy who had a Rottweiler he would let loose. It was a trained Rotto misnamed Yogi Bear — it was the fiercest thing on four legs I'd seen since that Hound of the Baskervilles in Isow's.

The cameras were set up to fire across two fields, as Paul's stunt double ran towards them, jumping over stone walls and pounding through the mud. Paul was hiding behind one of these walls, and at the right moment the double would duck down and Paul would come up over it, right into camera with us in hot pursuit.

Huston said: "We'll give you a hundred yards, Paul, then we'll let the dog off the leash." Newman looked a mite apprehensive, but he nodded and said: "Okay."

Cameras roll. The double ran like hell. The Rottweiler galloped along. Then we saw Paul jump up and over the wall — and the handler let the dog off the leash.

Well, I tell you: Paul ran like McDonald Bailey. He went over the second wall where the cameras were with the dog right up his fucking arse!

The handler yelled out: "Yogi! Here, heel!"

But the dog never listened. He was over the wall growling and snarling, and into the camera crew. He went for Paul, he went for John Huston, and they were beating him off with chairs and the clapperboard. I never saw such pandemonium!

In the end the handler hauled Yogi off, and dragged him away in disgrace. Paul Newman flopped into a chair, exhausted, and summed up the proceedings in one pithy sentence. "No fucking more!"

That old chestnut about never working with children or animals also held true for Victor Mature.

Victor was a big guy, but he always used to wear lifts to make him look bigger, and he had an ego to match. He was actually just six foot. But he played Samson, knocked over a temple, and never forgot he was a man of superhuman strength.

The lovely Anita Ekberg, who worked with him on a film, once told me that she always referred to him as "Victor Manure" — and when he found out, he actually laughed.

So the guy had a sense of humour, which was good news when I was hired to flex my own muscles on an epic called *Demetrius and the Gladiators*. I was playing — guess what? Well, I wasn't playing Demetrius. A gladiator again, complete with obligatory toga and sword.

This saga was actually the sequel to *The Robe*, in which Demetrius, a Greek slave, scoops up Christ's robe after the Crucifixion, and keeps it. But then he's sentenced to be one of Caligula's gladiators, a job without much chance of an old-age pension at the end of it. His chief reward is to be tempted by Susan Hayward, a ravishing redhead who was one of Hollywood's great actresses.

In one sequence Demetrius was to go to the mouth of a cave, and call out to a lion inside: "Leo, heel!" Now Leo actually is my birth sign, so my sympathies were somewhat with the lion.

They had got hold of a mangy beast that was supposed to come out of the cave on cue, and walk around Victor before squatting down by the side of him. This lion was so old that they actually made a set of false teeth for it, and fixed a hair ruff round its neck as a mane. I kid you not.

Even so, to Victor this was impossible. You've heard of the Cowardly Lion from the *Wizard of Oz*. Hail the Cowardly Gladiator! Victor was so terrified, I heard him tell the director, Delmer Daves: "No way am I going to let that cat get anywhere near me."

So the special effects boys created a piece of non-reflecting glass to drop down between Victor and the lion. They smeared some colourless meat essence on the lion's side of the glass, and prepared to film it. The director explained to Victor: "The lion is supposed to lick your hand, Vic. So you'll put your hand on the glass, and the lion will lick the meat essence so that it looks like he's licking you. Okay?"

"I suppose so." Victor was dubious.

"Then we'll cut, put a stunt double in your place, take the glass away and shoot it from the back. So we see the lion bounding out and actually licking the double. The next front view of you, we'll have a dummy lion in the foreground, but only some of it showing so no one will suspect."

"That's more like it," said Victor.

Well, it went okay, except that the lion was reluctant to leave its cosy cave and had to be prodded out with a pitchfork.

They tried it once, twice. Then Delmer Daves shook his head. Quietly he said to the stunt co-ordinator, Joe Canutt, son of the legendary Yakima: "We just can't get it like this. It doesn't look right. More important, it doesn't look real."

Joe said: "Leave it to me!" To Victor he said: "We're going to do that shot again, with the glass."

"Okay, kid," said Victor, his confidence now fully regained with two big sequences safely behind him, and not a toothmark to show for it.

Action! But on the take — the glass wasn't there.

Victor walked forward, calling the lion's name in stentorian tones. The lion bounded out, eager for meat essence. Victor felt for the glass — only to touch a large warm nose! And the lion goes sl-uu-rr-pp! right up his arm.

Well, all I can say is that Victor's face turned colour, and so did his toga! Victor Manure, living up to his name. Truly, he had to go and change it.

The upshot was that he demanded all the stunt men should be fired on the spot, because he knew we were all in on it. But next day he relented. He even saw the funny side of it — especially when the director told him that was the shot they would use in the final film.

I was saddened when I heard he died a month before this book was published. Another movie legend I'll never forget.

# 15: THE KRAYS

The name of the game is respect. Lose it in my line of work, and you might as well emigrate. I was brought up to follow this creed: *Do unto others — but do it first!* Meaning that if you've been done and you don't do them back you're finished.

It happened to me once when I got a knife in the back, and I had to settle things before the stitches were even taken out to keep my reputation intact. But that was to come.

Meantime, I had the Krays to handle. Now that may sound like something out of *High Noon*, because the Terrible Twins were at the peak of their power and only someone who was getting ready for the funny farm would dare to stand up to them. But we had a face-down, and I couldn't walk away.

It was a volatile time. The big London gangs were restless, itching for more territory. Their leaders met in private rooms above East End pubs to thrash things out, only to go away with nothing resolved. Some tried to form alliances, but these broke down within weeks. All the public knew about it was when a fresh body appeared on the pavement with its throat slashed open, followed by lurid headlines in the tabloids, then the curtain closed down again.

The Krays had honed the protection racket down to a fine art. If there had been an Open University course, those two would have come away with a master's degree.

It goes back a long way, protection. You can trace it back to the racetracks in the twenties, and probably before that, too. The first recorded racket was a method employed by a shifty Italian mob called the Sabini gang, who hailed from Saffron Hill near the City, an area known as Little Italy.

The king rat, one Darby Sabini, along with his five brothers, would approach the bookies and demand money to keep their pitch safe from trouble. If it was refused, the boys waited till the horses were being paraded around for the start of the first race, then returned — armed with wet sponges!

Why a wet sponge? Answer: they simply erased the chalked odds on the tote boards, leaving the bookies helpless. A decade later the Sabinis were muscled out by another bunch of thugs called the Black brothers, who in turn gave way to Jack "Spot" Comer when Spottie decided to try his hand at nobbling the racetracks. He took over a pitch costing two pounds a day, and charged the bookmakers seven pounds for the privilege of setting up shop.

I saw Spottie in action more than once, and his operation was formidable in its efficiency. His heavies went around below the stand, large men in huge-shouldered overcoats, carrying buckets and shouting, "Cards and slates!" as they approached a pitch.

It didn't mean a lot to anyone apart from the victims, who would drop pound notes into the bucket by way of a white flag, and keep their slates free from vandalism. Okay, we surrender. No trouble. Okay? And when the police, headed by the legendary Detective Superintendent Robert Fabian ("Fabian of the Yard") tried to get them to testify, the reply was always the same: "It's best to be like the three monkeys. See nothing, hear nothing, tell nothing."

Who can blame them? Not me.

The Krays moved in on Soho. Anyone with five shillings to spare, and a list of twenty potential members to back him, could open a "proprietory drinking club", no matter what his criminal record. Ronnie and Reggie seized the moment.

I knew their reputation and, in a curious way, I respected them. This legendary pair, born in the East End in 1933, built up a reputation that they should be avoided while still at school, and carried a climate of fear with them when they went into the Army — most of which time apparently they spent in the guard house. But I could talk their language.

I used to drop by the billiards hall they ran off the Mile End Road, even though I was a South London boy and you had to be careful where you stepped when you were in hostile territory.

But I was no threat to their burgeoning empire, and they knew it. Also, I wasn't one to tell tales out of school. I heard a lot, saw a lot and kept quiet. That way I stayed healthy, and was accepted by all of the big five mobs on both sides of the water. Ronnie even said to me once, over a drink in their club the Double R (for Ron and Reg): "You know, Nosher, you lead a charmed life. There's no one like you. I sometimes wonder how you get away with it!"

The implied threat was plain. I gave him my best smile. "By keeping my nose clean and my mouth shut, Ron. You know that."

He thought about it for a long moment. Then the pale face — someone once described it as the colour and texture of foam rubber — broke into a small smile. "Yeah, right." That was all, but it was enough.

But not now. This was Friday night, one o'clock in the morning, late, and the Twins had walked into Isow's with their usual swagger, as if they owned the place. I could tell at once they were the worse for wear — if not pissed, then both well over.

First off, they were rumpled and creased, and their hair, normally slicked back, was all over the place like an oil spill. Their complexions had the bleached pallor of too many nights in smoky clubs and pool halls, and it crossed my mind that they could have come straight from sorting out a spot of bother in one of their gaffs, except there was no sign of blood.

By now the boys were making a killing — excuse the expression — with Esmeralda's Barn in Knightsbridge, which was attracting the same kind of high-spending clientele as Isow's, and never any problem with the bills.

They were tieless, which didn't matter because, like most clubs with a dress code, I had a stock of ties hanging in the cloakroom, along with a few jackets, for any punter who came in without one. But with the Twins it was unusual. Ron and Reg were both sharp dressers, priding themselves on their appearance, usually in charcoal suits, white shirts and thin-knotted ties.

Normally they would have been the kind of customers Jack Isow liked in the club. That's if they'd had any other name but Kray. They stood in the middle of the foyer. Jack was up in his office. With more than usual reluctance, I knew I had to put the block on them. At least there was no muscle in sight — which was also unusual: they normally had a couple of minders around.

I said: "Sorry, fellers, but with respect — not tonight."

"You what?" they chorused.

"Not tonight, boys —"

"You fucker —"

That kind of language did not bode well for my health. I could have taken them there and then, because for starters I was fit and sober, and I also happened to be at least four stone heavier. But for once that was not a good idea.

Ron prodded me in the chest. "You know who we are, don't you?"

"Course I do, Ron. But do me a favour. I know all about you, and I know your family. Go home and sleep it off."

They started effing and blinding. But I stood my ground, staring them down. And in the end they walked.

Jack was sitting at his desk, his mouth open. "Christ," he said. "Do you know who that was? Fuck me!"

"No, Jack," I said. "If anyone gets fucked, it's going to be me."

Sure enough, next night in walks big brother Charlie. He was always the businessman, Charlie Kray, a smooth operator with a persuasive line in chat. This time he didn't mince his words. "Hello, Nosher. What the fuck happened last night?"

Word had got back. The actual words, it transpired were: "That c--t Nosher wouldn't let us in. What are we going to do about it?" Ominous.

I said: "Charlie, they was all over the shop. I had to show them the door. I don't have to tell you this, because you know I treat you with respect. Just as I want to be treated the same. But suppose you paid me a good wage to look after a top club, and you tell me that you only want people in who are properly dressed and sober — then I let someone in drunk and not properly dressed. What would you do? I'll tell you what — you'd cut my fucking throat! I'm only looking after what my boss pays me for."

Charlie looked at me for a long, thoughtful moment. Then he nodded. All he said was: "Good enough, Nosh. See yer. Goodnight." And he walked out. There was no comeback.

Respect, that's what it's all about.

I saw Reggie and Ronnie many times after that. Maybe I can count myself lucky, but I never had any more arguments with the Krays. I always like to say I've led nine lives, and I reckon that was one of them.

Something else had already happened between me and the Twins, which maybe showed them I'd got enough bottle not to back down.

I was twenty-one, fresh out of the Army, fit, tanned and just about to turn professional in the ring. One of my pals was called the Umbrella King — Joey Carver, who had stalls all over London selling umbrellas.

All the rejects, he'd sell them off for three bob each.

One day I was walking down East Street market, and saw him standing by a stall, looking as miserable as a cat that's just lost the canary.

"What's the matter, Joey?"

"I got fucked for four hundred quid." Now that was a lot of money.

"Who did it?"

"I gave these two guys a load of umbrellas, and they never paid me."

I said: "Well, fucking go and get it!"

He shifted his feet. "Nah. I don't have the time."

Like a prat, I stood it. "I'll go for you. Where are they?"

"The firm over at Vallance Road."

That meant the Krays. I said: "Lend me the van and I'll go and get it."

He looked at me as if I was mad. "You mean it?"

"Sure I do."

I took the van to Vallance Road, and found the place under the arches. These were early days in the life and murderous times of the Krays, and the Twins meant nothing to me then. I knew they were into things, but nothing to get the shits over, I mean.

I'd known them from my teens as a pair of young tearaways, and now they were moving up the scale, doing the long firm scam, selling goods for half-price, shutting the business down, walking away with a heap in readies.

The way it worked was this. From their warehouse under the arches, they'd put an order in to a leading manufacturer of, say, washing powder. Five hundred pounds' worth, paid straight up front. They'd sell the cartons cheap, for four hundred quid. Next came another order, this time for a thousand quid, which they'd pay on the nose, and sell for eight hundred. They were losing, but not a lot.

Then came the sting. They would put in an order for twenty grand's worth. They'd sell it for eighteen — and be gone, without paying the last bill. Vanish into thin air. That's how the Krays started, and the Richardsons too. They were all at it.

If any geezer was sent round from head office before time to investigate, he'd come away with shit in his pants, frightened out of his fucking life.

Knowing all this, I'd still committed myself. So I had to go through with it. I pulled up the van and jumped out, just as a little geezer I knew from the ring walked out, a flyweight named Nobby Clark I'd met in the gym.

His eyes widened. "Hello, Nosh! What you doing here? Thought you was fighting a war somewhere."

"I was, Nobby. But I'm back. And it's a bit embarrassing," I said. "I've got a partner in the umbrella business, and he tells me you owe him for four hundred umbrellas. I know your mob. You wouldn't knock me."

He shook his head vigorously. "Course we wouldn't, Nosh."

I said: "Well, I've come for the wages."

That's when the Twins walked in. Smooth, young, dangerous. "Hello," said Reggie. He addressed my little friend, who had started counting out the readies in fivers from a drawer. "What's he doing here?"

"I've come for the wages," I said.

"Oh, have you?"

There was the kind of silence you get in church, like a blanket settling over everything. Nobby stopped counting. We all stood very still, faces impassive.

At last I said: "That's what I'm here for. It's the umbrellas. You owe him."

The Twins looked at one another, and a kind of hidden message flashed between them. Maybe it was my size. Maybe it was my tan. But Ron gave the little guy a brief nod, and the counting started again.

The Krays stood watching him. At the end I stuffed the cash into a carrier bag, said: "Well, fellers, it's been nice doing business with you. Bye-bye!" And I was gone.

Back at the stall, Joey couldn't believe it. "You faced them down?"

"It's okay," I said. "But you owe me fifty quid commission. Otherwise you wouldn't have got fuck-all."

He paid it. Happily.

## 16: PARP! EXCUSE ME!

But we had our laughs. You could never call life at Isow's dull. Take the unfortunate episode with Orson Welles.

He was a regular. "Awesome" Welles was enormous in size and stature, with a presence to match that was like an aura you could reach out and touch. The night he had the big ruck with Jack Isow started off innocently enough for me, with no hint of the drama ahead.

Jack had called me into his office. "I want you in early tomorrow, Nosher. We've got a big night coming up."

"Boss," I said, "I get in at six. How early is early?"

"Listen," he said, "I've got a birthday party for a very important customer. He's in the road-haulage business, he's a big spender, and it's his granddaughter's birthday. It's a family affair."

"So?" I registered a blank.

"So I'd feel better if you was here taking care of the door. Besides, you know him anyway."

I did. The geezer was a half-bred pikey, part-gypsy, and he'd built his business up more by foul means than fair. "All right," I said reluctantly. "What time do you want me?"

"Five o'clock?"

"Fuck me, guv'nor —"

"Look," Jack said, "I'll make it worth your fucking while!" That's the way we used to talk, guv'nor and employee. Full of mutual respect and witty repartee. Actually, I loved the guy.

I thought for a moment. Why not? Nobody ever gets in before six, and a few more quid wouldn't go amiss. "All right," I said. "Five o'clock it is."

"Good boy, Nosh!"

Five o'clock next night I'm there, busying myself around reception, going through the guest list. A few minutes after five, in walks Orson Welles, a gigantic figure in a voluminous vicuna overcoat and Anthony Eden hat. It was the same outfit he'd worn in *The Third Man* fifteen years previously, and which he'd stuck to ever since.

"Good evening, Nosher," he says, in a voice that rumbled up from the grave. "How are you tonight?"

"Evening, Mr Welles. May I take your coat? Er — are you on the list?"

"What list?"

"For the party —" I realised I was digging myself into a hole, and stopped short. A road-haulage contractor and Orson Welles somehow didn't quite go together. "Have you made a reservation, Mr Welles?"

"Of course not."

Without further ado he marched off through the bar, and all the way down to the far end of the restaurant, where he plumped himself down in the chair with Muhammad Ali's name on it. No one had had time to search out his own seat, but Orson didn't seem to notice.

He ordered potato soup, with boiled chicken and split peas to follow. Half a dozen waiters, who were there to officiate at the birthday party, stood around the room in total silence, waiting for the jollities to begin. No one else had arrived yet.

Now the one thing potato soup does is to make you fart. Orson was wolfing his food down as if the place was on fire. He dispensed with a knife and fork, tearing into the chicken with both hands just like those films you've seen of Henry VIII, or the Vikings, where they throw the bones all over the place. At least he used a side bowl.

After a few minutes — oh dear. *Paarp!* An enormous thunder-clap broke the silence. No one said anything. The waiters tried to keep their faces straight. Moments later, Orson was in full flow, this time raising himself slightly from Muhammad Ali's chair to give vent to the full sonic effect.

*Br-room!* It was a symphony concert. But by now the aroma was starting to get a bit manky.

Now people were starting to drift in for the party, clustering in groups at the bar. One or two put their noses in through the door, but the moment they did so they'd go, "Christ! Ugh!" and make a fast retreat back to the bar.

Miguel, the head waiter, decided to take drastic action. A big mobile fan on wheels stood by one wall. He sidled up to it, managed to turn it round without drawing Orson's attention, and switched it on so that the odours would be blown back to source, so to speak.

Well, it worked — but only partially. Early customers were arriving, and reacted with similar disgust. They took one breath, paled visibly, and hastened off to join the birthday party behind the safety glass, even though they weren't invited.

One of them came back to reception, and asked testily: "Good God, Nosher, what's that smell in there?" I could only reply that I had no idea, but would do my best to find out. But soon the bar area was seething, while the restaurant was a desert of aching emptiness.

Meantime, Orson munched on, and the sound effects continued unabated. I know everyone breaks wind, even the Pope I imagine, but with Orson it was gale force ten.

An urgent message was flashed through to Jack, who realised he had to do something. I watched him stalk down the room, and approach Orson's table. His nostrils twitched.

"Good evening, Mr Welles. Er —"

Orson looked up at the rotund figure standing in front of him. "Isow! Fantastic place you've got here," he boomed. "The food is glorious," he gestured around the empty room, "but I can't understand why you don't do more business!"

Now Jack was a straight-speaking Yiddisher, and although he only stood five foot five, he wasn't frightened of anyone. This remark was like plunging a knife in his back, and then turning it. *"What?"* He looked as happy as a bulldog chewing a wasp. "Of course I can't do any business with you fucking farting all over the place!"

Now it was Orson's turn. He clambered to his feet, towering over his host. "Isow!" he announced sternly. "I will never eat in this restaurant again."

Jack responded in kind. "Then fuck off and let me get some customers in here." He was hopping up and down like a deranged flea.

Not many people talked to Orson Welles like that. But when the boss was roused he wouldn't be intimidated by anyone, even if the geezer was one of the greatest stars the cinema has produced this century. Orson threw some notes on the table and stalked towards the exit.

I saw him coming, and had his hat and overcoat waiting for him before he reached the desk.

"Going already, Mr Welles?"

"Yes." I helped him shrug his huge bulk into the vicuna overcoat.

"Thank you, Nosher," he said gravely. As he got to the door to the street, he paused.

*Paarp!* He let another one rip, turned to me with an exaggerated theatrical bow, and stalked off into the dusk without a backward glance.

I suppose you could call it one for the road, but I just went into the cloakroom and laughed my bollocks off.

One of the gimmicks at Isow's was the fish tank. Jack had installed a large aquarium in the wall between the cloakroom and the street, so it was visible outside. From the pavement, potential customers could see fresh juicy trout swimming temptingly around, just waiting to go on a plate with some tartare sauce and a bowl of chips.

When someone ordered trout, the waiter who took the order would trot off to the cloakroom, climb a short step ladder with a net, and fish around until he could whisk up his catch. At that time I had my own dog, Shep, a large Dobermann with a lively disposition, which I kept on a long leash in the cloakroom as back-up to discourage potential trouble-makers.

One evening a new waiter started work. Let's call him Mañuel, because that was probably his name anyway. No one bothered to tell him that there was a guard dog on the premises, or that he should ask me before he started fishing for trout. He takes the order: one fresh grilled trout. Comes into the cloakroom, climbs the steps, and leans over the tank, splashing around with his net as if he's stirring a bowl of soup instead of easing it along gently to nab his prey.

Well, Shep doesn't like the intrusion. He comes up behind the waiter, stands on his hind legs, and nips the poor sod in the backside.

I happened to be outside the main door taking a breath of night air, when I saw a commotion just along the street. People were staring into the window, laughing and pointing. I joined the crowd to see what the fuss was all about — and Christ! There's Manuel, panic-stricken and *inside* the tank.

He's on his knees and fully immersed in his dinner jacket, with trout swimming around him and sizing him up to see if he's worth a nibble. The waiter is gesticulating furiously at Shep, who is waiting for him, teeth bared, front paws up on the steps, quivering from nose to tail.

Well, I broke all records to leg it back inside before the guy died of fright or caught his death of cold. I hauled Shep off, and put a tight chain on him as Mañuel clambered out, and dripped his way back to the kitchens.

He handed in his notice that same night. But I'll lay a bet that I'm the only person ever to rescue a waiter from drowning in his own restaurant.

There's an old joke set in a monastery where the punch line is "It's your turn in the barrel!" I expect you know it, because it's one of the original chestnuts we all first heard at school. If you don't, I'll leave it to your imagination to work out the rest. Monastery, monks, hole in barrel ... okay? Yes, you've got it now.

But something just as bizarre happened one night, luckily well after hours when the shop had just closed and the restaurant was empty, though downstairs the club was still going strong.

A noisy argument started up in the foyer between two geezers who had been hitting the sauce too hard. When I tried to step in they both turned on me, giving me some lip, and using enough bad language to wind me up. I had to take them both out. While they were still on the carpet I heard the chef calling from the kitchen: "Nosh, there's someone in here. Come on, quick!"

My trusty Dobermann ally Shep was with me that night. I ordered him to lie against the main door, which meant no one would get out.

"Stay!" He lay down obediently, with one eye on anything that moved.

I went into the kitchen, and had a look round. George stood by in his white apron, head cocked. The ovens were still warm. I opened fridges, cupboards, even the man-sized freezers. Nothing. "There's no one in here, George."

"Nosher," he insisted, "I could swear I heard someone moving. Or *something*."

Okay, George was a nice guy. I'll humour him, I thought.

So we walked together the whole length of the kitchen. At the far end was a big table with a wooden block on it, raised chest high so that the chefs could chop their meat on it. Under the table stood two barrels, one for sweet gherkins, one for sour. Pickled gherkins were a must with salt beef.

I sensed a movement, bent down — and recoiled at a sight straight out of a *Carry On* film. Inside one barrel a bald-headed geezer was sitting up to his neck in sour gherkins and vinegar. All I could see was a pallid face staring back at me, frozen in terror.

"What the fuck are you doing in there?" I demanded. "Have you been drinking, or what?"

"Don't hit me!" His voice was tremulous. As he stood up, dripping vinegar, I could see he was shaking all over. "Please."

"Out!" I said. "And off upstairs!"

He climbed reluctantly out of the barrel and shook each sodden trouser leg so that gherkins came dropping on to the tiles like green insects. Then he squelched off down the kitchen.

I looked at George, and George looked at me, and we both shrugged in disbelief. "Your turn in the barrel, George," I said.

It turned out the punter had heard the commotion upstairs as I was laying out the two yobs, and was so frightened that he ran and hid. He thought some tearaway psycho was on the rampage, and took refuge in the nearest hiding place.

Yes, life at Jack's was never dull.

I was paid to protect Isow's, and be prepared to mix it with anyone who wanted a ruck. What I wasn't prepared for was to have to wrestle with a nine-foot boa-constrictor giving a damsel in distress a hard time.

But nearby up the alley was Raymond's Revue Bar, world famous for its exotic showgirls who came from all over the world to perform unusual and interesting acts on the stage.

The place was a "must-see" for jaded businessmen in urgent need of R and R, and for tourists fancying a spot of naughtiness, with style. They always got something different from your average cabaret, and that's putting it mildly.

Like what? Like Chinese girls juggling in the nude, for starters. Fire-eaters, naked, which made them extra careful where they stuck their flaming torches. Nude ice-skaters, nude animal acts with horses and dogs — even, on one memorable occasion, a nude female dancer prancing around a real live mountain lion!

The days when naked models had to stand as still as statues, as they did at the Windmill in the fifties, were long gone. Now, you will gather that a lot of mammary glands were on view, which was one reason for me to pop across the road during a break to take in the new acts.

I was always welcomed with open arms, and they let me in for free to catch the shows. Jack Isow owned the place, though Paul Raymond was the front man for all the publicity, and I'd got to know the boys and girls in Reception. One act they told me about was particularly intriguing.

Roy on the door showed me an advance poster. "What do you think of that, Nosh?"

She was billed as Miss Snake Hips, from Holland. "Jesus!" I exclaimed, staring at a busty blonde performing a sinuous dance — with a nine-foot boa-constrictor wrapped round her lithe body. "This I've gotta see!"

"She starts Monday," said Roy.

"I'll be there," I promised.

Monday night, around nine. I'm standing on my usual square foot of carpet in Isow's minding my own business when suddenly the street doors crash open. In tumbles Paul Raymond himself, and he is not his usual debonair self.

"Quick, Nosher!" he pants. "She's being killed!"

That sounded like trouble across the road. Murder, or what? "Hold the fort," I shouted to one of the waiters, and pelted out into the alley on Raymond's heels. What was it? Jealous husband, lovers' tiff, gangster's moll?

"Where's the fight?" I yelled at Raymond's back.

"On the stage," he shouted back. "With that fucking snake!"

I took the stairs three at a time, meeting a horde of panic-stricken punters heading the other way, and burst into the theatre. Then I stopped dead in my tracks. On the stage, Miss Snake Hips was writhing on the boards wrapped in what looked like coils of greyish-brown rope. Her face was purple, and she was gasping for air.

What had happened was this. The giant boa-constrictor was housed in a glass cage backstage, where it spent most of its time asleep, apart from being fed with the occasional chicken or rat. All snakes hibernate, but this one apparently liked its kip more than most, and remained in a semi-torpor throughout the act, which began with Miss Snake Hips, real name Karen, appearing with it entwined around her shoulders as she slid into a sinuous dance, using her pet like a phallic symbol. She wisely kept a strip of sticky tape around its mouth, just in case.

On this opening night the snake suddenly became wide awake, took a dislike to the noise and the lights, and swiftly coiled itself round her body. Then it started to squeeze. Panic. Screams from Karen, echoed by women in the audience. Exit Paul Raymond, rushing for help.

All this high drama I took in with one glance. Nobody else seemed inclined to help, and I wasn't too keen myself to behave like Tarzan. But Jane had to be rescued, and something had to be done.

I leaped on to the stage and grabbed hold of the slippery coils, tugging ferociously. That's when the great snake uncoiled like a whiplash — and wrapped itself around me. Over I went like a tree being felled, and now it's me rolling around the stage shitting bricks. At least I had my clothes on, unlike Miss Snake Hips.

Being crushed by a rampant boa-constrictor is not a lot of fun, I can tell you. Apart from the claustrophobic feeling of being unable to move your arms, and the terrible pressure on your rib cage, it becomes increasingly hard to draw breath.

I started seeing coloured flashes of light, which had nothing to do with the stage spotlights. Worse, I found I was looking at rows of small, sharp teeth grinning at me from inches away! Karen had omitted to tape the snake's mouth. "Help!" I tried to shout — but only a hoarse wheeze came out.

Suddenly there was a great *whoosh* of foam straight into the boa-constrictor's face, which wiped away the grin and loosened the coils in a trice. The reptile flopped to the floor like a slack rope unravelling, while I rolled away wondering who had sent in the cavalry.

One of the stage hands, thinking quicker than most, had grabbed a fire extinguisher and done the right thing.

Miss Snake Hips came round, and watched her precious pet taken back to its cage, where it swiftly revived. She even threw it a dead rat to eat, by way of apology for all the grief. I got a kiss of gratitude, and a free ticket for the late show.

Somehow, I gave that one a miss.

## 17: GUNFIGHT AT BATTERSEA PARK

When trouble happens, it happens suddenly. It might be in a pub, on the bus, in the street or, in my case, the club. From my vantage-point in the foyer I could see through a long glass partition into the bar and the length of the restaurant beyond it. I didn't miss a blink.

On this particular night there was a table in the bar with six people sitting at it, two of whom were the broadcasters David Jacobs and Pete Murray, along with their wives. As I was checking out the scene, the street doors opened behind me and in walked two geezers with two women.

"Hello, Nosh!" said the first. I recognised Georgie Glass, who ran a pub next door to Bloom's famous kosher restaurant in Whitechapel, and who had known me since my early boxing days. The other was a big feller, I'd say six two in his socks, weighing around eighteen stone and wearing a sour expression.

"All right to go downstairs, Nosh?"

"For you, George, any time." I made way for them and they trooped downstairs into the Jack of Clubs.

Ten minutes later, up comes the geezer who'd been with George. I'm standing in the middle of the bar area, keeping an eye on the clientele.

In a voice that could be heard all the way down the bar and into the restaurant, he shouts out: "*Oi!*"

I respond in kind. "What yer mean, oi?"

He says: "I mean *oi, wanker!* You don't remember me, do yer?"

"No," I say. "Should I?"

He scowls nastily. "You slung me out of here a while ago, you c--t. Do you think you could do it to me now?"

There are times when you know it's going to be one of those nights, and this was turning into one. But I tried. You've got to hand it to me, I really tried.

First, a deep breath. "You're having a joke, aren't you, chum? You're with my friend Georgie."

"I don't give a fuck," he said. "You try it now."

"Do me a favour." I'm still trying, though it's getting a bit ragged at the edges. But you have to go through the motions. "I don't remember you. Go downstairs and have a drink with George." The fact was that I'd had so many fights there, one more or less might pass unnoticed.

But with that, he goes *pow!* And slams me with a left on the jaw. I shake my head in surprise and disbelief, and find myself staring down at Pete Murray and David Jacobs at their ringside table. The whole place has suddenly gone dead quiet.

The big lug steps up the verbals. "Go on," he sneers. "Chin me!"

Now I always do what a customer asks, so I give him a light tap on the chin, the playful kind. "All right?"

"No," he says. "Go on. Chin me again, you c--t!"

So I tap him again. "That hard enough?"

"No," he says. "I'll show you how to punch." And he slings a right cross that would have taken my head off if it had landed. But, thank the Lord, the old reflexes are still there, and I move inside it, swing him round with my shoulder just like Joe Louis taught me a hundred years ago, and *whack!* I plant him with a haymaker of a right uppercut.

When I throw a punch, I don't go *pop!* As I tell anyone who's interested, you've got to go through the target — *pow! bam!* That's what I did, and down he went, all eighteen stone of him, with a cry of "*Oohmegawd!*" I'll always remember that shout, and then he was sprawled flat on his back, spark out.

At which rather tense point Jack Isow came out of his office. "Good boy, Nosh! Pick him up and sling him out." He had seen trouble coming, and called West End Central nick.

"Fuck him," I rejoined. I was all fired up. "I put 'em down. I don't pick 'em up!"

They got two waiters to lift Loudmouth into an armchair in the foyer, where he slumped like a customer snatching forty winks after a good dinner.

In the meantime, Jack had got on a direct line to the law, and two of London's finest turned up. "What's happened here? Who started it?"

"It's all right, officers," I said reassuringly. "They've gone — two geezers trying to get in without a reservation. They went that way." I gestured into the night. And off went the boys in blue in hot pursuit of shadows.

George appeared, looking for his man. He saw the slumped figure. Now, George was no slouch: he could tell what had happened. "Nosher, you bastard!"

"Georgie," I said. "Please don't. I've been your pal for years. This geezer come up and tried to assault me. I don't know what it was all about, honest I don't."

George ignored me, stepped outside and called a taxi. With the help of the two waiters we dragged his unconscious friend out, and they took off. When I went back inside, the whole restaurant stood up and applauded — but in truth I was heartbroken. Years went by before Georgie and I spoke again. Then one day he sent for me, from a hospital in the East End. He was on his deathbed, in the last stages of cancer.

"I've been wrong, Nosh," he said. "That bastard turned out to be a whore's son, always causing trouble, but I was too ashamed to come to you and apologise. But we're still pals, aren't we?" He held out a frail hand.

I took it gently, and patted his shoulder. "Course we are, George."

He died a few days later.

Back to the club. It took me an hour to calm down, and I was still simmering when out walked Pete Murray and David Jacobs with their group. David slid some notes into my hand. "There you are, Nosher. Twenty quid!"

"Cor," I said. "That's very generous of you." He'd always been a good tipper for the cloaks, a couple of quid here or there. But never this generous.

"Those mugs at the bar never knew the score," he said. "When that big guy grabbed hold of you, and we looked at the size of him, they all said: 'This is where Nosher gets his comeuppance!' I knew better, so I took a few bets. You've got half coming to you, so take it. And the rest of it paid for my dinner."

The fact that I can't even remember Mr Loudmouth's name isn't that surprising. It's like me asking you: "What did you have to eat last Wednesday?" Drunks, rough men and potential "situations" were so common I lost count of them. That's what I had to face every night, but I didn't lose any sleep worrying about it.

The problems came afterwards, when the last punter had taken his coat and gone home, and the doors were locked. That would be around three o'clock, and I'd walk out about half past.

But I wouldn't go home. I may have looked calm on the outside throughout the night's shift, often just standing there for hours on end imitating a lump of wood, but inside I was keyed up like a coiled spring, because I could never relax. Trouble erupts so fast, and it could come at any moment with whoever was stepping in through that door. So I had to keep my eyes peeled at all times, try to anticipate a problem and defuse it before anything went off.

So afterwards I would take a long drive, often as far as Brighton, to unwind with a long walk along the beach. Or I'd go to the stables behind Dad's house and take a horse out. If you saw a bloke cantering over Mitcham Common at dead of night, it would most likely have been me if it wasn't the ghost of Dick Turpin. I'd get home in the early dawn, drained and dog tired, and just flop into bed and sleep like a log.

Anybody who knows the minder's game will tell you the same thing: it's fine when you've got seven or eight of the big guys standing around, patrolling the large clubs like Mecca, say, with walkie-talkies, keeping everything nice and neat. You seldom get a problem. But when you're on your fucking own with no one looking after your back, that's when you need a bit of strategy.

Early on, I worked out my SP. A group would come in, and you'd always get the mouth and trousers, one mug, hollering and hooting, leading the pack. I'd get a phone call from Pino, looking after things downstairs in the club. "Can you come down, Nosher? It's getting a bit noisy."

Now it's off, and it's me who has to sort it out. But I know who the mouth is, and without any excuse-me, I tell him: "Belt up, or you're out."

Inevitably, the reply is the same. He'll say to his mates: "Come on, boys, let's 'ave him!"

That's when I give him my most belligerent stare, and say: "No! Hold it! Not let *us* have him — let's see *you* do it. You're the one with the mouth, and you want your pals to do the damage and get hurt. But let's see what *you* can fucking do!" It's face to face, like they do in the ring now. "Go on, throw the first punch!" And he does it, or swallows it.

I'd say nine out of every ten times they'd back down. Me? I never could. I've never backed down in my life — I just don't know how to. But one night it almost happened that I did.

It was a special occasion in the restaurant, a smart do for the toffs, black tie, invitation only. This big feller, around six five, fifteen stone and very athletic, shoulders as wide as a shithouse door, came to the door and wanted to get in. I barred his way. "Excuse me, sir. Have you an invitation."

He spoke with an accent. "No, but I'm waiting for my friend."

I noticed the lack of a dinner jacket, too. He was smart enough, but in a lounge suit. I said: "If you'd like to wait in the bar. I'll take your coat."

"Oh, thank you." Very polite. Warning bells rang. I thought: Watch it, Nosh, he's a big 'un.

The stranger sat by himself for a few minutes. Then suddenly he got up. "I think I'll go into the restaurant," he announced to no one in particular.

I moved quickly, barring his way. "No, sir," I said firmly. Just like that, brooking no argument. The effect was surprising. He swelled up the way a frog does, and I thought he was going to explode. Some people do that when they're angry, and if you're fifteen stone to start with it can be quite impressive.

Just then a geezer I knew from a South London sports club walked in, very elegant in a black tie and waving two tickets for the party. He greeted the other guy with a lot of back-slapping and mock punches, as sportsmen, stunt men and actors tend to do. Then, to me: "All right, Nosh? Long time. How are yer?"

"Your friend," I said quickly. "He's been waiting for you."

"Oh," he said, "let me introduce you. This is Jan van der Elste, all the way from Holland. He's the Olympic Games judo heavyweight champion."

"Christ," I said. "I was about to sling him out."

He chuckled. "Were you?" he said, "Nosh, you'd have gone right through the fucking window!"

Other times were not so amusing. One night I put the block on a bunch of young thugs trying to get into the Jack of Clubs. They were five-handed, noisy East End yobs — not particularly big guys, but loudmouths looking to barge in and create a ruck. They got as far as the reception desk.

Without messing with formalities, I said: "Out! I'm telling you now — you don't go down them stairs."

"Hey, asshole," said the leader, an olive-skinned kid who could have been Maltese. If so, they were probably running the vice in Soho, along with the Greek and Cypriot mobs. There were various small, dangerous gangs from the Mediterranean climate dotted around London, mostly north of the river, always getting into trouble, usually tooled up and always trying to prove something. Mostly it was territorial. This time it got personal. "What you on about?" Olive-skin demanded.

"There's the door," I said. "*Out!*"

Well, they went. It was quite early, before midnight, and they trudged off round the corner and out of sight. The leader looked back briefly, and gave me a hard stare before they disappeared.

The restaurant was still running, the cabaret was on downstairs, and I would be there till after three. Business as usual, but for some reason that stare worried me.

I always stepped out very carefully at closing time, but on this occasion I trod extra carefully. Don't ask me why, it was the old gutter instinct smelling danger. For some reason I had a suss that these guys would be waiting.

Before I left the premises, I went down to the kitchen, opened the cutlery drawer, and found a long salt-beef fork with two wicked-looking prongs on the end. This I stuck up my sleeve, with the handle against my wrist. Then I phoned Dinny at Smithfield Market, where he would be up all night working with the meat.

"Din? I think I got a problem. A mob could be waiting for me."

"I'll get over, Nosh. Hang about!"

But he didn't appear. It got to nearly four o'clock, and finally I left by myself. Shep was at home having a night off. Outside, I undid my bow tie as usual, looked up and down Brewer Street, then stepped out into the road, heading for the garage where I kept my motor parked. Lesson one: never walk along the pavement at that hour. Doorways can be dangerous.

It had been raining, and the streets were still wet. There were a few people around, even at that hour, because Soho never sleeps. Then I saw them. Two cars, loaded. Four or five in each car, parked fifty yards away. I knew then that they were waiting on me.

The garage was just beyond. I walked past the two cars without appearing to notice them, found my own Cortina estate, rolled it down the ramp, gave the geezer in the hut half a quid, and turned left into the one-way street. As I passed them, the two cars pulled out — and now they were on my arse. *Fucking hell*, I thought, not without reason. What now?

I didn't want to take them home to South London, so I had to think. *Get your head together, Nosher!* I headed down to Trafalgar Square, along Whitehall, on to the Embankment. My brain was going a hundred miles an hour. Turn in to Scotland Yard? They'd just drive on and away. This one I had to handle myself.

I kept her steady along Millbank, cruising through the slippery streets until the lights of Battersea Bridge twinkled in the distance. I took another look in the rear mirror. Sure enough, they were purring along fifty yards behind, not hurrying.

I put my foot down to go faster — when all of a sudden a voice growled in my ear: *"Go steady, Nosh!"*

I knew that voice. Dinny, my long-lost brother, had been lying doggo on the back seat all the time. Christ, was I glad to hear him!

"Where are we?" Dinny asked, keeping low.

"Millbank," I answered.

"Turn left over Chelsea Bridge," he ordered. "And, whatever you do, don't stop until then, even if it's a red light."

The lights at the bridge were green. I twisted the wheel, jammed my foot down on the accelerator and, even if I'm not Stirling Moss, I went over that bridge like a bat out of hell. The other cars grew smaller as they receded — then they were on to me again, closing up.

Across the river the road was deserted at that hour, getting on for four thirty. "Stop!" Dinny yelled from the back. I threw out the anchors, the estate slewed round in a shower of spray, the back door swung open and Dinny was out.

The pursuing cars were coming down almost abreast, going flat out. Then I saw that Dinny was clutching a Beretta shotgun — shit, where had he got that from? My brother stood in the middle of the road like fucking Gary Cooper in *High Noon*.

Then he pulled the trigger.

*Bang! Bang!*

He broke open the gun, slammed in two more cartridges, snapped it back. *Bang! Bang!* Two more.

Both windscreens shattered. The cars screeched round like a scene out of *The Sweeney* and went straight through the gates of Battersea Park, and into a pile of sand bins. Doors slammed open. Out they poured, seven or eight of them, all waving their hands and shouting: "Leave off, Dinny! No more!"

They recognised him because Dinny had a reputation throughout London. Not for starting fights but for finishing them. My brother, bless his socks, can be more than a little menacing when he wants to be, and he wanted to be now.

"I know who you are." He moved the shotgun along the row. "You ever come looking for my brother again, and I'll come after you.

And next time it won't be your windscreens — I'll go for your fucking pricks!"

"All right ... all right ..."

Dinny walked back to the estate. "All right, Nosh," he said quietly. "Home we go."

I never saw any of that mob again.

## 18: DINNY

Driving back through the streets of South London after the ding-dong with the Maltese mob, I glanced at my brother and remembered the first time I had seen him in action. He was all of fifteen, and had matured beyond his years while I was away in the Army.

On my first weekend back in Civvy Street, we went down to a pub in the Walworth Road to celebrate. Dinny had filled out, and was a strapping, red-haired lad standing six foot tall, with all the cockiness of a good-looking kid who can look after himself and pull the birds, too. He had suggested the Manor Place, adding: "I've got something that needs attending to."

It was a big pub, packed out, full of smoke and noise. A couple of pool tables were busy at the far end. In one corner a six-piece band was going full blast, a few couples were shuffling around, and lots of gorgeous, giggling young girls were standing in groups eyeing the lads at the bar and waiting to be asked. I ordered a couple of drinks, and looked around.

Something was wrong. It should have been great to be in the first English pub I'd set foot inside in two years. But I sensed a funny electric feeling in the air, as if people were waiting for something to happen.

Then in walked Freddie Foreman, with a couple of pals. We hadn't seen each other in all that time.

"Hello, Nosher. Where you been?"

"Doing my bit for King and country, Freddie. Like a drink?"

"No thanks, Nosh. Maybe later." He wandered casually away with his mates, and took up a position by the wall. That confirmed it for me. Something was up.

A voice said: "He's here."

"Who's here?" I asked.

At my elbow, Dinny said: "Tony Reuter."

Now Tony was an up-and-coming villain in South London, and his younger brother Peter was king of the local Teddy Boys. In they came, wearing the long jackets, bootlace ties, drainpipe trousers and winkle-picker shoes that marked out their gang. They pushed through the throng, and came straight over to Dinny.

It was Tony who spoke. "Well, I'm here," he said. "Where do you want it?"

Dinny said: "Over to the yard!"

There was a factory yard at the back behind the pub, and the whole lot of us surged out and through the gates. I found myself next to Foreman.

"What's it all about?"

He shot back a one-word reply. "Differences!"

To me, aged twenty-one and bigger than any of them, they were kids. But dangerous kids, like as not tooled up with knives, razors or bicycle chains, the favourite Teddy Boy weapons when they went spoiling for a fight.

In those days the most feared razor gang was the Angel Mob, who frequented the pubs and billiard halls around Islington in North London. They started young. Their ages ranged from sixteen to thirty, and they used cut-throat razors that were specially taped to maim, but not kill. Those bastards would slash their victims' faces to leave a cut that was anything from six to nine inches long.

They were also expert in daylight robbery on the Underground. Half a dozen of them would surround a likely mug, and crowd him while one deftly cut his pocket with a razor and whipped his wallet. They'd be gone before the victim discovered his jacket needed stitching — but he could count himself lucky it wasn't his face.

Razor slashing was part of the Teddy Boy culture, and thank Christ it went out of fashion along with the drainpipes. South London had its share too. There was even a gang of birds calling themselves the

Bermondsey Girls, who specialised in shop-lifting — but carried razors in their handbags.

Right now I was watching for any glimmer of a shiv as the crowd formed a makeshift ring in the yard. The only light was from a lamp-post in the street outside, but it was enough to see what was going on. I shouldered my way through, planted my thirteen stone in the centre, and bellowed as threateningly as I could: "Anyone tries to fucking interfere, they'll answer to me!"

Tony took his coat off, Dinny did likewise. Then they were at each other like two raging bulls. From the start Dinny had the edge. There were no rounds, and no rules, and Dinny just beat and kicked the shit out of his rival. They both went down in a heap, but Dinny was on top, and he got hold of Tony's ears and pounded his head on the cobbles like a madman.

Peter Reuter moved in to stop them and save his brother from further punishment. I barred his way. "Don't you make no fucking move. Let them fight it out!"

It probably only lasted two minutes. Finally Tony stopped struggling, and lay still. Dinny climbed off him, dusted himself down, and said to me, cool as you like: "Thanks for your help, Nosh. Now let's get back to that drink." And he went back inside as if nothing had happened.

Strangely, that was the end of it. Score settled. Just another teenage ruck. Freddie Foreman had been a pal of Dinny's for years, and remains so to this day.

We had a few more beers, even a dance or two with the girls for whom Dinny had become a bit of a local hero, stayed till closing time and went home. We never mentioned it to Mum or Dad.

But a lot of those young faces that night grew into real villains, put on the balaclavas, maybe spent some time as guests of Her Majesty's Government in various prisons around the country. Freddie was one of them. He combined muscle with skilfully planned high-take robberies, and ended up being brought back from Spain in handcuffs after doing a runner to the Costa del Crime. They learned young, and they were a tough crowd.

But we had our own code. All of five years later I bumped into Tony Reuter at the Good Intent, a pub near the Elephant that had been the scene of a murder the week before. We hadn't set eyes on each other since the ruck.

"Hello, Nosh." Then, after the briefest of pauses: "How's Dinny?"

"Dinny's fine," I replied cautiously.

"Ah." He nodded. Another pause. Then: "Good fighter." That was all he said, but it was enough. No hard feelings, that was the message. And Dinny *was* a good fighter, even as a youngster, and grew up to be a better one.

## 19: THE HARD MEN

Working nights at Isow's, I had the days to myself. I was getting extra work in films, but it was bits and pieces and I couldn't rely on it for an earner. So I spent a lot of time round the pubs and clubs in South London, even though I didn't drink a lot and usually stuck to orange juice. I liked the atmosphere and the give-and-take, even if every other face at the bar had villainy written all over it.

One day I was playing snooker at a club down near the Elephant, half a crown an hour. All the tables were busy. In walked Bobby Ramsey, a former boxer turned enforcer for the Krays, who ran the Stragglers Club at Cambridge Circus with the Twins. Along with Bobby were two big guys.

I was startled to see them. The Firm came from North London and Bobby was well out of his manor. I could smell trouble in the air like blood.

But he gave me a cursory glance, said, "Hello, Nosher," and looked round the room. "There he is!"

He'd spotted a geezer I knew as Italian Tony, who was a bit of a flash con-merchant around the Elephant. He was a big bastard, but a small-time villain who fought as a heavyweight in his early days before deciding there were more lucrative ways of using his muscle.

He wasn't all that clever as a boxer, even though they sometimes fixed his fights so that his opponents took a dive. Finally he came up against a Southern Area champion named Dennis Powell (no relation) who refused to go bent, and KO'd him after giving him a thrashing.

Anyway, Tony was bending over a table with his cue about to make a shot, when Ramsey came up behind him, picked a ball up off the green baize — and went *smash* on the back of Tony's head.

The crack was like a pistol going off! Tony went down in a heap. The place was deathly quiet. Everyone stopped playing, frozen in mid-shot. The barman stopped polishing the glasses. Nobody said anything. The two big men got hold of Tony by the legs and dragged him by his feet past me and up the stairs, with his head bumping on every one as if he was nodding goodbye.

Bobby strolled after them. "See you, Nosher."

"Er — yeah. See you, Bob."

They had a car waiting outside, and we found out later that Bobby took the wheel up to the roundabout by the Royal Eye Hospital, then drove round and round that roundabout while the two guys in the back beat the shit out of Tony, even though he was unconscious anyway. Finally they opened the door and flung him into the road. Then they drove off down to Blackfriars Bridge and over the river to their side of the water.

I never found out what Tony had done, but it must have been bad, or simply stupid. If he was ripping off the Firm, he was a very silly boy. A public lesson like that, in someone else's manor too, goes round the underworld like a brush fire. As someone remarked to me next day: "At least they were considerate enough to dump him outside a hospital."

Bobby ended up getting a five-year stretch — not for what he did to Tony, but for an attack with a bayonet on a guy named Terry Martin in an East End pub. Billiard balls or bayonets, it was all the same to him. Ronnie Kray was with him, and got three years for that one — even though Ronnie told the law when they found bloodstains in the car: "I had a nosebleed."

Tony'd had quite a colourful life. He once had an axe buried in his shoulder that could have taken his head off. A couple of guys marched into his flat and hit him with it while he was watching TV. He told me later: "I never even heard them coming."

Tony ran a clip joint in Soho. A mate of mine, another face who had done time, was Alf Melvin, a family man who ran a flower stall, and wore a flat cap over his bald skull-like head.

Alfie looked dangerous, the kind you wouldn't want to meet in a dark alley on a wet November night, which was why Tony chose him to go round all his gaffs picking up protection money from the one-arm bandits.

Alfie ran a fruit-and-flower stall, which was owned by Mullah, in Covent Garden, and the two had been pals for as long as I knew them. Alfie was totally trustworthy: if he was sent round to collect four hundred quid, he came away with four hundred quid. That's why what happened shook the whole of Soho.

One day Alfie was having a quick drink with me in the Bus Stop Club, and he opened up a little. "I've got to tell you, Nosher, Tony's getting to me. He just ain't polite any more. Fucking do this, and fucking do that! Who does he think I am?"

I sensed a loss of respect in the air, and said: "Well, why don't you have a little chat with him? Tell him how you feel."

Alfie stuck me with a gaze that was suddenly chilling and devoid of all friendliness. "I intend to," he said. "We're having a meet tomorrow. I've got to settle a little argument."

I heard about the settlement next evening, after both of them were dead from gunshot wounds and there was a lot of blood spilled on the pavement outside the Bus Stop Club. Alfie had taken a gun in as a frightener, and bullets started flying.

Personally, after all those years, I don't think Alfie meant to shoot Tony. I think he just meant to scare him. But the gun was on a hair trigger — and bang!

Tony staggered down the stairs and out into the street, where he collapsed on the pavement. Alfie ran down after him, saw what he had done, and turned the gun on himself.

That was it. Both of them dead. And Soho had lost two more of its own.

The Firm were arrested in the famous dawn swoop on 1 May 1968 by Chief Superintendent Leonard "Nipper" Read and his merry men, so that was the main source of Bobby's income dried up. But he came out of jail — and next thing I knew, there he was at Pinewood, sitting outside a caravan on the back lot, large as a life sentence, with a smile on his face and a wad of notes in his pocket.

"Hello, Nosher! Long time ..."

"Christ, Bob. What are you doing here?"

"I've gone into showbusiness, that's what."

And, in a way, he had. Bobby had opened up an agency for film extras, and he would head the crowd scenes himself. Especially at Pinewood, his favourite studio. The boys and girls got paid on a daily rate, in cash, so there was a big queue outside the pay-out caravan at the end of the day.

Fifteen quid here, maybe a pony there. Bobby always went straight to the front of the queue, so he was first in and first out.

It wasn't so much intimidation, more that he was known as the guv'nor, even if it was a fine line. He had got them in, and he expected his cut.

At the end of the day he would take his percentage. The kids would count out a few quid and press it into his hand as they came out of the caravan. He called it "my agent's fee", and nobody seemed inclined to argue.

It was payola time. Bobby had simply gone from illegal extortion to legal extortion. Me, I never paid him a penny. I got all my extra work — and later, stunt work — through my original agent Gabbie Howard, and then by myself.

The last time I saw Bobby Ramsey was in the summer of 1998, in a nursing home in Epping. He was frail, thin as a scarecrow, and hardly recognised me. I had heard he was a very sick man, and because he had never done me a mischief I went to pay my respects. I wish I could say I joined a long queue, but there wasn't even a single flower by his bed to cheer him up.

In his prime, with the Krays out of the way, Bobby's controller had been Charlie Richardson, later to make headlines in the notorious "torture trial". Now Charlie, five years younger than me, was a hard man — and his kid brother Eddie was harder. Charlie was the brains, Eddie the brawn, and together they ruled their South London empire with a mixture of intimidation and brutality.

Charlie had started early. He escaped from approved school at fourteen, and after some minor villainy became a scrap-metal merchant, proving himself a shrewd businessman and organiser. He was even into gold in South Africa, and would tell me lurid stories about how the local labour some mines employed to maintain the machinery at the top of the lift shafts came to a grisly fate.

"Those shafts go down half a mile and more. The guys stand on a bridge across the top to oil the wheels, and they're supposed to fix a safety-belt to the rail. Often they're just too lazy, and can't be bothered. What happens? They overbalance and topple down the shaft. They're never found, because by the time they've bounced off the sides for half a mile there's nothing left to bury!" And he'd laugh uproariously.

By 1956 he was worth £250,000, huge dosh in those days. Funny thing, when I knew Charlie early on around the pubs and clubs, he was actually the go-between with the Krays and the Nashes, from Islington, whose six sons were once dubbed "the wickedest brothers in England". If there was a problem, it would be Charlie and Eddie who were called in to sort it.

I knew all the mobs controlling everything from protection to prostitution, but in the end it all came down to greed. Not just money and territory but the so-called "aphrodisiac of power" that kept the adrenalin running.

Charlie's brother Eddie, two years his junior, was tough, two-fisted — and a thorn in his side. All Eddie had was muscle. Where Charlie would talk to a man and try to negotiate, Eddie would go in with his fists flailing.

When I first knew him he was working for fifteen quid a week round the back of Covent Garden. He was swarthy and aggressive, with curly black hair and dangerous dark eyes. He could put the fear of God into people if he came after them.

At the end of the day the market workers used to get together for a game of dice. Eddie would take the bets. "Eddie, fifteen quid on six coming up!" Next day, he'd expect the money to come in. If it didn't, wallop! No further arguments. I saw him do people several times in the market, leaving them lying on the cobbles.

It's very rare you get a guy who's good in the street and good in the ring, but Eddie was both. In the ring you step back after a clinch. In the street you go in — *whack!* You nut him, smash his eyes wide open, and keep smashing. Not nice, but necessary.

Maybe I was unwise to mingle with them, overhear whispered secrets, be seen drinking and joking with them. But, remember, they were all family in the sense that their folks had been friendly with my folks, and we all grew up together.

In fact, I was talking to Buster Edwards once and he said to me: "That job was cursed, Nosh." He was talking about the Great Train Robbery, what else?

And now it can be told: when the GTR was being set up, I was sounded out to be a getaway driver. I was approached by a bloke in a pub, who said he was looking for a co-driver for a "special job". "We know you can handle fast cars, Nosher. Can't tell you much, but there's plenty of dosh." That's all he would say.

"Thanks, mate, but leave me out," I said. But so as not to hurt his feelings, I added: "Maybe another time."

They did the job and, of course, they had no idea there was going to be that amount of money on the train. Then they drove a few miles to Leatherslade Farm, and hid up. In all, fifteen villains spent several days counting out more than two million quid and realising they had hit the jackpot, before heading off with suitcases stuffed with loot.

The job of getting rid of any evidence was given to a small-time thief named Ginger Marks. He was a tall, amiable cove with red hair and glasses, and the only reason I know more about him than most is because I was so often mistaken for him.

Ginger was hired to wipe the farm clean of prints then burn it to the ground. The way I heard it, he was paid up front, went around with a cloth, lit a lamp, threw it inside, and scarpered in a hurry.

But ... the lamp just flickered, and went out. Of course, there were fingerprints all over the shop, and the boys got rowed in. Bad luck for them, and even worse luck for Ginger, who was gunned down in Stepney in January 1965, his body spirited away, never to be seen again.

While the heat was at its height for him, I was minding my own business watching TV in the South London flat I shared with Pauline soon after our marriage. The knocker went on the front door.

I answered it — and next minute they were all over me. The Old Bill. Plain clothes at the front, uniforms backing them up. There wasn't even the courtesy of an "Excuse me, Mr Powell, but we have a search warrant here!" They kicked the door in, and then there were just fists and truncheons flying — and me fighting back like a demon.

I had one advantage: it was a small flat, and the passage was so narrow that they couldn't get at me more than one at a time. I laid six of them out before going down under sheer weight of numbers.

Suddenly a voice was shouting: "Hold it! Hold it!" The superintendent, in peaked cap and crisp uniform, stared at me. My face was cut and bruised, and my right eye would be black in about an hour. When you get the heavy mob jumping on you, they tend to make an impression.

Pauline was screaming her head off in the kitchen, poor girl. We hadn't been married that long, and to have the full majesty of the law smash into your home and jump on your husband doesn't bode well for a long and happy union.

The super eyed me more closely, then looked away rather hastily. "We've made a mistake, lads. This isn't Ginger Marks! I know him. It's Nosher Powell." To me: "Mr Powell, I have to apologise."

I exploded: "Apologise? You bastards! Just look at me!"

"Can we have a talk?"

I calmed down just enough to allow two of them in to the living room.

"I'm sorry, Nosher." First-name terms now. "But we had a tip that Ginger Marks was hiding out in here, and we couldn't afford to take any chances. If you want to take it further ..."

"Naw," I said. "Forget it." I suppose these days I could have sued them for a million, but it was an honest mistake. We shook hands.

"Please don't do it again," I said.

From that moment I found I had unknown friends in the force. Little things in my favour: an assault charge arising from a fracas at Isow's was dropped; parking fines never got issued. Suddenly the force was with me.

And if you're wondering about the real Ginger Marks, you might want to look under the Hammersmith flyover, inside the second concrete pillar heading west out of London.

So you can understand why, as far as I could, I kept my nose clean, but I trod a dangerous line with all the villainy around me. Like a high-wire walker without a safety-net, I managed to be part of their world without getting sucked down the plug.

Like the Nash family. I knew them all — Billy, the eldest, then Johnny, Jimmy, Ronnie, George and Roy, who had made his own mark on society with a manslaughter conviction after knifing a youth in a dance hall fight when he was only sixteen.

Johnny Nash was the guv'nor. They called him the Peacemaker, because he was the brains behind the outfit and called the shots. They were feared, they were vicious and they could all fight. The Nash motto was: "You come out with a knife, we come out with an axe. You come out with an axe, we come out with a gun." Sean Connery's character said something like it in the film of *The Untouchables*, and the message is the same the world over.

But in the end they thought they were above the law, and it was when Johnny was sent down for five years for GBH that their reign ended.

I used to find Jimmy at Johnny Romaine's garage at the top end of the Angel. The two were like blood brothers. I'd be in there when Jimmy and some of his pals would materialise from the yard. "Johnny, I want to talk to you. Oh — Nosher! Would you mind ...?"

That was my cue to make myself scarce for an hour, while they talked up a bank job or a contract on some luckless geezer who had strayed on to the straight and narrow and tried to screw them. Mine not to reason why, if I wanted to stay healthy. Their name was a legend around North London, which was their patch. Jimmy always watched Johnny's back, and Johnny did likewise. If one of them ever got hurt, which occasionally happened, a lot of other people got hurt.

I once saw them in action, and that was an education. Mind you, I was part of it too. Cup final night in the West End, and triumphant

Sunderland fans were on the rampage after beating Leeds one–nil. I was having a quiet drink with Ronnie Nash in Jimmy Humphreys's club off Charing Cross Road, and Johnny and Jimmy Nash were at a table at the back.

All of a sudden the doors crashed open and a mob of soccer fans from up north burst through.

"Aw, fuck you!" seemed to be the general greeting, as they started knocking over tables and smashing glasses. I looked at Ronnie. Ronnie looked over at his brother. We all nodded in unison. It was time to go to work.

We all steamed in, the Four Musketeers — but it was more like something out of a John Wayne movie. Slam-bang-wallop! The place was a shambles, but one by one we slung the lot of them out. Then we had a drink on what was left of the house.

One funny PS to the Nashes: I was invited to Johnny Romaine's barmitzvah. The rabbi had no idea who was in his audience, but midway through his sermon he looked up all of a sudden, peered over his glasses and intoned: "There are some of us who have obtained money by false means." Half the congregation shrivelled up. "They will have Jehovah's vengeance on them!" he thundered, getting into the spirit of it.

The boys were sliding further and further down their seats. Afterwards, as we headed for the food, Jimmy Nash said to me: "What's that wanker doing, talking like that about us?" He took it personal.

I've certainly encountered many types of villainy in many different circumstances. You meet up with it in unexpected ways. Once I was contracted to do a threatening job on *Emergency Ward Ten*. Another actor and I had to walk in through the swing doors to a doctor's surgery and intimidate the doctor.

The actor I had to work with was Johnny Bindon, a powerfully built tough guy who was part of a protection racket around West London. He was a looker. We did the rehearsal two or three times. Then came the take. We were given the cue by the first assistant. Just before we were to move, the first assistant held up a hand. "Stop," he said. "I've given you the wrong cue."

I stopped, but Bindon went on walking. He went through the doors, up to the assistant, grabbed him by the lapels, and growled: "Don't fuck with me. Next time you give a cue, make sure it's fucking right. Okay?" It all went on film — and he meant it.

The director was frightened out of his life. I said to Johnny: "That was a bit strong." But he just shrugged.

Another time we were rehearsing in Putney, outside a hotel. We had a break, and were standing in the car park enjoying the sunshine when a sports car rolled in. Out got the most gorgeous blonde.

The doll walked straight up to Johnny and gave him a big tonguing — I'm talking about a real tongue-down-the-throat. This was Vicki Hodge, model and show-girl.

Later that afternoon Johnny showed me a photo of himself in Mustique on a beach with Vicki.

He was known for the size of his whopper, and he had his costume pulled down, and there was Princess Margaret, standing right beside him, smiling and laughing. I know it's hard to believe, but they made photocopies of that picture and it's been round every film studio in the country. Johnny showed me the photo himself. "How about that, Nosh?"

She had her hair pulled back tight in a bun. I said: "That's Princess Margaret!"

"Yeah," he said. "How about that!"

Later he told me his place was raided twice after he got home. Princess Margaret had been on the cocktails, and when she sobered up and realised what she'd done, the shit hit the fan. She knew the photograph was floating somewhere, and the Special Branch moved in.

Johnny finally got cancer, and he couldn't muster the fear that he used to strike into people. He faded away. In his heyday he had been in great demand at celebrity functions, and he had the breath of scandal attached to him. He had been charged with murder. He was a violent man, and could overreact on the spot. Witness that little episode with the first assistant.

## 20: TROUBLE AND STRIFE

Someone had to keep an eye on me in the midst of the high life I was living and the low-life I was associating with. That someone turned out to be my darling Pauline, last heard of here sharing a pram with me when I was one year old and an innocent in the wicked ways of the world.

Pauline went on to have a convent education, and I lost touch with her for twenty years, though I did see photos of her that Mum showed me. After the war she worked in the social services section on an American Army base, before returning home to South London to become manageress of the Carlton cinema in the Haymarket. Bright girl, Pauline.

I happened to be standing outside the local dance hall at the Elephant when I noticed this striking looking redhead emerge from the tube station.

As she passed me, she said: "Hello, Nosher!"

I looked more closely, realised who it was, and exclaimed: "Good Gawd alive!" I was always ready with a sparkling chat-up line.

That's how it all started. My first date was at her cinema, where I sat in the royal circle, best seat in the house, to watch Jane Russell in *The Outlaw*, before taking Pauline out for a drink afterwards.

We went dancing at the Lyceum, and I found she was just so easy to talk to that I've been doing it ever since. We've known each other a lifetime, and that girl has been friend, lover, confidante, everything to me. The only problem I can't come to terms with is that she's better at cards than me. I often told her: "You'd have made a brilliant croupier."

I should have known because the first time I took Pauline home, she said: "Let's have a game of cards. Rummy." We played for a penny a point, and she cleaned me out. It's taken me fifty years to try to get it back. We were married on 27 July 1951 at St Jude's Church by the Elephant, and the bride looked a picture in white.

Pauline only ever saw me box once, and that was early on at Manor Place baths. I won on points. Every time I looked at her in her ringside seat for an encouraging smile, she had her face buried in her hands. She hated me getting in the ring. But I still tell people the most dangerous stunt I ever try to pull off is borrowing a quid from the wife!

The fact is that I never wanted Pauline to see the other side of my nature, and I've always tried to protect her from the people who bring out the worst in me.

I'm still called on to help out. Only the other day a guy rang up and pleaded: "Nosher, for friendship's sake ..." He was running a club in the Old Kent Road, and having protection problems.

My son Greg had been stunt co-ordinator on *Mission Impossible*, and been over to California to stay with Tom Cruise for the world première. That was a movie full of stunt action, and Greg used to bully Tom as if he was a schoolboy.

I saw it for myself on a visit to Pinewood, when Greg walked on to the set to find Tom balanced on top of a train without a harness. If you saw the film you'll remember the cracking fight they had aboard the EuroStar — that was Greg at his best, and what a wonderful climax to a film that had been non-stop action all the way. But now Greg saw his star living too dangerously, and reacted accordingly.

In front of the whole unit, he bellowed out: "Oi, you, get your arse down from there!" And Tom obeyed, meek as a kitten.

But it's that word again. Respect. They became great mates, and Greg brought back with him from the US an 80,000-volt stun gun. "This may help you in your occupation, Dad!" he said drily, handing it over discreetly in the living room so Mum wouldn't see.

At the time I was quite offended. I've never used a weapon in my life, although my Fist of Numbness, like the fists of any heavyweight boxer, is officially classed as a lethal weapon. So, legally, you have to watch what you do when you wave them about.

But I took the gun along to this club, because I wasn't too sure of the SP, and tucked it away out of sight under the counter. Lucky I did. We were three on the door, the place was a seething mass, with God knows what being smoked or swallowed inside, and the music was deafening heavy metal.

All of a sudden a heavy mob, twelve-handed, descended on us. Early twenties, brash, threatening. They refused to take no for an answer.

The first one faced me arrogantly across the desk while the rest milled around outside. "You think you're strong enough for us?" he said loudly. "Well, we'll go through them" — he jerked a thumb at my team on the door — "then we'll have you on your own!"

"Okay, sunshine!" I rejoined. "But remember one thing. You can only get in through that door two at a time. And for every two of you that get in, two will be going out feet first."

But this yobbo turned and yelled at his mates, and in they came like a solid wedge. By which time I had the gun out, and was able to give them 25,000 volts apiece as they came within reach.

A stun gun has two prongs. Touch it anywhere you like, it goes through the clothes and they drop. If you give them the full voltage, that can be a bit risky, so I kept it reasonable. *Whoom! Whoom! Whoom!* The bodies started to build up, lying there twitching like a hospital casualty ward. The best place to administer this summary justice is on the back of the neck if you can get to it, and the stomach's a good place because it makes them shit themselves, even while they're lying unconscious on the carpet. But keep away from the heart, because that can get a bit dodgy.

When that mob came to, they were in no condition to carry on the argument. We shoved them out like so many sheep, and I fancied I could see sparks trailing behind them as they trudged off into the night. Privately, I had a word for my son. *Thanks, Greg!*

But the night wasn't over. The scent of marijuana wafted through like a postcard from Lotus Land. I took my boys on the hunt, and we found a cocaine school going strong in the gents' toilet. Lines of white powder by the basins — sniff, sniff! Welcome to Cloud Nine!

"All of you out. *Now!*" They grumbled, but they went. I blew the remnants away into dust, then noticed one of the cubicle doors was closed. There were no locks on any of them, and when I pulled it open, sure enough, a geezer was sitting there with a line of coke on top of the cistern, and he was still sniffing it.

"You prat!" I brushed it off down the toilet, pulled the chain — and that's when he lunged at me. I caught the flash of steel and saw the knife in his hand.

Well, let's not mince matters. His arm was broken inside three seconds. It went *snap*, and he was squealing like a stuck pig. Then he fell, with his head down the toilet. Just to make the point, I had a slash all over him. I took him, groaning and half-conscious, back to the entrance, and made my announcement to anyone who cared to listen. "I'm twice as old as you lot, but I can still take you! Now just behave. Anyone want to argue?"

Not surprisingly, there were no takers. I phoned for the ambulance, and they took the user-turned-loser to hospital. I saw him again a week later, and he was walking along the street with his arm raised in plaster like a Heil Hitler salute.

I hate to say it, but sometimes you have to play dirty.

Another night, at Isow's, I was on the door when in walked the Nashes.

"Evening, Nosher!"

"Evening, Johnny, evening, Jimmy!" They were eight-handed.

"See you when we come out, Nosh!" I knew that meant a tenner in my hand.

Twenty minutes later, in came the Regans. Six of them, headed by big Mickey himself. "Hello, Nosh."

Now I have to tell big Mickey: "The Nashes are downstairs."

"Thanks. Don't worry."

I called the head waiter and told him: "Pino, put them on opposite sides of the room."

Next thing: in come the Richardsons. "Hello, Nosher! How are yer?"

Christ, I thought: this could end up like the St Valentine's Day massacre! I was shitting seven bricks. There was twenty-two of them all told, and all in one room. I'd never heard of anything like it before.

If the place had gone up in flames, London's gangland scene would have changed overnight. To my relief, there was no punchline to this particular story: the boys started sending drinks over to each other, though that was as far as the goodwill went.

Speaking of the Richardsons, I witnessed an interesting moment at a pub near the Old Vic, when I was doing a bit of business with a mate of mine. All of a sudden the door opens, and in they come, six-handed, including Frankie Fraser, a Richardsons' enforcer and hardest of the hard.

He sent me down a drink. "Okay, Nosher," he calls. "This one's on me!"

They're all laughing and joking down the other end of the bar, then Frankie said something, and the next minute one of the geezers with him, a bit of a loudmouth, passed a comment, a little too noisily: "Leave off,

Frankie. Don't be a c--t!" Now there are different ways of saying that word. Humorous, and not. Frankie took it the wrong way. He stuck a back-hander whack! in the geezer's face without so much as looking at him.

Christ, the place went quiet. But Frankie carried right on talking as if nothing had happened.

It was time to head for the door.

We moved. "See you, Frankie!"

"See you, Nosh!" All very matey, while this other bloke is still holding his face wondering what he'd said. That's one argument where you don't get involved.

Two nights later I had a particularly heavy time with two big lugs who came into Isow's, young but nasty, with a bad attitude. I took one look at them, and I knew it would all end in tears. They were in jeans and combat jackets, and there was no way I was going to allow them downstairs.

At which moment in walks George Cornell, who at that time was an enforcer for the Richardsons. Neither he nor I knew it, but he only had twenty-four hours to live.

I knew him well. "Hello, Georgie. Sorry to be abrupt, but I've got two fellers here causing me grief. Let me take your coat, then I'll have to do the business." The two geezers stood by the counter, waiting.

George was short, around five seven, thick-set and dark. He had a steely look about him that made people tread warily in his presence. "What's the matter, Nosh?"

"Nothing, really. I'm just trying to tell these two that I can't let them in dressed the way they are. I can handle it."

But he turned on them like a Rottweiler. "You c---ts! This is Nosher you're talking to. Let's have a bit of respect. Fuck off!"

And you know what? They ran. Out into the street and out of sight. As the doors swung shut I said: "Thanks, Georgie!"

"That's all right, Nosh. I know them, and they know me. Think nothing of it."

But I did think. Here's me, six foot four and seventeen stone, and there's George, five seven — and they'd run like scalded cats. In that moment, I realised there's more to doing the business than mere brute force. Respect or fear, take your pick.

It didn't help George Cornell. Next night he was shot dead by Ronnie Kray as he sat on a stool at the Blind Beggar pub in the Mile End Road. Apparently he'd insulted the Firm by calling Ronnie a "fat poof". Very unwise. I'm told his last words were "Look who's here!" as Ronnie walked up and shot him at point-blank range with a Luger pistol. There are times when you should know when to keep quiet.

But there are also times when you have to speak out, and hang the consequences. Jack "Spot" Comer was an underworld tsar, a burly hood built like a Mafia mobster, with dangerous eyes, rubbery lips and a long nose. He always wore a grey trilby hat with a band round it, and he led a chequered career as the "Caesar of the Soho gambling dens".

In fact, Spottie's proud boast was that he had been stabbed nine times in different encounters, hit on the head with an iron bar, and hospitalised with a shillelagh. After one attack that reached the courts, with up to thirty men raining blows on him, the prosecutor remarked drily: "Very much like the murder of Julius Caesar."

In August 1955 he was involved in a famous knife duel with Albert Dimes, challenging him for control of Soho's sleazy nightclubs, that ended with Jack having 280 stitches, and onlookers sluicing the blood off the Frith Street pavement with buckets of water. As someone remarked: "Jack had hand-stitched shirts and a hand-stitched face".

They were both regulars at Isow's, though either by design or chance they never checked in on the same night. Which was just as well, because the hatred simmered between them for months before it finally erupted in the daylight battle that became part of Soho's gang land folklore.

It became personal for me when I took Pauline for a night out at the London Palladium to see Frankie Laine top the bill. What a singer! "Rawhide", "Gunfight at the OK Corral", "Cool Water", "Ghost Riders in the Sky". You name it, I've got the record. I idolised that guy.

We were in the bar, ordering drinks, when I heard loud voices from the far end. A foursome clustered there were knocking back champagne and laughing a bit too loud for my liking. The faces were familiar. Billy Haward, one of the hardest of the hard men, who with his brother Harry ran several clubs in South London and had been a friend of my father's since I was a kid. And Jack Comer. Both with ladies in tow.

I should mention here that I take a size twelve shoe. At which point I hear Spottie passing a loud comment at my expense: "They're not shoes. They're fucking Thames barges!" And he bellows with fruity laughter.

I turned round, and slid up the bar to face him close up. "You fat c--t. You can't even see your shoes!" But I made sure the ladies didn't hear it.

Spottie gave me the hooded fish eye. "What?"

Billy Haward stepped in, smartish. "Hold it, fellers." To Spot: "You! Keep your mouth shut!" And to me: "It's okay, Nosher. No problems."

But I was seething. "It's not okay. I've got the wife here. I don't like that kind of language when we're out together." Which was true. Maybe I was being over-protective, but in another age you might have called it chivalry.

"You're right," said Billy. "It won't happen again."

Spottie might have owned Soho and made his name in the headlines, but Billy Haward called the shots that night.

I've been hurt more times than I can remember, and for a lot of different reasons. Sometimes in the ring, when you go in expecting it. Other times outside it, when you don't. That can be nasty.

I could live with the occasional wallop when I was on the door at Isow's, or acting as a minder. But not to be knifed in the back. That is an experience I do not recommend.

It happened in South London. Jack Isow had finally decided to call it a night and retire from the club scene. He'd made his pile, and wanted to ease off for a quieter life. A spot of golf, slippers by the fire, that kind of thing.

I had been five years at Isow's, and in all that time the worst thing to damage my health was probably the cigarette smoke. I never got seriously injured, though I sometimes came home with a few lumps and bumps to show for a lively night.

Jack, bless his old boots, put the word out, and found me a job at the Peacock Club in Streatham run by an old customer of his, a bloke named Peter Chaplin. He put me in charge of security, which meant I had two minders with me on the door, and another couple wandering around inside to keep an eye on things.

This was the time when everything on the club scene was changing. In Pete's old place you could talk above the music and hear yourself think. He had a live group, cabaret twice a night, and the kind of dancing where you actually had some form of body contact with your partner.

His son Terry took over. He wanted to attract the younger element, and that meant head-banging music blasting out from a glass box with a DJ in it, and kids turning up in jeans and trainers for their big night out. Once you get that sort in, you encourage the kind that get two gins inside them and want to fight everybody. They were just kids, but I still had to keep order.

The DJ was good, I'll give him that. He was a bright spark named Guy, who called himself Guy Fawkes for the crowd, and his patter always included his personal catchphrase: "Let's go with a bang, folks!" He was a pal of Pete Tong, a top celeb DJ.

Unknown to me he had fallen foul of a mob from North London —

what the argument was, I never did find out, and it wasn't my business anyway. But I made it my business after a Saturday night, always the busy one, when a group of them turned up, ten-handed, like a soccer team having a night on the town.

I was standing outside with my two blokes, controlling the queue. The group pushed to the head of it, and I spotted our Guy Fawkes in the middle of them, looking pale and frightened.

The mob started shoving him around, with a lot of shouting and swearing to steam themselves up. I didn't like what I heard.

I stepped forward. "Leave it out," I ordered. "And leave him alone."

The leader, a weasely guy with bad skin and an attitude to match, turned on me. "Fuck off, you big four-eyed c--t," he said loudly. Four-eyed? I wasn't even wearing glasses.

"That's enough of that," I said. "All of you, piss off!"

Now at this point I'm afraid I forgot the first rule of being a minder: *don't turn your back.* I was always good in a rumble, because when a mass brawl really gets off it's like a John Wayne movie. Bodies flying everywhere. All I do is stand there, and just whack 'em. You don't stop to ask questions, or say: "Excuse me, you're on my foot ..." You just lash out. It could be your best friend you flatten because he's got in the firing line by mistake. Then apologise later. If it's in a club, I'd shout: "*Clear the floor!*" And to all the waiters: "Keep away from me, 'cos I'm going to hit everything that fucking moves!" If it's outside in the street, same SP. It's called self-preservation.

But on this night I made my big mistake.

I made a grab for Guy Fawkes, dragged him out of the mob, and turned my back on them to get him inside. Next thing — *thump!* I felt a sharp, searing pain in my back, right between the shoulders. One of the bastards had stuck me with a knife.

I managed to hustle Guy Fawkes inside, and slammed the doors shut, jamming the heavy bar down to stop anyone busting in. I felt warm, sticky liquid running down my back, and I knew something bad had happened. In fact, I was bleeding like a stuck pig, and starting to stagger a bit.

Through the glass I saw the mob running away, scattering up the street. They were gone before the law got there.

I was helped on to a seat, and slumped there till the bloodwagon arrived. I was fading in and out of consciousness, lying there listening to the jangling bell, and still I couldn't work out what had happened. Only when I was in casualty in the Mayday Hospital at Norbury, face down on a trolley, did I realise how close I'd come to snuffing it.

My back was one mass of red, soaking through my shirt and jacket. They pulled the curtains around the trolley, peeled off my clothes, and a doctor examined me.

Finally he said: "Mr Powell, you're a very lucky man. You've got such strong back muscles that the blade has glanced off instead of penetrating a vital part. Otherwise I'd be writing out a death certificate, it was that close. But we'll stitch you up and keep you in for the night."

He put in six stitches, because the blade hadn't been that wide, gave me a pain-killer, and I slept like a baby.

Two nights later I was back at work. The first thing I did was sort out the DJ. There was some unfinished business to attend to.

"Guy," I said. "Who are your friends?"

"Leave it, Nosh," he muttered. "I can handle it."

"That's not what I'm asking. *Who are they?*"

Finally, with more than a little reluctance, he spilled it. There'd been an argument in a club in North London, and someone had got the hump. A rival DJ, the weasel, had brought his mates over to settle a score.

"Oh, yeah," I said. "Where's he working now?"

Guy told me. "He's got a little club near Oxford Street." He gave me a name and an address. "It's in the basement."

I got on the phone to three of my pals, and gave them the SP. "I don't want you to do nothing. Just watch my back. Okay?" I still had the stitches in.

"Sure, Nosher. Whatever you say."

They were good boys. Three husky stunt men who could take care of themselves — and, on this Friday evening, take care of my shoulder-blades if they had to. Around seven thirty, when the place opened, we wandered in like ordinary punters off the street, paid two quid each at the door, and walked down the stairs into the basement.

The room, small and intimate with discreet lighting, was empty. But there was Weasel Face, up on a small stage, fiddling with the record console. I strode across the small floor without a word, and as he looked up — *whack!* I buried him.

I slammed my fist into his face, knocking the extension mike off his throat. If there'd been a beam I'd have hung him from it. I was mad as hell, but in a cold, controlled way.

I slung the records all over the shop, kicked his chair to pieces, and up-ended the console desk on to the floor. There was a small cocktail bar, which I pulled over on him, and left him thrashing about underneath it.

The club minders, two of them, came running down the stairs, but my boys stopped them. "Hold it. This is personal! Don't get involved."

They saw sense, and stepped back.

One of them knew me. "Okay, Nosh. We know what it's all about."

As a final gesture I got the extension mike and wrapped it round the Weasel's neck as he lay amid the shattered glasses, groaning and holding his face.

"Listen, c--t," I said, without preamble, "I don't know you from shit, and I don't want to. But if you ever try to stick a knife in me again, just make sure you finish the job. I don't use tools, I use hands. And I'll fucking kill you."

And *whack!* I hit him again, to put him out.

I never heard a whisper from them after that. But next night when Guy Fawkes came into Streatham, he said: "Nosher, I don't know what happened last night, but whatever it was, thank you. They're never going to touch me again."

I gave him my old-fashioned look. "Let's get one thing straight, sonny boy," I growled. "I didn't do it for you. I did it for me."

I'd gone in, done the job, and walked out. That was all that mattered.

Because if word had gone round, "Nosher got fucked the other night", then all the people I'd done over the years might start thinking: Ah, Nosh could be slipping a bit! This is my chance to get back at him. And before I knew it I'd be back into all the fights again. It's the old law of the jungle at work, and I'm talking about the urban jungle.

But for now, as far as anybody knew, I'd done it on my own. I'd walked into the lion's den. Nobody else did anything, they just stood there.

The word did go round, of course. Like Chinese whispers, it grew in size and lessened in credibility with every telling. After a month of it, I was probably wiping out an army.

Either way, truth or consequences, I got respect.

## 21: GOING POTTIE

Out of the blue came a call from Jack Solomons. I hadn't seen the old promoter for a while, and it was good to hear the familiar gravel voice down the phone. "Nosh? What are you doing for the next couple of weeks?"

"Working nights, but I'm free during the day. What can I do for you, Jack?"

"I'd like you to go down to Southampton tomorrow and pick up a guy who's arriving from South Africa. He's fighting for me in a couple of weeks, and I'd be grateful if you'd look after him while he's in London."

"Well ..." I still needed my beauty sleep.

Jack's timing, as usual, was impeccable. "I'll pay all your expenses, plus a hundred and fifty pounds a week. Just keep him happy, and maybe spar with him a bit."

I weakened. That was a good bonus for my finances. "Okay, Jack. Who is he, and what do I do?"

"His name's Evart Potgeiter, he's coming in on the *Edinburgh Castle*, and you'll be collecting a furniture removal van in Walworth to meet him."

"What?" It must be a wind-up. "You want me to pick up a guy in a furniture van?"

"You'll need it," Solomons assured me. "Just do as I say."

So there I am next morning, bright and early at the firm in Lorrimore Square, and sure enough a massive removal van is waiting for me, bigger than a double-decker bus. The driver jerked a thumb inside. "Take a look," he said.

In the back of the van was a king-size bed, but not just any old king-size bed: this one could have been made for Henry VIII. It was enormous. "We added two feet to it," said the driver proudly. "Special request from Mr Solomons."

Presumably somebody knew what was going on, even if I didn't. Without further argument I hopped up beside the driver, and settled down to enjoy the ride.

When we arrived at the dock the vast bulk of the *Edinburgh Castle* towered above it. I waited at the foot of the gangplank as the first passengers began to disembark. An officer in a white uniform was at the foot, wishing everyone farewell.

I went up to him. "Do you know a Mr Evart Potgeiter, skipper?"

He looked at me. "Certainly do, sir. You can't mistake him."

"How will I recognise him? Can you identify him for me?"

"When the sun is blotted out, that will be him!"

Funny man, I thought. But then, all of a sudden, the horizon did get darker. The biggest man I'd ever seen was lumbering down the gangplank. He stood seven feet four inches, weighed twenty-two stone, and made me look like Charlie Drake.

"Mr Potgeiter?"

"That's me!" The man mountain bestowed a friendly grin from on high. My head came to just below his shoulders.

I introduced myself, passed on Jack Solomons' regards, and told him: "Your transport's waiting."

There was no room for him to squeeze into the driver's cabin, and I couldn't leave our guest alone for the drive back. So we sat together on the king-size bed, and it was like one of those kids' bouncy castles whenever the van went round a bend. I've never had a journey like it before or since. Half-way to London, he suddenly felt hungry.

We stopped off for lunch at a Little Chef on the A3. Pottie ordered soup, chicken, chips and vegetables. "Make it double portions of everything," he said. "And a whole chicken. With two bowls of prunes to finish with." Pottie, I learned later, loved his prunes, and couldn't get enough of them.

That man turned out to be a gentle giant, a farmer from the Transkei, and one of the nicest guys I ever had the pleasure of knowing.

Heart of gold. He told me how his great-grandfather had led a trek across the Transvaal. "We've got the pioneer spirit, man," he declared. "It's in my blood."

Jack put him up in a flat in the Haymarket, and over the next two weeks I took him under my wing. That meant picking him up in the morning and taking him across the road for breakfast: six rashers of bacon, three poached eggs, sausages, mushrooms and half a loaf sliced into toast. Plus a pint of hot sweet tea. "Got to keep my strength up, Nosher!"

Then it was off to Hyde Park for an hour's road work, followed by sparring sessions in the gym. Most important of all was to keep him in the right frame of mind for his upcoming fight. His opponent would be Noel "Bull" Reed, a big strong Jamaican who tipped the scales at nineteen stone. Pottie would have his work cut out — and that worried me. Because this gentle giant was just that: too gentle. Up to then he had won every fight he had ever boxed down in South Africa. But now he had moved up a league.

I reported my fears to Solomons. "He just isn't vicious enough, Jack. He'll get slaughtered."

Jack's answer was brief and to the point. "Well, wind him up, then, so he gets vicious!"

Well, I tried. I outran him on the road, setting a punishing pace until he was gasping for breath. I ridiculed his boxing technique, making him miss so often that he ended up hitting air. I even took a poke at his most precious possession: "Bet you've got a prick the size of an acorn! All big guys like you have." This, in fact, wasn't true. Pottie was hung like a horse.

Well, he didn't get mad. He just got dejected. I felt so sorry for the guy that I came clean. "I'm just trying to save your hide, Pottie, that's all."

Relief flooded his face. "I'm glad to hear it, man," he said, in his guttural rumble. "I kept wondering how I'd upset you."

I lost a stone in weight, and was as fit as I'd ever been. We even played leapfrog in the park to break up the monotony. When I went over him, it was like going over Becher's Brook in the Grand National. When his turn came, his feet never left the grass. But we got a laugh out of it, and so did the passers-by.

On the night, to my surprise, Pottie took out the raging Bull in eight with a TKO. Fight stopped. Glove raised. We celebrated at Isow's; Jack Solomons joined us — and signed the bill.

A week later, the phone rang. Jack again. "Nosher, I need your help.

Evart is staying with us for a couple more fights. And he needs a fuck."

"Don't look at me!" I said, witty as ever.

"It's serious, Nosh. He's getting all wound up."

"I thought that's how you wanted him," I said. "Lean and mean —"

"Not that way," Jack said testily. "He deserves a bit of ... let's say relaxation. You know all the clubs and bars. Can't you get him a nice girl?"

I sighed. A nice girl for a nice guy. Why not? "All right, I'll try. How much will you pay?"

"It's got to be at least a pony. Look at the fucking size of him. She'll have to be a big girl to survive!"

Well, I did know a girl who fitted the bill. She was a hostess at the Jack of Clubs, a strapping wench named Mary with a personality that matched her bra size. That night I cornered her when she walked in. The conversation went like this:

Me: "Mary, can I have a word?"

Mary: "Sure, Nosher, what is it?"

Me: "I've got this heavyweight boxer, a lovely feller. Trouble is, he's getting too fit, he's going off the boil. What he needs is a bit of ... relaxation."

Mary: "What you mean, Nosher, is that he wants a fuck!"

Me: "If you put it like that, Mary, yes, he does." Pause. "Er — you know, take him to a show, get to know him, let things take their course. Everything will be paid for." Emphasis on the word "everything".

Mary: "All right, Nosher. Why not?"

Next day I escorted her to the flat in the Haymarket, and up two flights of stairs to his front door. "We all call him Pottie. I'll leave you to it. I don't want to be in the way. See you tonight." Then I rang the bell, and hurried off.

On the way downstairs it occurred to me that the one thing I had omitted to mention to Mary was the size of her blind date.

That night I was in the foyer as usual when the main door opened. Mary came in, walking slowly and carefully. She came up to the desk, put her face close to mine, and whispered: "You ginger-haired bastard!" Then she smiled. "What a fuck! That man's built like a rhino."

I could have said something about a horn, but I resisted. Instead I grinned back at her. "I'll tell you something, Mary. I'll bet you're the only bow-legged hostess in the club tonight!"

Three days later Mary moved into the flat, and Pottie became the happiest heavyweight on the circuit. Brimming with energy, he won both his fights, and kept the smile bright on Mary's face too.

He even bought himself a second-hand car as a runaround for the summer, mainly because he wasn't keen on public transport. You try getting on a tube in the rush hour when you're over seven foot tall and weigh twenty-two stone!

"Look at that, Nosher. Isn't she a little beauty?" He'd parked it in Brewer Street, outside the club.

"Umm," I said. To me it looked like a beat-up old banger, a family saloon that had seen better days. But it was obviously his pride and joy, so why should I give offence? I looked closer. Something was missing.

"Where's the front seat?"

Pottie stood to his full height, beaming. "Oh, I had to have it taken out. It was too small."

"So how do you drive it?"

Silly question. "From the back seat. We'll go out tomorrow." And with that he squeezed his massive bulk into the rear, stuck both legs out to reach the pedals, grasped the wheel from the back seat, and took off.

Next day we went for a spin in the country. Pottie sat in the back with Mary, driving in supreme comfort and ease. Guess who sat up in the front passenger seat by himself, like a lemon, trying to avoid the disbelieving stares of everybody gazing in?

I taught him "The Boxing Blues", sung to the tune of "There's No Business Like Show Business", and we gave it the full works as we headed down the A4 to a pub lunch by the Thames.

> *There's no business like the fight business,*
> *They smile when they're hit low,*
> *All the managers are great schemers,*
> *Twenty-five per cent is all they know,*
> *Managers go on for bleeding ever —*
> *But where, oh where, do fighters go?*
> *There's no racket like their racket,*
> *Cigars are all the vogue,*
> *After every match they come and take their whack,*
> *Into their limos to count their jack,*
> *While the poor old fighter*
> *Tries to make one more comeback.*
> *On his bike he pedals for home —*
> *What a game this fight game has become!*

The idyllic summer couldn't last, and we all knew it. Eventually Pottie had to go back to his farm in Transkei. He bade farewell to a tearful Mary, then paid a final visit to the club when she wasn't there. "Thanks for everything, Nosh. I'll never forget you."

I shook the huge hand of friendship. "I can be sure of one thing myself, Pottie. I won't either."

Another fighter for whom I had to perform escort duty was Sugar Ray Robinson, one of the true legends of the ring. For fifteen years that guy was a world champion, first at welter, then middleweight.

He was such a great fighter that he could actually position photographers from the ring as he mesmerised his opponents. Look at pictures of Sugar Ray knocking someone out, and he was always facing the camera, always flashing that 22-carat grin of his. I've watched him walk them around — then *pop!* Down they went.

Sugar Ray dropped by London, courtesy of Jack Solomons, during one of his famous European tours when he took on the cream of every country and gave them all an object lesson in ringcraft. I had a week in the gym sparring with him, and the tricks I picked up from that genius were gold-dust.

But his personal life, from where I saw it, was something else. He was a good-looking dude, unmarked in all his fights, yet when it came to a casual night out, Sugar Ray loved slags! He could have pulled any bird he wanted but, no, he had to have the worst. He went for blonde, blowsy tarts, the ones wearing rouge and lipstick as if they'd been painting the Sistine Chapel.

It was weird. And, for me, embarrassing. At the hotel by Marble Arch, where Jack Solomons put him up, the champ would come prancing through the swing doors with a real dog on the leash, and whisk her through the foyer and up to his room. My nightmare was that someone with a camera would catch sight of him, but miraculously he stayed lucky.

Lucky, that is, up to a point. Inevitably with such a surplus in rough trade, Sugar Ray caught a dose. The first I heard of it was one evening when we were heading into the West End in his pink Cadillac for a night on the town. The Cadillac was an integral part of the Sugar Ray entourage, and accompanied him on his whistle-stop tour all the way across seven countries. The man was a showman outside the ring as well as in it.

In the back of the car, his personal manager George Gainsford, who was dressed like a senator, handed me a slip of paper. "Nosher, I've got to get this." I looked at it. It was a prescription for his boss's ailment.

"Boots," I said. There was one open all night in Piccadilly.

"Boots?" echoed Sugar Ray from up front. "I don't want fucking boots, man!"

"No, Boots the Chemist," I told him shortly.

At the prescription counter, you can imagine the line-up. The senator, two black minders, a couple of hangers-on, the star of the show and me. Sugar Ray handed the prescription to a young girl assistant. She took one look, flinched visibly, then said: "For you, sir?"

Sugar Ray reacted with his usual lightning reflexes, jerking a thumb at his manager. "No, for him!"

George recoiled."I ain't no poxy black man!" he shouted. He pointed at me. "It's for him."

Okay, so I took it. The man was a guest in our country, after all.

## 22: SHOW TIME!

I actually got my first break into movies through boxing. I was at the peak of my fighting career, training every day like it was a second religion. On this day I was down in Joe Bloom's gym preparing for a fight at Haringey Arena with Don Scott, who hailed from Derby, for the handsome purse of forty-five quid.

I was a muscular lad in my mid-twenties, tip-top condition, full of myself and a bit flash with it. Suddenly I noticed two geezers standing quietly in the doorway, watching me. They'd come from nowhere, and I had no idea how long they'd been there. But I've always been a bit of a ham when it comes to putting on a show for the punters, so why should today be any different?

When I'm training and there's no one watching, I take it seriously. But once I've got an audience — oh dear, that's when I start getting a bit lemon.

The speed ball, for instance. I moved on to it as if I hadn't noticed them, and started slapping it around. I can hit that spinning lump of leather like no one else, making it jump on its chain as if it's alive. *Tuckety-tuckety-tuckety-tuckety!* And skipping — I was using that rope like Sugar Ray Robinson. *Zip! Zip! Zip!* Flash bastard, that's me!

When I finished, I could have done with a round of applause.

Instead, silence. So I stalked back to the dressing room to sit down and get my breath. I was rubbing the sweat out of my eyes with a towel when there was a light knock on the door, and the pair walked in.

The first, a compact, dapper man with a pleasant smile, said: "Mr Powell? Could I have a word with you?"

I said: "Sure, guv, what's your problem?" I thought maybe they wanted something taken care of, if you get my meaning. The other guy was a sharp-featured man who just stood there, watching and listening.

"My name is Lewis Gilbert. And yes, actually we do have a problem." Mr Gilbert was a B-class director in those days, before he went on to greater things like *Alfie* and *Educating Rita*, with Michael Caine, and two of the best James Bond movies: *You Only Live Twice*, with Sean Connery, and *The Spy Who Loved Me*, with Roger Moore, both of which I would work on with him. He went on: "I've got a young actor, and I want him to look like a light-heavyweight champion for a film I'm directing. It's called *Wall of Death*, and his name is Laurence Harvey."

I registered a blank. I'd never heard of this kid, and neither had anyone else. So I gave it to Mr Gilbert straight.

"You've got a problem all right, guv. You can turn a boxer into an actor, but you can't turn an actor into a boxer. Not inside a year."

He said: "We've got three weeks. Will you have a stab at it?"

I said: "Not really. I'm fighting next week. Sorry, I'm not interested."

Undaunted, Mr Gilbert pressed on. "I'll give you a hundred pounds a week."

I said: "What? You'll do *what*?"

He said: "All right, one fifty."

I said: "You've got to be joking!"

He said: "Two hundred — and that's my final offer!"

I think my jaw must have sagged. I was getting forty-five quid, and training for a month just to get my block knocked off. At that price, I would have said yes to the weather! Sometimes it pays when you *don't* keep your mouth shut!

"All right, you're on!" I said. I figured I could still do the fight and keep fit while training this unknown kid for the cameras.

A week later I took the train from Waterloo down to Nettlefold Film Studios in Berkshire. I didn't have a car so I used public transport.

The journey took over an hour, but I felt the excitement rising in my throat as I saw the sprawl of the studios like aircraft hangars behind a high wire fence. My name was on the gate, and when I got to the set the first person I bumped into was Lewis Gilbert himself. He was sitting in a canvas chair with his name on the back, immersed in the script.

*Wall of Death* was a small-budget affair set in a circus. The stars were Harvey and fellow heart-throb Bonar Colleano, with a blonde chick named Susan Shaw, a former model and Rank starlet, hired for the glamour.

"Good morning, Mr Gilbert!"

He looked up. "Lewis, please. Make yourself at home. Larry will be out in a few minutes." Sure enough, I found myself face to face with a tall, good-looking young actor who looked as if he had stepped out of the pages of *Debrett*. His aristocratic manner was heightened by an overcoat with a velvet collar, and a tie with a fat Windsor knot.

"Hello, Nosher," he drawled in a voice like cut glass. "Delighted to meet you." He extended a slim hand.

I thought: *Bloody hell*! What's this willowy wisp doing in a boxing ring? Aloud, I said: "Me too, Laurence."

"Larry, actually."

"Right — er, Larry. We've got to start working out, and I have to see what you look like."

How wrong could I have been about Laurence Harvey? And who would ever have guessed that he was actually Lithuanian, born Lauruska Mischa Skikne in a place called Yomishkis that I couldn't pronounce, and only spell after looking it up? Larry told everyone that he'd been born on 1 October 1928, and emigrated with his parents to South Africa. But he had joined the Army in 1943, and had been in the South African Union Defence Corps — at fifteen? I always reckoned he was a good seven years older than he said he was.

But they found us a quiet corner on another set, away from prying eyes, and I told everyone: "I don't want anybody here, no one at all." I piled some boxes in a square to create a makeshift ring. Then we went to work.

The kid was good, and keen as mustard. He shaped very well indeed. So much so that I had to put the block on him, because he would have carried on for hours. "Show me this way, Nosher, show me that way!" I was showing him how to *appear* to fight, but he started wanting it for real instead of just faking it.

So I got him standing with the correct posture while I did the moves. "All you've got to do is stick that left hand out — *jab, jab, jab* — and leave it to me to make you look good. Okay?"

"Okay, Nosher. Anything you say."

I had three weeks to get him ready.

I put him through the mill. Weights, shadow-boxing, pushing each other around the ring, building up muscle and bulk. Everything went fine for ten days — then suddenly it all went to pieces. Larry was just not working with the same venom that he'd had in him before. He looked tired — Christ, he *was* tired.

But why? When you're a trainer you know when your fighter is not doing as he should. As a fighter, you can't hide anything from your trainer, because he sees everything. Every muscle. Even — as we say in the business — down to your prick! You see him stripped naked, physically and emotionally. That's why a good trainer can make all the difference to a fighter.

I couldn't understand it. Harvey should have been getting fitter by the day, putting on more weight with the way I was training him. His co-star Susan Shaw had turned out to be a lovely little thing, blonde and bubbly, and the thought occurred to me: maybe Larry's knocking her off.

But she was actually going out with Bonar Colleano, whom she later married.

Finally I decided to take the bull by the horns and ask him straight out. I took him aside. "Larry. It's not going right, son. This is the chance of a lifetime for you, and you're going to blow it."

At that time, I might mention, Laurence Harvey was under contract to Associated British Cinemas, and getting the magnificent sum of thirty quid a week. Me, I was getting a hundred and fifty!

Finally he came clean — and it was a real shaker. Playing the part of a gypsy fortune teller in the film was none other than Hermione Baddeley, known to one and all as Lottie. She was a distinguished actress who would go on to be nominated for an Oscar in 1959 for *Room at the Top*, which by happy chance was the film that made Larry an international star.

Now, Lottie had been born in 1906, which made her a lot older than Larry, and without wishing to be unkind she wasn't the best-looking bird in the world. In fact, as someone remarked at the time, without intending any malice, I'm sure: "Lottie could play a witch very easily — without any make-up."

Bless her, she was a very nice woman, a real trouper specialising in "ribald character roles". Her sister Angela went on to make her own name as Mrs Bridges, the cook in *Upstairs, Downstairs*.

But Lottie also had an explosive temper.

Larry held up his hands, and confessed all. Miss Baddeley had started filming on the next set. One night after his workout with me, he had offered to take her home — and the inevitable happened.

The fact was that Larry owed money everywhere. He was living way above his means, ordering suits worth £200 apiece, slurping down champagne by the bucketful and spending money like there was no tomorrow. He was a great appreciator of the finer things of life.

Out of the blue comes this bird from an élite theatrical family, loads of dosh behind her, with a beautiful Georgian house in Belgravia, a woman with influence and class. So what's a handsome unknown actor, twenty-two years younger, going to do?

Answer: He's going to give her one, and make her fall for him. And that's just what Lothario Larry went and did. The result was that he started going to places he had only previously dreamed about, like the Caprice and the Ivy where, over the caviar and bubbly, Lottie introduced him to all her rich and powerful friends — while paying all the way. As Larry admitted to me: "Once you get the taste, Nosher, it's hard to stop."

He would walk into a restaurant where she was a regular customer with his own friends, looking and acting like the Duke of Windsor. Afterwards he'd sign the bill with a flourish, and tell the *maître d'*: "She'll pay later!"

Lottie had everything that Larry wanted. But in a funny way he also thought a lot of her. He wasn't just on the make. He told me as much. "I really love her, Nosh," he would say later, after the crisis happened that could have cost him his career.

But Lottie's temper was a matter of legend, to be talked of in hushed tones. And you must remember that at this time I'm just starting out in the business, and needing to tread a bit careful. So it was with some trepidation that I summoned up my bottle and headed for her dressing room. Not to put too fine a point on it, I was shitting bricks.

But I knocked on the door, put my head inside at the imperious command of "Yes?" and said: "Lottie, can I have a word with you?"

She knew me because I'd been working out with Larry, but we'd only exchanged the odd hello.

She responded: "Yes, Nosher, what is it?"

Her dresser was there, so I said: "Can I talk to you on your own?"

"Very well." She dismissed the dresser with a wave.

I took a deep breath. "Lottie, I've been given the job of making Larry look a million dollars. He started off well. But all of a sudden it's all gone to pieces. He's knackered! I can't get anything out of him any more." My voice faltered to a halt.

She looked at me for a long moment, extracted a cigarette out of a box, and took her time lighting it. Then she said: "In other words, Nosher, you want me to stop fucking him?"

Well, I nearly fell down on the spot. But now she was talking my language. I said: "Since you put it like that, ma'am, yes."

She said: "Nosher, I love that boy. In no way would I jeopardise his career. I want him to succeed. But perhaps I have let my feelings run away with me, and I forgot what he was supposed to be doing. Maybe I did tire him out a little."

"A *little*!" I exclaimed. "You're damn near killing him! He's supposed to be a light-heavy, but the way he's going he'll wind up a fucking flyweight! I'm trying to train Larry — and I don't mean on the couch."

Lottie actually looked penitent. She said: "Very well. You've got a deal. No more fucking — until the boxing sequence is finished." She paused, and took a drag on her cigarette. "But, Nosher, for heaven's sake get it over and done with just as quick as you can, will you? Because I'm a randy old cow!"

She extended a manicured hand, and we shook on it.

I noticed the improvement immediately. Larry was getting his sleep, and he was sharp and fit again. I don't know what that dame told him, but he came in prompt each day to our private corner in the studio, and he started to flourish. By the time they started filming, he was the dog's bollocks.

When the final scenes were in the can, Larry came up to me. "I'm really glad you said what you did, Nosh. Let's face it, she's no chicken — but she was fucking the life out of me!"

Another problem on *Wall of Death* came up. The guy in the ring with him was an actor called Dennis Vance, who unfortunately wasn't all that clever with his fists. He was supposed to be the world champion. After a lot of to-ing and fro-ing, Lewis Gilbert asked me if I'd play the role of the champ, the guy Larry's taking on.

I said: "No way!"

"Why on earth not? It's a great role."

I told him: "I'm sure it is. But I've never trod on anybody's toes in my life. If I take this man's job, he's got nothing. I've got work to go back to. He hasn't."

Then the producers started chipping in, two men in dark suits who, up to then, had always stayed in the background and kept quiet. "Won't you reconsider, Mr Powell? It's vital for us. You know how to work with Larry, you make him look good. Have a think about it."

So I had a think. It was true, I did make Larry look good. Finally I came up with an answer. "I'll do the role, providing ..."

"Providing what?"

"Providing you give Dennis Vance a part in this film. *This* film. Not a later one, where you might forget. This one, okay? Then I'll play the role."

They found a job for Dennis as a speedway manager, and I can't remember whether we ever saw it or if it ended up on the cutting-room floor. But for me, it turned out to be one of the smartest career moves I ever made. Why? Because Dennis never forgot it. He realised what I'd done, and he also realised that his career lay not in front of a camera — but behind it.

He rose through the showbiz stratosphere to become head of ATV. And over the years, as Dennis climbed the ladder, I'd be getting phone calls. "Nosher, I want you to work with Morecambe and Wise ... work with this show, and that series ..." For that small gesture he paid me back a hundred times over.

Meantime, through the years that followed while he climbed his own ladder to stardom, Larry and I kept in touch. In many ways he was a no-good bastard, all self, a bullshitter, but I couldn't help liking him. Time and again he'd call me up to get him out of a spot.

I'd get a call. "Nosh? Larry."

"What's the matter?"

"Got a problem!"

"Where are you?"

He'd tell me, and I'd go out and settle it.

Once, he chinned a gendarme in Paris. Now, you don't go around doing that to the local constabulary in a foreign country, especially if you're only earning fifty quid a week and can't pay or bribe your way out of trouble.

Larry had got involved in an argument over a car that had suffered a bit of a bang, and they slung him in jail. The problem was that he'd caused the bang after downing a few too many strong brandies — his favourite tipple, along with Pouilly Fuissé white wine — and he was behind the wheel when he shunted into another car.

Not a clever move. A gendarme appeared, and after an exchange of unpleasantries Larry made his second mistake: he clocked the *Vieux Guillaume* one. So — into the slammer he went.

It was ten days before I sorted it. I hopped across to Paris, found an interpreter, signed a bit of paper, handed over fifty quid and bailed him out. Then we did a fast runner for the ferry before they changed their minds.

It was several years before Larry ever set foot in France again, or he'd have been arrested. It was only when he finally became famous and had a few quid in his pocket that he was able to clear it all up.

Another time he got into an argument in a pub in Chelsea, in a watering-hole frequented by the acting fraternity. Larry was in there one night holding court, as was his wont, to a bunch of cronies — luvvies, we'd call them today. By now he was determined to become another John Gielgud, up there with the acting greats. He even told me he'd changed his name to Laurence to take some of the shine off Laurence Olivier! I had to believe it.

But actors and villains are never far apart, because traditionally one attracts the other. It was always thus, and always will be. There was another type who used the same pub. One of them was a guy I knew quite well named Big Mike, who ran a used-car business down the road in World's End.

Of course, dear Larry has to get a bit flash and start mouthing off, insulting him as only Squire Harvey could when he'd downed a few. This geezer gets the hump and pops one on Larry, smack on the chin, flooring him. Larry went down, not out — but he was hurt in more ways than one.

His pride, for a start. In the boxing scenes for *Wall of Death* I had trained him to look like a fighter — but I had never actually landed one on him. After all, the star can't be damaged goods. I would throw punches at him — *pow, pow, pow*. But they always landed a fraction of an inch short, in thin air. He had never been hit. So when it finally happened, he wondered where Nosher's training had got to!

To make it worse, right in front of all his mates, Big Mike poked a finger at him, and said loudly: "Don't you ever come into this fucking pub no more, or I'll throw you right out through that fucking window!" So you can imagine Larry was a bit put out.

He gets on to me, pours it all out — so okay, I take a trip into Chelsea to see the man. I found him propping up the public bar, and he gave me a cautious nod of recognition. He was big, but I was bigger.

"Look, Mike, this guy's a c--t. He believes in everything that he's been taught by me, but he couldn't swat a fly and kill it. He don't really mean the tough talk.

"Let me fetch him in, and the two of you have a drink and sort it out. I'll be there, standing by." And just to make the point, I added: "You'll realise that although he's a c--t, he's actually quite a nice feller."

Mike said: "All right, Nosher, if you say so. In my book he's a right fucking stupid bastard, trying to insult me and take the piss. But I'll go along with it."

I said: "Thanks. And listen, this boy is growing up, and going places. Just you see."

Larry was still in the saloon area, rubbing his jaw. I went up to him. "Listen, I've made a meet with this man, and you've got to see him."

He started to sweat. "Nosher, I can't afford to have my face marked."

"Don't worry, son." I took him into the public bar, and the two of them faced each other warily. I stood close by — very close. I said: "Right, Larry, you've got to say it."

He swallowed. Then: "Okay, I'm sorry."

And Mike said: "That's all right, son. 'Ave a drink."

You know what? Six weeks later Larry ended up buying his first Jag from that guy, which was more than I'd have done! It was an old 1950 model and guzzled petrol no end, but he was as proud as punch of it, and insisted on taking me for a spin.

"After all, Nosher," he reasoned, "if it hadn't been for you, I'd never have bought it, would I?"

## 23: OH, LARRY!

"Oh Gawd, Larry. What 'ave you been and done now?" I lost count of the number of times I said that when the phone rang and his voice was on the other end, languidly requesting a favour, or merely slurred. The message was always the same: *"Come and get me out of trouble!"*

But one morning the drawl wasn't quite so clipped and confident as usual. "Nosher, I'm in deep trouble."

Wearily I said: "What is it now, Larry?"

He said: "I've just killed a man!"

*"What?"* That made me sit up and take notice.

"I was in the Jag, motoring up to Stratford. I'm in a Shakespeare here. I was just into town when this chap stepped off the pavement straight in front of me. And I hit him."

My first thought: "Have you been drinking? Tell me straight!"

"Not at all. I promise you." The voice was pleading now. "He came out from nowhere. You've got to help me."

"Where are you?"

"At the theatre."

I told him: "Don't say no more to no one. I'm on my way."

I broke all records up the A40, and made it to Stratford ten minutes before the curtain was due to go up on *As You Like It*. Larry was in his dressing room. He was still trembling like a leaf, but he had to go on. The police had taken a statement, and let him go.

I hurried round to the nick, and had a few words, arguing Larry's case. They told me that when they picked the guy out of the gutter he was still alive, but by the time they got him to hospital he was dead. The verdict was accidental death. The post-mortem showed he had enough alcohol in him to send a rocket to Mars.

At the inquest Larry appeared under his own name, Lauruska Skikne, and somehow nobody picked it up. The case came on late, I hid Larry in a side room, and by the time he stepped into the box all the local press had gone. It never got into the papers or the tabloids would have had a field day.

Afterwards he pumped my hand, the old Larry, bright and breezy, who believed he could get away with anything. "That's one I owe you, Nosher."

"You mean another one, my son," I told him wearily. "If I was charging you by the hour, I'd be a rich man."

Talking of riches, Laurence Harvey was now rich and running. From fifty pounds a week he found himself earning ninety thousand pounds a film, and then into six figures. His portrayal of the ruthlessly ambitious womaniser in *Room at the Top* opened the floodgates on his career — and it went to his head. With films like *The Alamo*, *The Manchurian Candidate* and *Walk on the Wild Side* under his belt, our Larry was flying high.

The top restaurants and bars saw him walk on his own personal wild side, and didn't like it, even as they laid out the welcome mat to a big spender. Larry would saunter in as if he owned the place, call for the best table, and ooze charm — but you never knew which way he'd go when he got a few drinks inside him. As he said to me once: "The great thing about having money, Nosher, is that you never have to look at the right-hand side of the menu." Pursuing that creed to its logical conclusion, he revelled in Dom Perignon champagne and his favourite Pouilly Fuissé — and left it to darling Lottie to go back next day and sign the bill for the food, the bubbly and the broken crockery.

Larry moved in with Lottie, putting his slippers under the table in her elegant flat in Chester Square, one of the great addresses in Belgravia: trees outside the windows, a church at one end, and a lot of chauffeur-driven Rollers in evidence.

He had reached a peak in his own ambitions — just like his character in *Room at the Top*, grubbing up the ladder. Only Larry made it happen in real life.

But one day something happened that could have put the skids under his career for ever. Late morning, the phone rang in my South London flat. Larry's voice, tense and urgent. "Nosher, you've got to get over here, quick!"

"Where are you? What is it?"

"I'm at Lottie's place. I can't tell you on the phone — just get over here. Now!" There was real apprehension in his voice.

I hurried over in my old rattler of an estate, found a parking spot, and took the steps two at a time. The door opened while my finger was still on the bell-push. Larry had been waiting, and his face was pale and tense. Without a word he simply beckoned me to follow him up a wide staircase and into a bedroom. I stood in the doorway not believing what I saw.

There was Lottie lying on the bed — and hardly recognisable. Blood had soaked into the pillow, her eyes were all over the show, and her face was puffed up and swollen. There was a slit under her right eye, a cut above the other one, and she was a right mess, poor girl.

I turned on Larry in sudden blind rage, grabbing him by his shirt. "You did this?" He nodded wordlessly. God help him, he'd punched seven colours of shit out of her. "You fucking dirty bastard!" I stormed. "After all she's done for you —"

He started mumbling: "Please ... I'm sorry, Nosher. I had too much to drink ..." His voice tailed away.

I shouted: "Don't you make fucking excuses to me!" My knuckles were white, and I could have laid him out then and there on the bedroom carpet. But there were more urgent matters to take care of, and I had to cool off.

Although I know the fight game backwards, I'm not an expert on cuts — but I knew a man who was: Danny Holland, the best cuts man in the country. I phoned his gymnasium in the Old Kent Road, and by luck he was just opening up the shop.

"Danny? I need your help." Danny had been Henry Cooper's trainer, — and our 'Enery would not have got anywhere without Danny because he cut easily, like a bit of tissue paper. And, you remember, that's what robbed him of stealing the world crown from Muhammad Ali, then plain Cassius Clay.

Remember? Who can ever forget it? Certainly none of the thousands of fans who packed Highbury Stadium that June night in 1964 when Cooper fought Clay for the heavyweight championship of the world. I was shouting with the rest of them, " 'Enery! 'Enery!" fit to bust a gut to cheer our boy on to glory.

But that was the one night Danny should have been there, and he wasn't. Not his fault, I have to say. He'd fallen out with Henry, so Danny's brother George Holland was in the corner instead. The way I heard it, they used to give Danny a hundred quid for training 'Enery up to scratch, and this time Danny thought he was worth more because it was a world fight.

We all know what happened that night. I can still see the blood gushing from our great white hope's cut eye — and so, I reckon, can our 'Enery, living with it all these years later.

But right now I said urgently down the phone: "Danny, I need your help. I'll make it worth your while. Can you get over here?"

Danny, bless him, didn't ask questions, and he made it from Battersea to Belgravia in half an hour. He walked in, took one look at the pitiful face on the pillow, and reacted accordingly: "Cor, fuck me!"

Then he turned on us. "Right! You two — out!" The door shut.

Every now and then Danny would emerge with a bowl filled with hot water, crimson at first, then pink, then just water. It took three hours before the door finally opened and he said: "Okay, you can come in."

Lottie was beginning to look human again. Danny had put a clip on her left eye, and a stitch under the other. The swelling had gone down, and she managed a weak smile. I turned on Larry. "I should fucking mark you up the same as you marked her."

But from the bed came Lottie's voice, weak but audible: "Leave him alone, Nosher. He was drunk. Please ... don't touch him."

Danny looked at Larry. "You, young feller," he said coldly, "you want to get your head examined. Now listen to me carefully. Every two hours she has to have a hot compress on her face. I'll be back at the same time tomorrow. Understand?" Larry nodded mutely, and hung his head. He looked like a whipped dog, but this was one time I could never feel sorry for him. Any man who beats up women is beneath contempt, and should crawl under the nearest stone.

Three days later the swelling had gone, though both Lottie's eyes stayed black and blue for days. But, best of all, her sense of humour had returned. "Nosh," she said. "I can't go out looking like Quasimodo!" So she stayed in the house, ordering hampers of food to be brought in from Fortnum and Mason, which Danny and I demolished with gusto. Slowly she got back her looks and appetite, and her lover-boy was forgiven.

Larry gave Danny a hundred quid. In my book it was worth a whole lot more. And, like the true blue South London gentleman that he was, Danny never breathed a word of that episode to anybody. He's dead now,

God bless him. But I can tell you this: without him, Lottie would have ended up marked for life.

So Larry had his dark side, like all of us, but perhaps darker than most. Yet, despite it all, I liked him. He could be warm, witty and utterly charming. He spoke in that marvellously clipped accent — which he'd worked on from a long time back — and he could pass for royalty.

On the lighter side, one of his failings — if it was a failing — was that he was so outspoken. Larry just couldn't keep his stupid mouth shut. Like the very first time he met Margaret Leighton to discuss a film he was going to make with her, *The Good Die Young*, a mail-van robbery directed by our new-found friend Lewis Gilbert. I'll never forget the moment their eyes first met.

Lewis performed the introductions in the Green Room at Pinewood, during a small private party to let the leading members of the cast get to know one another. I was standing with Larry when this elegant lady was brought over to meet him.

His first words were: "Really, you're too old to be working with me in this part!" And that for openers! Tact was never Larry's strong point.

Maggie was six years older than he was, if you believe the official records. She was a lovely redhead, almost as tall as him, and they struck sparks together in the film. She must have forgiven him his social lapse, or maybe she was fascinated by his directness and rose to the challenge — because three years later they were married. That union lasted four years before Larry moved on to another older bird and married Joan Cohn, the widow of Columbia Pictures boss Harry Cohn.

The good die young? I don't know about that. The last time I saw Laurence Harvey, I'd popped into Shepperton Studios to do some business, and there he was in the bar holding court to a group of acolytes around him, the usual bees-to-a-honeypot hangers-on. But now I hardly recognised him — until he spotted me and waved me over.

"Nosh!" I tried not to look shocked at how gaunt my one-time sparring partner had become. The handsome face was haggard, but his eyes lit up, and he gave me a big hug. "Nosh, how are you?"

It was the last embrace we ever had. A month later Laurence Harvey was dead, from cancer, at the too-young age of forty-five. At least he had lived his life to the full.

I still miss the silly sod.

Nosher as Home Secretary? Don't scoff – it happened!

Ride 'em cowboy! That's me on my beautiful rearing horse Alamarante, an eight-year-old I kept stabled at Boxhill, Surrey.

*Top:* A whole new meaning to bare back riding ... me, minus shirt and my brother Dinny on location in Turkey for *You Can't Win 'Em All*.

*Bottom:* On a wing and a prayer – Nosher does his own dangerous stunts in *Eat the Rich*.

*Top:* The gang's all here. I'm surrounded by the entire stunt team on *Brannigan* – and there's John Wayne in the middle!

*Bottom:* Facing up to an altercation with Ron Tarr in *Eat the Rich*, he's a well-known character actor from film and TV. Maybe you've seen Big Ron in *EastEnders*?

Nosher in his element with two wenches as a warm-up to my jousting tournament at the Tower of London ... and as a jovial Cap'n Red Beard in the spoof TV series, *Pirates*.

'Have you got a problem, Ollie?' Well, yes. The problem *was* Oliver Reed, and I had to throw him out of a celebrity party when things got nasty.

*Inset:* My son, Greg, stunt director on *Mission Impossible*, with Jon Voight and Tom Cruise on the set at Pinewood.

*Top:* Oi, stoneface! All right, which is which?

*Bottom:* Me with ring legends Terry Spinks and Henry Cooper.

## 24: SINATRA

It doesn't take much to get hooked on showbusiness. Some of us get that way from childhood. Others take a little longer. I realised now that I was a sucker for the excitement, the uncertainty, the drama, the weird and wonderful people you meet every day at the studios or on location.

In short, I'd been bitten by the bug, and I knew there was no cure for it. So — whoopee!

I came at it from three different paths. Film extra, stunt man, and as a minder to the rich and famous. And you don't get much richer or more famous than Frank Sinatra, who was about to become my boss.

Looking to make a few waves, my brother Dinny and I had taken a cheap flight to Los Angeles, and started making ourselves known. I don't mean we went about smashing up bars. But we put it around that we were tasty with our fists, and could be relied upon in a tight corner.

The first time we had to prove ourselves happened in a club owned by Sinatra's corporation, a place called Dino's, located off Sunset on Ventura Boulevard and named after his friend Dean Martin. Frank himself, of course, always liked to be known as the Chairman of the Board by his pals in the Rat Pack, Dino himself, Joey Bishop, Sammy Davis Jnr and Peter Lawford.

So, would you believe it? Two Limeys over from England have to wind up this joint with the tables and bottles flying, and the whole place in uproar. We could hardly have picked a more unhealthy place to start shifting the furniture and leave our business card.

"I can assure you, sir, it's very unusual for a fight to start in a Sinatra club," the head bouncer told me later, as he helped me wipe blood off my cheek. "People usually have too much respect."

Not tonight. It started over by the bar. I was sitting with an agent named Marian, who was trying to find extra work for us and hosting some of her friends from casting. Dinny had gone to the toilet. I heard raised voices, the crash of glass — then a large bloke in a loud check jacket came hurtling backwards over our table, knocking everything flying, before collapsing on to the carpet. Marian went over too, and so did several of her guests.

I was up in a flash. The place was in pandemonium, with everyone taking sides or settling old scores. Following my usual policy in such unsociable situations, everything that moved, I hit!

Next minute I'm grasped from behind by someone I mistake for Guy the Gorilla. He has my arms in a vice, and I can't move. "Steady, feller," says a voice as deep as the tomb. "Take it easy!"

When I managed to turn my head, I glimpsed this huge guy standing there — and this was one impressive gorilla all dolled up in a monkey suit, complete with black tie. We recognised each other in the same breath.

"Nosher!"

"Christ, it's you. Hello, sailor!"

What else could I say when I found myself facing Tami Moriella? The heavyweight who had once been the pride of the US Navy, last seen toppling through the ropes of the USS *Valley Forge* at the wrong end of my gloves off the coast of North Africa.

That was all of fifteen years ago. Since when Tami had fought a draw with our Bruce Woodcock, and even put Joe Louis on the floor before losing a world title collision with the Brown Bomber.

Now he was Frank Sinatra's personal minder.

"Well, you haven't changed," the big man said wryly, surveying the wreckage around us as order was restored. "Let's you and I have a little talk." They mopped me up in the rest room — or gents, to you and me — and I went back to the bar after making my excuses to Marian and what was left of her table companions. Most of them had fled into the night.

Dinny came steaming up, furious at being caught with his trousers down, so to speak, and missing the action. I introduced them. "Dinny, huh? Dinny as in Dino's! Why not?" The big man found it funny, and that was good enough for us to echo his chuckles.

I followed him over to the bar, treading carefully so as not to grind broken glass into the expensive carpet. The riot had finished as swiftly as it had begun, which tends to happen in a general fracas, with no apparent hard feelings and a lot of drinking time to catch up on, though I couldn't help noticing a few more empty tables.

Tami pulled out a stool. "I like the way you handle yourself," he said. "You've done a bit since we last met, haven't you?"

"Here and there," I said. I was still trying to work out how I'd beaten him all those years ago. This great lug had arms of steel, a barrel chest, and his lantern jaw had that blue tinge that makes a chin still look unshaven seconds after running the Gillette safety razor over it.

Moriella was certainly one of the toughest characters I'd ever come across, which is saying a mouthful in the Nosher Book of Life. He could have stepped straight out of *Guys and Dolls.*

"How long are you here for, feller?"

I was up front with him, straight. "Next week. The money's running out, and I've got to get home."

Tami thought about it. Then he said: "I've got a deal for you."

"What sort of deal?" Knowing the kind of guys frequenting the neighbouring tables, I was careful with my words.

Tami said: "How would you like to go home in style?"

"Go on."

"I'd like you to look after young Frank, the boss's son. He's doing a British concert tour, and leaving on the *Queen Mary*. First class. You can go with him. First class too, of course. We want someone to look after him, someone who knows the business and can *do* the business if they have to."

The upshot was that a week later I flew up to New York to join Frank Sinatra Junior on board the *Queen Mary*, no less. First-class cabin, and all the trimmings. In the intervening days Dinny and I were honoured guests at Dino's, wining and dining every night without a cent changing hands and not a fist thrown. I left Dinny making his own way in Hollywood among the film crowd, and headed home just as Tami had promised — in style.

But once back in town, it all went pear-shaped. I tell you, that kid led me a dog's life!

He was handsome, he was twenty-two years old, he drew the birds like a magnet, and he thought he was above the law. Fair enough, he had a good voice — but he was Frank Sinatra's son and, from where I stood at his elbow day and night, it was glaringly obvious that he was poncing on his old man's name.

For the first week he stayed at the Dorchester, and things were fairly calm while he surveyed the scene. He explored the night-life, and must have seen the inside of every club in the West End, from Tramp in Jermyn Street to Annabel's in Berkeley Square.

Then we moved to the Cumberland Hotel at Marble Arch, which overlooks the spot where they used to hang highwaymen and other misfits at Tyburn. And from then on, for Nosher the Minder, it was another form of murder.

To cite an example. One night I put young Frankie to rest as usual, playing the Dutch uncle and seeing him safely to his room. Inside, I ran through the schedule. "Okay Frank, bedtime. You've got an early start tomorrow. Half seven. We're off to Bristol for an early-morning band call. You'll be on stage at eight that night. So get some rest."

"Okay, Nosher, whatever you say. I'll just take a shower, and get my head down."

I busied myself with some paperwork until I heard him call out: "All right, Nosher? See you in the morning."

I stuck my head round the door, and saw his face on the pillow, nicely tucked up. "Good night, Frankie."

"Night, Nosher."

Downstairs I said cheerio to Pat the doorman, a good Irish guy I knew well, and headed for home and an early start in the morning.

Next day, bright and early, I turned up at half past six, let myself into the suite with my own key, walked into the room, and there was Frankie — with two girls under the sheets with him, all three fast asleep!

Jesus! I raced downstairs to Pat, who was still on duty at the door. "Pat! Where the fucking hell did these two birds come from?"

Pat shrugged hopelessly. "Nosher, two minutes after you walked out, Frank walked out after you in his dinner jacket!" The bastard had been lying there fully dressed under the bedclothes.

I dashed back upstairs. Frankie was half asleep, just coming round from a night's activity in the sack.

"Out! Out!" I shooshed the birds out of bed, handed them a few quid from the kitty, and told them: "All right, girls, he'll phone you later." Then I gave that kid the biggest bollocking of his life. He was knackered, and just kept grinning at me with a Cheshire Cat smile that told me he'd had the cream and didn't care what I thought.

In that whole first month, I could not control him. Frankie was girl mad. Every night in his hotel a different bird would flutter in, and stagger out. How that boy ever got to his feet to sing, I'll never know, but the concerts were a sell-out up and down the country. All I could do was keep him out of trouble.

Then, early one morning, I got a call at home from the States. Tami on the line. "Nosher, the Don arrives the day after tomorrow. He's staying at the Dorchester." The Don was Frank Sinatra Senior. "Get the kid over in the evening. His father wants to see him. Is everything okay?"

"Sure, Tami, everything's fine."

I passed on the glad tidings, and watched with some satisfaction as Frankie went pale. "Now listen, sunshine. I'm going to give it you straight. If you don't behave yourself between now and then, I'm going to tell him everything!" From that moment he was like a little baby, and never put a foot wrong.

Now I'd never actually met Sinatra. Two days later I escorted his son round to the Dorchester. There was a minder down by Reception, who took us to the lift. Another heavily built geezer showed us to the Oliver Messel Suite, where a third guard stood outside, equally unsmiling. The corridor felt like Fort Knox.

Tami opened the door. Frankie said loudly: "Hi, Tami, how you going?" But you could see the kid was nervous: he was actually trembling in his patent leather shoes.

We walked into the room, and there was Sinatra. The Man was smaller than I expected, but his presence filled the room. He was wearing an open-neck shirt and slacks, and he had a slim gold band around one wrist. He also had the brightest blue eyes I'd ever seen on anyone, and they fixed me with an unnervingly direct gaze.

"Hi, Nosher. I've heard all about you." We shook hands. He merely nodded at his son. Then: "How's it been going?"

"Okay, Mr Sinatra." I'd been warned: never "Frank".

Then Tami put his spoke in. "He's a fucking liar, boss. Your son has led Nosher a dog's life."

Now I hadn't said a word to anyone. But someone else obviously had.

Sinatra looked at me, then at Frankie. And without warning — whack! He gave his son a savage backhander across the face that sent young Frankie literally catapulting backwards over the sofa. He landed out of sight on the carpet, and all I could hear were frantic scrabbling sounds from behind the settee.

Silence. The kind you can cut with a knife. Frankie slowly climbed back to his feet, shaking his head. Then Sinatra said quietly: "I heard."

He faced his son. "You c--t!" And repeated it. "You c--t! Pack your grips. You're on your way home."

I have to say I thought that was a bit strong. After all, Francis Jnr was in the middle of his tour. But who am I to get in the middle of a family squabble?

Sinatra cancelled the tour on the spot. It cost him a small fortune to pay everyone off, close down all the dates, take care of the band and the entourage. But he ended the contract there and then, everything.

When the mire had finished hitting the fan, Sinatra summoned me back. "Nosher," he said, "on behalf of Nancy and myself I want to apologise to you for my kid's behaviour."

I stuttered a bit. " 'S all right, 's all right. It's nothing I couldn't handle ..."

"I'm sure it isn't. But I'll make it up to you."

All I know is that young Sinatra was on the private plane back to the US that night, a very chastened young man.

A week later I got another phone call. Would I look after Sammy Davis Jnr at the Palladium? I had fourteen months with Sammy — and that's a good long time to be in a well-paid job with all the perks attached. Then Shirley MacLaine, when she came to London for a TV show. The same with Joey Bishop and Dean Martin when they were over.

Suddenly I was minder to the Rat Pack.

Who said Frank Sinatra didn't look after his own?

## 25: SAMMY DAVIS JR

S ammy Davis Jnr had a favourite gag. "I go to the fridge, the light comes on — and I do four minutes!" That was Sammy. He came over to London to star at the Palladium in *Golden Boy*, a social-conscience drama about a guy torn between being a prize-fighter and a violin player, if you can believe that. No strings attached, they'd already made the movie, based on the original thirties play, in 1939 with William Holden and Barbara Stanwyck.

It was an unlikely vehicle for Sammy. The son of vaudeville hoofers, the "one-eyed Jewish Negro" was the least likely looking entertainer the century has thrown up — and among the most talented. I rate him close to genius. I used to look at that crouched figure, hang-dog jaw, glass eye — the result of a car crash in 1954 that almost ended his career and his life with it — and marvel at the volcanic energy running riot through the man.

In his youth Sammy had been a bit useful in the ring himself, and *Golden Boy* struck a personal chord with him. He put body and soul into making it catch fire, and gave a fantastic performance with rave reviews to show for it.

Sammy had arrived with a bodyguard called Joe Grant, a top karate man with a shining pate like a black billiard ball. Sammy immediately asked for me — courtesy of Frank Sinatra's suggestion, the kind you don't refuse.

We had a meet at Sammy's apartment above the Playboy Club in Park Lane, and the ground rules were spelled out. "If a white man comes up and gives us trouble, you look after it, Nosher," said Sammy. "If a black man comes up, Joe will take care of it. We live in sensitive times."

Very diplomatic, if a trifle unrealistic. What if Joe got clobbered? Was I supposed to stand back while my new boss got it, too? But I kept the thought to myself. If it happened, I'd know what to do.

So each night Joe and I stood behind the curtain on either side of the wings, and we carved ourselves an imaginative line on the stage beyond which Sammy must never venture. If he set foot there, he'd be out of our POV (point of vision). Which meant our faces would have to peer out from behind the curtain, and people would wonder if we were part of the act. As it was, we became known backstage as the Black and White Minstrels.

We emphasised to Sammy: "*Never* go beyond that spot. You're safe with us, as long as we can see you. Okay?"

"Okay, boys. Now just enjoy the show."

And we did. It was a cracker.

No one knew it till later, but it was during this tour that Sammy discovered he had cancer in his vocal chords. At that point the only sign was a bad throat, which gave him trouble throughout the run of *Golden Boy*, though being the total pro he went on night after night without giving anyone a hint of it. My own view is that Sammy might have been alive today if he had listened to the doctors.

Well, he listened, but he ignored their advice. A year into the show, he finally admitted to me: "You know what they told me, Nosher? They can cut out my vocal chords, but it would mean I'll never sing again. I told them: 'I'd rather die.'" Sadly, in the end, that's what killed him.

On one particular night, there was no sign of it. Sammy seemed in fine voice, and took curtain call after curtain call. Joe and I nodded approvingly at one another from our vantage-points, and prepared to get back to the star dressing-room.

But then what does Sammy do? He walks forward out of our sight. I put a cautious eye round the curtain, and peer out into the auditorium. Sammy is sitting down on the edge of the stage, his legs dangling over the orchestra pit.

"Who's got a cigarette?" He's all fired up, loving the adulation as fresh waves of applause break over him like a wild sea. What's he doing?

He's asking for a cigarette, that's what he's doing. He gets it from someone and lights it, nice and easy, talking to the audience. They love it. Laughter and affection fill the air. "Any requests? What do you want me to sing?" They're all throwing numbers at him.

Someone shouts louder than the rest. "What Kind of Fool Am I?" Sammy starts: "What kind of fool am I, who never falls in love ..." Singing away, smoke dribbling out of his nose as always, milking every moment. And from the wings I'm hissing to Joe: "Can you fucking *see* him?"

"No, I can't. Can you?"

"No."

Now, it's easy for a minder to get lulled into a false sense of security, especially if there's a friendly feeling in the crowd all around you. But in any crowd, there's always one.

There's a spot in the song where Sammy gets to his feet. "Why can't I fall in love ... like other people do ...?" That amazingly deep, courageous voice flowed out from the footlights, holding them all in a trance.

And that's when a guy in a dark suit sitting in the front row stood up and took a running jump on to the edge of the orchestra pit, then a flying leap on to the stage itself like a fucking stag ... to slap a writ into Sammy's hands!

Sammy stops singing. The music comes to a grinding halt. Pandemonium backstage. I'm bellowing like a maniac: "*Bring the curtain down!*" And I shoot out in time to glimpse the geezer haring up the main aisle, running like the clappers, to disappear behind the back row. I did chase after him, but he was gone. I think they must choose Olympic sprinters for this kind of work.

By the time I got back to the stage, the curtain was down and Sammy was in a head-to-head argument with Joe. I heard him say: "You black bastard! I pay you two grand a week, and that c--t could have killed me."

Joe looked at him and said quietly: "Number one, I'm not a black bastard. Nosher and I told you never to go beyond that spot. But you fucking did — *you* black bastard."

The writ turned out to be about some costumes Sammy had ordered for a children's charity concert, and had never paid for. It could have been ugly, or worse, but in the end I defused it with a slap on the back and a laugh — even if there was a hollow ring to it. "Just don't do it again, Sammy!"

Sammy was keeping himself busy. Several nights a week after the curtain rang down on *Golden Boy*, he hared back to the Playboy Club to put on his own show for the punters.

I suspected it was part of a deal he'd struck for his luxury apartment, but it was all in a good cause. He called it Sammy Davis and Friends Entertain for the Children of Biafra Fund.

The place would be packed out. Sammy would spot celebrities like Harry Belafonte, Buddy Greco, Joan Collins, Tom Jones, even Ava Gardner in the audience, and invite them up on stage with him. Every time was a surprise. You just never knew who'd be stepping out into the spotlight. It was great for business and the punters loved it. Sammy always had his own table for his personal guests.

They'd given him a luxury suite two floors above the club. Some time after midnight, he would step down from the small stage, wiping his glasses clear of the perspiration and his hair shining with sweat. He would gesture to me and say: "Nosher, take my guests upstairs." Next thing, there'd be not two, four or even six but up to twenty people trooping towards the lift to take advantage of Sammy's legendary largesse. It's called freeloading, and it's the largest club in the world.

I would check with his black minder. "Going upstairs, Joe."

"Okay, Nosh!" That meant he knew I was among the missing, and he would have to stay extra close to the boss. My job was to take the guests upstairs and serve the drinks until Sammy made his appearance.

This particular night went as usual, with no hint of the drama to come. Around a dozen "friends" crowded around the small bar lashing into Sammy's booze, most of them finger-snapping black dudes dripping with gold, with gorgeous chicks hanging around their necks. The usual following.

One bird had to be awkward: she wanted a special fruit cordial that we didn't have in the bar. So, okay. I called out: "I won't be a moment. Enjoy yourselves," and headed for the door, leaving the other magpies to it, just as Sammy came in.

"Where you goin', Nosh?"

"Some bird wants a special drink, Sammy. I'm getting it for her."

"Fine," he said. "And order steak and chips for everybody while you're down there." That was Sammy, keeping them fed as well as watered.

In the kitchen I called for steak and chips for twelve, found the bottle of fruit cordial the girl wanted, and took the lift up again. I happened to be holding the glass bottle down by my side as I stepped out — and the first thing I saw was this huge figure poised outside Sammy's flat. I stopped dead in my tracks.

He was an awesome sight, I have to admit, a towering shaven-headed bruiser filling the corridor with his immense bulk. From where I stood, none of it looked like fat and all of it looked like trouble.

I went through my personal memory file, and drew a blank. No, squire. Never seen you before. I don't forget a face, and you wouldn't forget this one in a hurry, with its piggy eyes and flattened features, as if he'd had an argument with an iron, and come second.

The piggy eyes watched me as I sauntered casually along the carpeted corridor, and it seemed like a long walk. Finally I reached the flat, took my key to put it into Sammy's lock — and that's when this geezer grabbed me by the lapels, and swung me round. Now I take a lot of swinging, especially when I don't want to be swung, but he made it seem effortless.

Luckily my reactions were in top nick, and I used the momentum to whirl the bottle and crack it on to that shining bald head. Well, he'd started it. His head crashed back against the door, and down he went, arms flailing. Once he was down, I put the boot in.

The principle of street fighting is to do it first, and keep doing it until the other guy has lost interest in the world. It's nasty, it's messy, but it's essential. While he can still get up, he's dangerous.

That guy must have weighed all of twenty stone, and he'd been standing six foot four, so I couldn't take a chance. We went for each other like maddened bulls. But I had that initial advantage. I clubbed him again with the bottle, and finally he stayed down. After that I never stopped kicking him until he was unconscious.

The din sounded as if the place was being raided. When you're in a brawl like that, you don't keep quiet. Half of it is shouting in anger, the other half is to goad yourself on. Every time I kicked him he went crashing back against the door, which added to the sound effects.

Then it opened, and there was Sammy, open-mouthed, surrounded by a load of people gawping behind him. He stared at me through his glasses, then looked down at the huge bulk sprawled at my feet. "What the *hell* is going on out here?"

"Trouble, Sammy," I panted, trying to get my wind back. "This c--t went for me. And if he's going for me, that means he's going for you."

At which point another guy, not much taller than Sammy, poked his head through the throng. He was fastidiously dressed, wore an Astrakhan hat and a wispy beard, and I recognised him at once. "Black Malcolm" Malik, later to call himself Malcolm X when he got involved with the black Muslims, along with a load of weirdo names like El Shabazz, Detroit Red and even Satan.

I seem to remember he was assassinated in 1965 after falling out with his old mates.

But now here he was, with a stare that drilled holes into me through thick-rimmed glasses, pointing down to the prone figure lying unconscious on the carpet. "Hey," he said furiously, "that's my minder you've just put away!"

I was aware that I was treading on dangerous ground. This guy was a hothead with a creed of violence, whose own father had met his Maker in suspicious circumstances after being crushed under a tram. His mother had been certified insane. Not the best start in life for a geezer who later became, in my book, the original Yardie.

Sammy's reply came back in a flash. "Couldn't you do no better?" he inquired. To me, out of the corner of his mouth he muttered: "Take an early night, Nosher. You're not going to be very popular around here. These are all his friends."

It didn't worry me none. Home I went. And slept like a baby.

It didn't quite end there. Two weeks later Sammy was invited by Malcolm to visit a community centre at Ladbroke Grove in West London. Several of us went along to keep him company — myself and Joe Grant to watch his back, an actor named Al Boyce, his dresser, who I knew as Murphy, and a couple of others, all of us fitting into a stretch limo, and all of them black except me.

There were crowds of black people there, so I stood out a bit, which didn't worry me. I've always got on well with ethnic groups, probably because I've boxed so many good black heavyweights.

But as we were standing inside the crowded community hall, the door at the back burst open, and in came a black youth, laughing and giggling and out of his skull on dope. I shot a glance over, wary for trouble — and kept looking.

The kid had a dog lead in one hand with a collar on the end, and the collar was round the neck of a leading Member of Parliament, crawling on his hands and knees! Christ! What kind of community was this? Now there were two honkies in the room, and one too many for my liking.

It was time for us to make our excuses, as they say in the tabloids, and leave. "Move, Sammy!" I said sharply.

"But —"

"*Move*, damn it!" Joe and I seized an elbow each and hustled our reluctant boss through the gathering, which was getting rowdier by the minute. "If there's a bust and you get caught in here with this lot, you're finished!"

Sammy got the message. Black Malcolm was at the door as we rushed him through, but our boss had time to stop and say tersely: "I came here with the best of intentions to meet my brothers and sisters. I don't know what's going on here, but whatever it is, I don't like it. Don't ever invite me anywhere again. Now get out of my way."

In the car, we relaxed. Sammy said to me: "That guy with the collar? Do you know him?"

"Not personally," I said.

"Maybe we could find a place for him in the show," said Sammy. He saw my face. "Just joking, Nosher. Just joking."

## 26: LOOKING AFTER SAMMY

At that time, flush with cash, I ran a Mercedes. Sammy had been given a Rolls-Royce while he was in London. The Roller, a beautiful maroon Silver Shadow, was parked outside the stage door round the side of the Palladium.

After the show his star dressing room was always full, resounding to the clink of glasses and the sounds of back-slapping and brown-nosing. After a suitable time he'd give me the nod. "Number five, Nosh. Ten minutes."

That meant number five exit. Ten minutes later I would be waiting outside in *my* car, and away we'd go with Sammy crouching down in the back, out of sight, past all the people milling round his Roller waiting to mob him.

The man never slept. His energy was astonishing. After the show he was on a high, and we'd head into Soho for dinner, finding ten or a dozen waiting to have a meal with him in a pre-booked restaurant. More often than not it was the Trattoria Terrazza in Dean Street.

This was the place that made their fortune for Mario and Franco when Frank Sinatra was photographed by the *paparazzi* after dropping in unexpectedly for a dish of pasta late one night. Who tipped off the wolves? Why, the opportunist M. and F., of course, and good luck to them.

But it became a favourite watering-hole for Sammy, and stayed open into the early hours to accommodate him. Afterwards he'd be out clubbing until five in the morning.

Me, I always chose the cheapest dish on the menu and stuck to beer. I didn't want to be a ponce. Others were less altruistic, meaning that they were greedy bastards who didn't give a shit, and went through the menu like a forest fire.

At the end Sammy would call for the bill. He always paid in pound notes, counting them out carefully one by one and adding a generous tip.

One rare night just the three of us ended up at the Terrazza — Sammy, Joe and myself. I called the head waiter over and spoke quietly in his ear. "If no one else joins us, let me have the bill." I figured I owed the boss one.

Sammy was chatting away, high and happy, and the dishes kept coming. One a.m., and finally we were through. The head waiter muttered into my ear. "Eighty-seven pounds, Mr Nosher!" In those days, that was heavy duty. But I paid it without a murmur, and the tip brought it up to a ton.

Sammy beckoned for the bill. The *maître d'* bowed. "The bill has been paid, Mr Davis."

Sammy exploded. "What? Who pays Sammy Davis's bill?" He turned on me. "Did you pay my bill, Nosher?"

"Well, yes."

He shouted: "Don't you pay my fucking bills, Nosher!"

The few tables left had suddenly gone quiet. I bellowed back: "Bollocks! If I want to pay a bill, I fucking will. I'm not a ponce like all them other yes-men you've got licking your arse!" And out I stormed. You will gather I was genuinely upset.

I sat in the Merc, talking aloud to myself. "Bollocks to him ... Bollocks to him ..." It may sound like a stuck needle on a seventy-eight, but that's how I felt.

A few minutes later, he emerged from the trattoria, and climbed into the Rolls. Joe saw me, and jerked a warning head: *Follow us!* I was still on duty, so I had to go along with it. Sammy had hired a private cinema off Brewer Street for the night, starting at one o'clock, finishing whenever.

A whole lot of his mates were waiting, plus birds galore. They were showing *The Dirty Dozen* for starters, after which I reckoned it was going to get more lively.

Since soft porn flicks don't interest me that much, I sat in the bar by myself. To the barman: "Give us an Old Granddad!" And another one, while you're about it. Along with a few Scotches. I had the right needle, I can tell you.

Three hours later we were off to the Playboy Club, and Sammy's flat. I went up first, checked it all out. "Okay, send him up."

In strolled Sammy, with a bird on each arm. Joe Grant had his own room down the corridor, and had turned in. Sammy jerked a thumb at me, and turned to the girls. "Okay, ladies, which of you is going to fuck the two of us first?"

I affected not to hear. "Right, Sammy. What time in the morning?"

He waved a languid hand. "Pour yourself a drink, Nosher."

"I don't want a drink," I told him. It had been a long night, and I was ready for home.

"Don't fucking sulk," he said. "Pour yourself a drink!"

So okay, I had a big dash of old Granddad from his bar. Why not? He was paying, and I figured he owed me for the very public ruck.

Then Sammy said: "Nosher, I love you. I think the world of you. You're the only white man who's got the keys to this flat, do you know that? Not even Dean Martin's got them."

I was still smarting, and he could see it. He went on: "Listen, Nosher, there's something you should know. The only reason I tell you not to touch any of my bills is that I don't actually get *paid* at the Palladium — but I do get twenty-five thousand pounds a week expenses!

"If I don't spend twenty-five grand in a week it goes back to that fat mother, Val Parnell. I'm having a hard job spending twenty-five grand. Don't make it any harder for me!"

After that little confessional, what could I do but pick him up and give him a big hug. Next night he took me to the White Elephant in Mayfair, another ritzy showbiz haunt. I sat as usual at a table by myself watching the clientele coming in, and I ordered lobster Thermidor, which alone was thirty-two quid on the menu.

Sammy passed me on the way to the loo. "Have another one, Nosh," he said. "On me."

When I was minding Sammy, I never knew who I would find myself sitting next to at dinner after the Palladium, when he was winding down and holding court.

One night I was part of the crowd at Alvaro's, and found myself seated next to Harry Belafonte, a singer I've always had a lot of time for. We spent more than two hours over dinner in lively conversation, and I told him what a wonderful voice he had.

"Harry, I particularly like your 'Banana Boat Song' and 'There's a Hole in My Bucket', I told him, warbling a few bars as the evening progressed.

"Why, thank you, Nosher," he responded like a true gent.

Finally, he rose to his feet and announced to the table: "Sorry, folks. I have an early plane in the morning to LA. With great reluctance I have to bid you all goodnight. But it's been a great time, God bless you Sammy, and I thank you all."

Applause all round, as he went from chair to chair, shaking hands with everyone. Finally, he got to me, and squeezed my hand. "Goodnight, Nosher."

"Cheers, Harry," I said. "Have a good flight."

He bent low and murmured in my ear. "Actually, Nosher, I'd prefer it if you called me Sid." And off he went.

Funny, I thought. I said to my neighbour: "Why did he want to be called Sid?"

"Because he's Sidney Poitier."

Sometimes you don't know where to look.

Another time, I ran into Michael Caine. Now he used to live just around the corner from me. His dad was a porter in Billingsgate fish market, and we knew the family well. Mike himself was five years younger than me, and I always looked on him the way you treat a neighbour's son.

He was tall, around six two, good-looking, fair-haired, and not a lot of meat on him.

I was starting to make my own waves in the business, and the word was getting around. One day I was walking down the street when I bumped into Mike. In his broad Cockney accent he asked: "Mr Powell, 'ow do yer get into this acting game?" He was very polite, and hadn't acquired the middle-class monotone that has become his trademark.

I told him straight: "Forget it!"

Why was I so blunt? I'm tapping my nose now. Survival, that's why. Mike was six foot two, fair, same size as me bar a couple of inches, if a little less muscular. A man like that could do me out of work! Yes, I was that selfish.

So I put him off. At least, I thought I had. "Your dad's got a good steady job, you can do the same. Fifty-two weeks a year, the money's coming in. Stay with it, my son."

He listened intently. Then said, seriously: "Thanks, Nosher. See you around."

Fast forward ten years. Michael Caine has made *Zulu*, *Alfie*, and carved his own unique niche as Harry Palmer, the "antidote to James Bond", in *The Ipcress File*. I'm sitting in the Arethusa restaurant in Chelsea, haunt of the arty set, with Sammy Davis Jnr hosting a crowd of us for dinner. It's a busy-busy table with everyone talking this way and that.

In saunters Mike, with his gorgeous wife Shakira and a group of friends in tow. He gives Sammy the glad hand, nods to the rest of the table — then his eye lights on me.

For a moment he stares through the famous spectacles. Then he bends down, and whispers in my ear: "Better than fucking Billingsgate, Nosher!" before moving off, with a tight smile of satisfaction.

Serves me right. Mike has a memory like an elephant. He never forgets a compliment — or an insult.

But we would work together on *The Italian Job* and an African kidnap adventure called *Ashanti*, and he never mentioned it again. Well, he didn't have to.

Incidentally, I wonder if any of you who saw *The Italian Job* worked out an answer to the last scene? Remember, the coach carrying the stolen gold bars was teetering on the edge of a cliff, with the bullion stacked at one end and the villains up front at the other, not daring to move in case they went over.

Michael Caine's final words were: "Anyone got a bright idea?"

Well, someone had. Years later they were thinking of a sequel, and sat down to work it out. The answer they came up with? Leave the engine running until the petrol tank is empty, then the rear of the coach will be lighter, and swing up. And everyone gets off.

Smart. But quite what the Italian fuzz would be doing in the meantime they never did say.

We had a lot of adventures, Sammy Davis and me. It dawned on me pretty quick that he was the easiest touch in the world. Anyone could take him if they talked it up enough. That man died potless. When he finally chucked in his tap-shoes at the age of sixty-four, he never had a penny piece to his name.

One time I saw it for myself, and felt I had to do something. We'd gone to dinner in Soho after the show — at the Terrazza, where else? The place had become the hottest joint in town. As far as I know, Sinatra never went back, but his friends did.

They were a party of twelve, with Sammy picking up the bill as usual. The group were loud and noisy, with one guy named Marco, an Italian–American out of New York, louder and noisier than the rest.

Bill paid. Ready to go. At the door the loudmouth gave Sammy the high fives. Slap! Slap! "So long, Sammy!" Slap! Slap! I can tell a wanker when I see one, and I just pushed past him and walked out into the fresh night air.

We got to his apartment. Inside, Sammy said: "Pour yourself a drink, Nosher." He looked troubled. "You know that punk you saw back there? He just had me for a thousand bucks."

I said: "What?"

"A thousand bucks," Sammy repeated. "Yeah, but forget it. It's not worth bothering about. We did a bit of business that went sour, that's all. But I don't want any trouble, okay?"

I didn't like my boss being taken for a ride, and I made a mental note. Aloud, I said: "Okay, Sammy. Whatever you say."

Two days later I drove out to Pinewood. I used to drop by from time to time to chat with the boys and maybe drum up some work. Now I strolled into the restaurant — and there was this Yank sitting there large as life having lunch with two women, knocking back the bubbly.

I walked up to the table. "I want a word with you," I said quietly, giving him my gimlet smile, which shows a lot of teeth and no humour. He looked startled, but rose obediently and followed me through to the bar at the back.

The bar was full of lunchtime drinkers. I knew some of them, and most of them knew me. But this time I ignored the nods and the greetings as I made for the far corner, away from the throng but still visible to everyone.

That's when I grabbed him and slammed him up against the wall. He gave a strangled squawk, followed by a weak smile. Normally intimidation isn't that obvious in a public place: the enforcer usually blocks his victim from running, then steps on the guy's instep with a size fourteen boot, grinning pleasantly all the time — which is all the more unnerving. When he says, "I'm going to cut your heart out!" it's no higher than a menacing whisper.

Not me. I spoke in my normal tones, which can carry across a field and send the cows into a stampede. "You dirty rotten bastard!" That for starters. Now the main course. "You can wipe that fucking smile off your face right now." The smile went. "You've fucked the best guv'nor I ever had!"

I can still see Peter Rogers, the producer of the *Carry On*s, gaping at me from his own favourite spot along the famous mahogany bar.

Peter propped it up daily to dispense champagne to his chums, and we always used to say he had left his footprints in the carpet like the prints outside Graumann's Chinese Theater in Los Angeles. That day, he must have thought he was witnessing a scene from one of his films.

The rest of the bar seemed to be holding its breath. Actors, extras and everyone who works in movies all love a drama, and they were seeing one unfold in front of them. It would give them something to gossip about for a month. One thing for sure: no one was going to interfere.

I gave the unfortunate Yank the full Nosher verbals. "Turn out your pockets!"

He started to mumble something, but I shouted him down. "I said turn your fucking pockets out!" Reluctantly he fished in his jacket, and brought out a bulging wallet. He had five hundred pounds on him, cash. I counted it out. Then I threw the wallet back. "That's mine, to give back to Sammy Davis." Then I turned my back, and walked out.

Marco hadn't uttered a word. And I never did get his other name.

That night I knocked on the door of the Playboy apartment. Sammy opened it. I pushed a brown envelope into his hands.

"Here you are, Sammy. Five hundred quid."

He gawped at me, his single eye blinking in disbelief. "What are you talking about? What happened?" He opened the envelope, examined the contents. "Jesus! How did you do it?"

I told him, and he put a hand on my shoulder. "Nosher, I've got to tell you something. Your heart is where your head is — but your head is in your arse!"

"Yes, guv'nor." I looked suitably contrite, but inside I felt good. You win some, you lose some, and this was one time I knew I'd won.

One time I lost it happened with Sammy in the Arethusa. My fault, because for once my self-discipline deserted me.

After the show, Sammy was whooping it up with his pals in the corner while I had taken a breather to have a drink at the bar. I got chatting to Rod Steiger, who was standing there too, and we were having a nice old palaver when I saw Sammy get up from his table and head for the door.

I didn't realise until later, but one of the Italian waiters had been at the sauce. The owner, Alvaro, had put him out in the street to sober up. As Sammy emerged, the waiter made a grab for him, and hung on. Some guys get very strong when they're drunk, maybe it's fuel injection that does it, but Sammy couldn't unlock his grip.

Well, I could. I started to ease his fingers away, and said: "Take your hands off him, and take it easy, pal!"

But he hissed at Sammy: "You fucking black bastard!" Then he turned — and spat full in my face.

Now no one had ever done that to me before, and I can tell you it's not very pleasant. It was a right gob, and I had an aroma of garlic and alcohol in my nostrils for hours.

So I hit him with a right, and he went flying back through the door into the arms of his fellow waiters, and three of them went down in a heap. I was so mad I forgot my own golden rule, and went after him. Sammy and two of his retinue jumped into the waiting car, and left me.

Suddenly I'm surrounded by hostiles. A whole motley of Italian waiters all making unpleasant gestures and threatening noises. Alvaro came steaming up before they actually laid a hand on me, or it would have been Monte Cassino all over again.

Out in the street I hopped a cab quick, and followed Sammy to the Playboy. He waved an admonishing finger. "Tch, tch!" he chided. "Never do that, Nosh."

I said contritely: "I know boss, I'm sorry. I should have walked away."

We had one area of constant discord. To put it bluntly, Sammy Davis Jnr had the pox about me because he could never introduce me without the other person saying: "Oh, I know Nosher!" or some such greeting. If I have one claim to fame, it's that I'm going to be recognised somewhere, anywhere, in the world. Usually when I least expect it.

On this night Sammy fancied a bit of clubbing. "Annabel's," he said. We headed for Mayfair, and Mark Birley's high-octane, low-lit spot which promoted itself as Europe's most exclusive nightclub. Certainly every blue-blooded aristocrat, movie A-star, model and politician gave their milk teeth and probably more to set foot in that basement club on the west side of Berkeley Square.

Personally, as far as I could see it was the haunt of the rich, the famous and the unemployed jet-set, but that's just an opinion. The entrance was deceptively modest. No sign, a discreet doorman in the shadows, and passers-by doing just that — passing on by.

You could walk past the wrought-iron gate leading to a wooden staircase, and never know the club was down there beneath you. The steps were so steep and narrow that you couldn't even squeeze past anyone coming the other way.

"This is a very exclusive place, Nosher," said Sammy, as we climbed out of the Rolls. "You've got to be special to get in."

"I know that, Sammy." We clustered by the gate to descend the steps as the doorman saluted — then stood back to wait for a couple who had already started the long climb up. Sammy recognised the tall, emaciated figure close behind an attractive blonde as they came level.

"Hey, Nosher." Out of the corner of his mouth. "I bet you don't know *him*." Meaning that he doesn't know *me*.

It was Paul Getty. As he drew level, his rheumy eyes lit on me. "Good evening, Nosher," he said, with a nice degree of warmth in his high-pitched voice.

Two years before, when I'd worked for him, he had told me I could call him by his first name.

"Good evening, Paul," I replied gravely, as he passed on into the night.

Sammy watched the millionaire's back retreat into Berkeley Square. Then he looked at me, taking a lot of time to pick his words.

"That *fucks* it!" he said.

I don't think he ever got over it.

## 27: PAUL GETTY

Ah, yes, Paul Getty. I've mingled with the very rich and the very poor, and sometimes it's quite hard to make out which is which. It was Peter de Savary, the property millionaire and sometime owner of the St James's Club, who once told me: "I go to work on a bicycle, cycling down Piccadilly. When you see me arriving in my Rolls-Royce, you know I'm in trouble." If you don't have to make an impression, or bullshit a prospective punter, then why bother?

Paul Getty belonged to this school of thought.

I was in the kitchen at home making myself a snack when the phone rang. "Pete here, Nosh. What are you doing right now?" Chief Detective Superintendent Peter Cooper of West End Central had been a mate for years. We had a thing going, Pete and me, where he'd put the occasional job my way.

"Boiling myself an egg," I said. "Three minutes. Otherwise, not a lot."

"I've got a little job for you. Very discreet." Pete was a good bloke, and especially good today. "I've got the world's richest man for you," he said.

John Paul Getty had just bought Sutton Place near Guildford. The place was being done up, and he lived in one wing. "Come with me and meet him."

Who am I to turn down a date with the world's richest man? We motored down the A3, and turned into the estate through tall iron gates flanked by two red brick lodges. I have to say I was less than impressed.

Sutton Place was a rambling Elizabethan manor house with a gravel drive, leaded windows, a high vaulted vestibule, and dark panelled walls that had been painted over by Hugh Casson, no less. Its new owner had taken over the west wing, which had been renovated to accommodate him and felt oddly out of place.

The overall effect was more of a museum than a home. And, yes, Getty really did have a red telephone box in the hall for his guests to use if they wanted to make outside calls — and were prepared to pay. My dad always did say that's how you get rich and stay rich, looking after the pennies.

The Master of the Manor, on the other hand, was the total opposite of the home he had chosen to make his base in Britain. Most people thought of him as a shrivelled prune, a tired old man with too much money and a mean streak. Let me tell you, this wasn't the person who came striding purposefully out from the kitchen to greet me, a tall, spare man approaching seventy yet exuding the kind of strength and authority that comes with enormous wealth.

The kitchen, I would find, was the place where the world's richest man actually felt most at ease. It was a spacious area with Mediterranean tiles, wooden table, Captain's chairs and a homely lived-in air. I might have been in a French farmhouse, and there was even an aroma of fresh bread baking to complete the illusion.

"This is — er — " Getty looked at Pete. His voice was a thin reed.

"Mr Nosher Powell, sir. Your private security."

"You recommend him?"

"I do, sir." Good for Pete.

"I won't ask for references, then." A brief, dry handshake, and I've got the job. "Welcome to the family — Nosher."

I couldn't help thinking: Christ, I've shaken hands with a billion dollars. That's about a hundred million a finger! My mind tends to go like that. Now what?

Basically the job was to watch out for trouble, and keep it away from my new boss. I had moved to Wimbledon and bought a pub, the Prince of Wales, right next door to Wimbledon dog track. Every day I drove down to Guildford in the Mercedes with my new Dobermann guard dog Leo, named after my birth sign, to report for duty by eight a.m. After which I simply hung around the house.

You haven't met Leo yet. He was as good as gold with me and

Pauline, and our two boys, Greg, born on 13 May 1954, and Gary, born on 10 September 1964. But all teeth and snarls for anyone who gave me the hump. All I had to say was one word, "Go!" and he was away like a streak of lightning. Leo is no longer with us, I'm afraid. He ate his last bone in 1981. So, as I told everyone: "You can sleep easy in your beds at night."

I struck up a friendship with Getty's chauffeur, Terry. He was as important in the equation of keeping our master alive and well as I was. He was a good boy, hot as mustard behind the wheel, and knew the game, too. We used to work out on a police skid pad near Aldershot when the boss wasn't around, just to keep our hand in.

I tell you, that's an experience that can give you grey hairs before your time. But it pumps up the adrenalin like nothing else as you spin round and round on the oiled tarmac, especially in a heavy Merc. When that baby started to go, you just had to keep your foot off the brake, go through the gears to slow her down, and pray!

Over the first weeks I got to know the intriguing, complex and charismatic man that was John Paul Getty in our early morning stroll round the grounds. It was more a ritual than any major keep-fit exercise, but it got the day off to a good start and I know we both looked forward to it because he told me as much.

Each outing would last ten minutes. Not a minute more, not a minute less. Getty would walk along, with his tall angular frame bent almost double, his hands clasped behind his back.

One day, when I was chucking a ball for Leo, he suddenly said: "Nosher, do you mind speeding it up a bit?"

"Certainly, Mr Getty. I'm just taking my time with you. But may I ask, what's the hurry?"

He frowned at me. "Let me tell you something. I earn one thousand pounds a minute, twenty-four hours a day. Ten minutes I can afford. Eleven I can't. So let's *move!*"

After the first two weeks, Getty seemed to relax with me. "Call me Paul," he said in that reed-like nasal twang. I compromised with "Mr Paul", like the rest of his staff, and I would stay a year with him before moving on. I wish I could say that I learned how to get rich quick, but he never gave any secrets away, and I can't say I blame him. He was a canny, astute man, and nobody's fool.

In the third week of my employment, I was called on to show what I was made of. I had been up in Mayfair, waiting for him in the plush corporate offices in Grosvenor Street. This was a late session, and after midnight a message came via his personal assistant: "Mr Paul will drive back with you, and wishes you to stay overnight in Sutton Place."

I knew there was a permanent room for me in the east wing if ever I needed it, complete with a four-poster bed that was so big my toes couldn't even feel the end. I called Pauline from Reception to tell her I wouldn't be home, and the boss appeared just as I put the phone down.

There was no reason given. He sat up front beside me as I pointed the Mercedes south towards the A3 and let her rip, always with one eye on the mirror. And he started talking, as if on a couch to his personal analyst — talking but never waiting for a reply or a comment.

First thing, he was slagging off some executive in his company. "Why am I giving this asshole sixty grand a year? I could do it better myself." Pause. Then: "Do you want the job, Nosher?" And before I could say, "Yes, please, I'll take it," he was off on another tangent.

I realised immediately that he was using me to let off steam. And the fact is that if you're a personal minder there are no secrets between you and the guv'nor — or very few. There can't be too many, because my job is to know where you are twenty-four hours a day, seven days a week. Even if you're behind closed doors and closed curtains.

At which point my attention was diverted. There *was* a car on our tail. I had spotted him soon after leaving Grosvenor Square, a black saloon with two men in it, hanging back but always there.

Over Putney Bridge, up the deserted high street, and right at the roundabout on to the Kingston bypass. The road was practically empty, but the headlights were still there behind me.

We stayed that way until Cobham, at which point I said: "Mr Paul, get yourself ready to hold tight. We've got company, and I think we should lose them." Then I hit the accelerator. We touched a hundred in seconds, then I braked abruptly and slewed the car into a side road that I knew was coming up. Getty rocked in his seat, but kept his lips tight shut.

I hit that bend at seventy, with the other car right up my exhaust pipe — but he missed the turning and hurtled on down the dual carriageway.

Unfortunately I lost some Brownie points by bumping over the kerb and shunting the car off a tree, which didn't do the bodywork any favours. But at least I'd lost the pursuers, whoever they were.

Getty never opened his mouth all the rest of the way back, but I was too intent on watching the side roads and lay-bys to indulge in idle conversation. It was only when we were safe back inside the gates at Sutton Place that he nodded in satisfaction.

"Great driving, Nosher. Great driving!" Amazing. He hadn't turned a hair or said a word.

I had to ask: "Any idea who they were?"

"I have a lot of enemies, Nosher," was the enigmatic reply. "That's why you're here."

As he climbed out, he glanced at the dents and scrapes along the side, and said brusquely: "Get it done!" I had the whole car repaired, serviced, resprayed, and he paid for the lot. After all, he could afford it.

For a while after that we laid on an extra two cars as escort, with SAS-trained drivers, one in front and the other behind. But the roads stayed clear of trouble, and eventually we called them off. But I still made sure I took a different route into town each day, and out again at night.

Getty was an early riser. To get to him in the morning I had to leave home at five-thirty to be sure I was there by seven o'clock. He ate a spartan breakfast, and I would find him in the dining-room toying with a single Weetabix and a drop of milk, immersed in the *Financial Times*.

After the first two weeks of this routine, I ventured: "Can I have a word with you, Mr Paul?"

"Sure," he said. "What's your problem?"

We were walking across the gravel drive to the car. "Well," I was a trifle tentative, "I get a hundred and seventy-five pounds off of you for being your bodyguard. But I'm using my car, and what with the petrol, it all costs money."

"Oh," he said. He got into the car. "Remind me at the office." I thought it might mean another tenner a week. When we pulled up in Grosvenor Square he was out and gone before I could say anything.

That evening I took him back to Sutton Place, and it had slipped my mind. I was having a quick cup of tea in the kitchen when Sally the maid appeared with an envelope. "Oh, Nosher, this is for you."

Inside was a blue credit book, which meant I could get petrol anywhere in the country, any time, and it would be charged back to the Getty organisation. And that, I have to say, improved my finances no end. It isn't too many people who can say they scored in a business deal with Paul Getty.

Some evenings we would sit in the kitchen together, just the two of us, chatting over a cup of tea. Getty was 99 per cent a gentleman, courteous to his staff who knew him as "everybody's uncle", and sensitive to their needs. Like: "Take the night off, Sally," to the maid, "and give my regards to your husband."

It was the one per cent I didn't like, and the language that went with it. There would be a bellow of rage directed at the poor girl, for no apparent reason. "Fuck off! I don't want anybody here!" And to me: "Not you, Nosher. Sit down!" The man's moods swung like a weather-vane, and you never knew whether the sun was out or storm clouds were swirling over Sutton Place.

I would have to sit and listen to a tirade about an oil strike on one of his rigs, or a problem with something in the ocean that had "gone to fuck and cost me three million dollars". Sometimes I would be the object of his wrath, but I never let it get to me — so it was like water off the proverbial duck. I pretended to hear, but inside I just cut off.

When we had finished, the boss would apologise, and there would be a brief silence. Then: "How about a game of Kaluki?" And out would come the cards.

Kaluki, for the uninitiated, is an American version of Rummy, in which you are dealt thirteen cards and have to make up four sets of the same suit or numbers. Once you get forty points in your hand, you can put down.

And there on that plain kitchen table we used to play for pennies. If you went down with one line, that was ten pence you had to bet. If you got the lot, you shouted, "Kaluki!" And your opponent had to pay up. Pretty simple stuff, you might think.

But, like any inveterate gambler, with Paul Getty every game was like the Third World War had broken out. I saw him play in casinos like the Ritz Club, Crockford's and the White Elephant, and lose a bucketful. Me, I used to beat him regularly and took him for a nice few quid in his kitchen.

Finally, one night, his composure cracked. It was around one in the morning when he threw down his cards on the table, and growled at me: "You know, Nosher, you're a fucking crook! I'm going to get some new cards."

After which he would come up with four new packs every single night, and say with that lopsided grin: "Now, these are *not* fucking marked, Nosher!" At least I got the once-used ones, as good as new, to take home next day. I've still got a drawerful.

The world's richest man had one good suit to his name, his favourite, made by Frank Diamond of Wardour Street — back in 1936! It was as good as the day he bought it, and on special occasions out would come that grey herringbone with the tight waistcoat, which meant the boss had never put on an ounce of fat in all that time.

One such occasion was when a gilt-edged card dropped through the letterbox at Sutton Place from Buckingham Palace inviting him to attend a formal luncheon with the Queen and Prince Philip. Getty hadn't met either of them before, which surprised me.

That night, he left the cards lying on the table, and seemed preoccupied. Finally, he said: "Nosher, I've got this invitation. I don't want to put a foot wrong here, because I may get a gong."

I said, politely: "Oh, yes?"

"Yes," he echoed. A pause, then: "So tell me — how do I address your Queen?"

"For myself, I would call her Your Majesty," I told him, "but as you're not one of her subjects, I suggest you could call her Ma'am."

He slept on it. The following afternoon, safe back from Buck House in the plush corporate offices in Mayfair, Paul Getty summoned me into the inner sanctum. "You know," he said, looking up from behind his massive desk, "that Queen of yours, she's a good little Ma'am!"

I said: "Yeah?"

"Yeah," said Paul Getty. "But that husband of hers — what a stuck-up bastard!" And he allowed himself a flinty smile. He never did get that gong.

His son did, though. John Paul Junior was awarded an honorary knighthood in 1986 and became John Paul Getty KBE. If the old man was aware of it beyond the grave it must have irked him no end.

Getty, of course, had a reputation for being a tight-wad — witness that red phone box in his hall — but I saw him do funny things with money. One weekend he laid on a party at Sutton Place, with a hundred guests taken from the great and the good. Champagne flowed. Caviar and canapés set the tone, and the buffet was the best I'd ever tasted. Whatever you wanted, just ask.

But without warning the pendulum would swing the other way, and the shutters would come down on his hospitality. Suddenly he would go very mean. Who knows why? Maybe the shares had dropped. The boss would have the same gang back in again — and this time they'd only get red and white wine, and a meagre selection of canapés. No spirits. Not a single bubble of champagne. It wasn't my place to ask, but I could hear the murmurs of the guests. "I rather think we picked the wrong day," I overheard one illustrious member of the House of Lords complain as he bit into a sausage roll.

Getty was a stickler for punctuality. If I was a minute late, I would be in for one right bollocking — and the boss didn't mince his words.

In that year, I was his sole minder for five months. But other things were happening in my life, and the workload finally got too much. I was away from home all the time, and I wasn't seeing enough of the kids.

Being at Paul Getty's beck and call twenty-four hours a day took its toll. He was at endless meetings, from the West End to the City, and all too often I would sit outside in the car doing the crossword or brain teasers for up to four hours, sometimes more.

Socially it was the same, even though the insides of the best joints in town became a second home to me. One night Quaglino's, the next the Ivy. Then an embassy party, or maybe a concert at the Royal Festival Hall and even Westminster Abbey. I was with my guv'nor all the time, watching his back. How about the River Room at the Savoy? Or the Connaught Grill? You name it, I've been there.

And there was Nosher sitting by himself at a corner table, bored out of his skull, with the world's most sumptuous dishes passing under his nose, a wine list he had to turn away and call for fizzy water instead — and all he wanted was to go home and have egg and chips with the missus.

It all came to a head one night in the City. I had been sitting outside an office block by the Mansion House for almost five hours. Finally my bladder could stand it no longer. I also badly wanted a cup of coffee, and had spotted a pub round the corner where I could satisfy both needs.

I was gone no more than ten minutes — but you've guessed it. Sod's law came into its own. In that time Getty emerged — to find his driver missing. I came back to see him literally dancing in the street with rage. I reckon the noise of the bollocking I got went all the way to Wall Street and back.

Enough is enough. I can take a lot of shit if I have to. But on the drive back to Guildford — in brooding silence on both sides — I remembered the story of the mushroom: they keep you in the dark all the time, and once a day someone opens the door and throws a bucket of manure over you! That's how I was starting to feel.

In the kitchen at Sutton Place, I said: "Mr Paul, I have to talk to you."

"What's your problem now?" he demanded. "And cut out the mister. It's Paul, remember?" I told you he was canny. He sensed something was up, and now the old soft-soap was being used.

I said: "I've got a wife and two kids. I've been working seven days a week for the past five months. I think I've got to call a halt here."

He interrupted. "Don't you like me, Nosher?" I wonder: how often did Paul Getty say that to anyone?

I said: "Paul, I love yer. Even after what happened tonight. You're a good old guv'nor." For once I left out the mister.

He brightened. "I like that. Good old guv'nor! Well, then — you don't really want to leave, do you, Nosher?"

"No, I don't, guv'nor. But I've got to get a life."

He held up a hand. Then he rose silently and left the room, returning a few minutes later with a brown envelope. "Pay off time," he said. "Two thousand pounds. Okay, Nosher?"

I looked up at him. "You're a doll!" I said.

Now that I think of it, I don't suppose many people called Paul Getty a doll either.

When he died in 1976 at the age of eighty-four, I couldn't help the passing thought that I might be remembered in his will. I wasn't. He didn't leave me a penny. But to me, he'll always be a doll.

And now it was time for Nosher to head where his true calling lay ...

## 28: ENTER THE STUNT MAN

I've always said that stunt men have got to be crackers! They say we're a bit East Dagenham — four stops to Barking — and maybe we are, to get away with some of the things we do.

But the real truth is that we stunt men consider ourselves the élite, the chosen ones. Does that sound arrogant? Not 'arf! You need to have physical strength but, believe it or not, you've got to have brains too. We're not just lumps of meat falling out of the sky at the whim of some guy with a baseball cap and a bullhorn. We have to be able to interpret what the director is trying to get on the screen, and give it the most spectacular shot we can.

Speaking personally, and admitting this for the first time, there's never been a moment when I haven't been frightened out of my fucking life when I'm doing a job. But I like to say I keep thinking of the pound notes, and that gets me through.

The first time I ever knew there was such a thing as a stunt man was when I met Paddy Ryan. Paddy was the granddaddy of them all. To me, he would always be the first and the best. He was in his forties when I first started in the business, and the fight arranger on the Laurence Harvey film where I first faced a camera as Larry's trainer.

Paddy couldn't tell me anything about boxing, but he could tell me everything about stunt work. He did the high fall in *Richard the Lionheart*, with Dermot Walsh in the title role, all 160 feet off a tower, landing in three layers of boxes and four mattresses. Over the years we would become great mates, but those early days were make-or-break for an eager young kid starting out in the business.

Paddy became a guru to me. He had the right attitude to life, he liked to have fun, and he liked a drink too.

Typical scene: the woods outside Denham studios. We're filming *Sword of Sherwood Forest*, adapted from the hit TV series starring Richard Greene as Robin Hood. As one of Robin's Merry Men, Paddy had to climb up a tree and be on the lookout for the Sheriff of Nottingham.

Merry? I'll say he was. Paddy was so drunk that day he leaned back on his branch as if he was in an armchair, and plummeted right through the tree into the leafy glade. The drop was at least twenty feet.

He lay there winded, like a squashed insect, in his Lincoln green costume. Then he shook his head, got up, and said very clearly: "How's that for a fall?"

They don't make too many of them like Paddy.

But first, there were the walk-ons. I signed up with an agent named Gabbie Howard, a lady who specialised in athletic types, if I can put it like that. She was a small, bird-like woman with an office in Wardour Street from where she spent hours on the phone finding work for extras.

Gabbie decided I should cut my teeth in TV and commercials. She found me spots in the Michael Bentine series *It's a Square World*, then other comedy capers with Eric Sykes and Dick Emery — and, okay, if you blinked, you missed me. But I was learning. Commercials for fish fingers, various soap powders and toothpastes followed — I was the cleanest guy on the block.

Then one day I got a call from Madrid, inviting me to play a character called Billy Chocolata. Since I would be in Spain anyway as a cowboy on the spaghetti Western *A Fistful of Dollars* that launched Clint Eastwood into orbit, I accepted.

Billy Chocolata was an Indian type of guy who wore a big black Stetson with a feather up one side, and he was forever doing people favours. Every time he did a person a favour, they would give him a chocolate. He would push it up under the brim of his hat and say: "Gracias, y adios!"

At the end I would add: "*Adios, amigos!*" take my hat off and a cascade of chocolates would pour out. The message was simple: I'd done all those people favours, so they should buy the brand name.

On the first day, filming on a bull ranch in Segovia, an hour's drive from Madrid, I turned up in my black Stetson and feather to await instructions. The Spanish director said: "We have to do a sequence with some cattle."

They showed me the script, and gave me a horse to get used to. I climbed into the saddle, started mouthing him this way and that, spun him around to show who was master here. No problem. Nice horse, obedient with it.

I was introduced to a handsome young feller named Cordobes, who shook my hand, spoke quite fair English, and said it was a pleasure to meet me. Likewise, I responded. The director called over: "Señor Nosher, we have the bull here for you!"

I looked past him, and there in a paddock was this huge black bull, staring ominously back at me. The director waxed enthusiastic. "Cordobes 'ere, 'e is going to be wrestling with the bull, trying to get it into the paddock. Uppa you come on your horse, slide off, getta hold of the bull by the horns, and help him wrestle it into the paddock. Okay?"

I don't know how many tons that bull weighed, but it was a lot of hostile meat and muscle glowering at me.

Cordobes said soothingly: "It is very easy, Nosher. All you have to do is walk up behind the bull, put both arms around his horns and hold him, and I will do the rest."

"Okay," I said, not knowing quite what I was doing, or why. The camera started whirring. Someone called out "Action!" — or something like it. At which point Billy Chocolata cantered up to the paddock in his finery, slid off his horse, walked up to the bull, which was standing there looking remarkably docile, smiled at the camera and put his hands on its horns.

And that was the moment that Cordobes lifted the bull's tail, and fired a fucking air pistol right up its arse!

The noise and the blast of cold air up its backside had a dramatic effect. The bull took off with me hanging on, bounding half-way across the paddock. Talk about being stuck on the horns of a dilemma! My feet never touched the ground.

"What the fuck — ?" Now it dawned on me at last why they'd employed a stunt man to be Billy Chocolata instead of some good-looking actor dude. I was dragged this way and back to kingdom come. Finally I was flung off, and the bull was persuaded back to its stall by a lot of guys waving colourful capes and shouting in Spanish.

El Cordobes, of course, was the world-famous matador. He had supplied the bull. "I am sorry, Señor Billy," he apologised. "The bull was too quiet. We had to wake him up."

At least I became the hero of the hour.

"What *cojones*!" they shouted, as I was helped back, sprinkling chocolates from my hat.

I like to think they were referring to Nosher Chocolata, and not to the bull.

Then I found myself in TV plays with actors hoping to make a name for themselves: Sean Connery, Windsor Davies, Stanley Baker, Bill Kerr, and a beautiful young wannabe named Joan Collins.

I also appeared in *The Quatermass Experiment*, which was one of the most thrilling serials ever to go out on TV, a foretaste of so many sci-fi dramas to come, and I'm proud that I was part of it. Who can ever forget the poor guy turned into a cactus-like vegetable clambering up Westminster Abbey?

But one real-life horror story almost happened below the Abbey, in the crypt. Another guy and I were chasing a young stunt actor named George through the stone-flagged dungeon, actually a studio set, of course — and the guy was on fire! The crypt was draped with cobwebs, which were supposed to be flameproof. At the far end two assistants were waiting with an asbestos sheet to wrap around him and put out the flames.

The cameras churned, we raced off, and at the far end — high drama! They wrapped the sheet round the wrong way, and poor George was rolling on the floor, burning from head to foot. The cobwebs had caught fire too. The guys with the fire extinguishers were nowhere to be seen. The flames wouldn't go out.

Thinking quickly, I produced man's best friend — and I don't mean his dog. I piddled on George from a great height, directing the stream up and down his body until the flames were doused. Amazing. They went out just like that, which could be a useful DIY tip in an emergency.

George sat up, shaking his wet head, and looked up at me gratefully. "Cor," he said. "Thank you, Nosher. Thank you for pissing on me!"

"Any time," I said. "You were just lucky I'd had a few beers beforehand."

And all the while I was practising for my real ambition: I wasn't going to win an Oscar by reciting 'To be or not to be', so stunt work became my personal Holy Grail.

I took myself off to Mickey Woods's gymnasium in Oxford Street, where I taught myself the basics of falling and head-on impact for car crashes in an unusual way.

Learning to fall: the hardest stunt you can do is to stand on the floor and fall flat forwards on your face. It sounds simple, but crashing down on your face contains all sorts of dangers, including the obvious one of a broken nose. You have to breakfall with your forearms, getting it just right.

I trained at my local swimming pool, doing the "dead man's fall" from the six-foot diving board, forwards and backwards. The first lesson you learn is that a belly-flop can be quite painful, too. In the end I was able to stand on a chair, and fall full-length backwards on to the mat without breaking anything.

Sudden impact: I used to hang around the dodgem cars at fun-fairs on Mitcham Common and other places, until they slung me out. Reason: I had to know how much I could take in a head-on bang. So if you saw a big ginger-haired git squeezed into a dodgem and bearing down on you from the wrong direction, sorry for the shake-up.

I'd put my foot down, zoom round the wrong way, crash! And the conversation was always the same: "Ooops ... sorry, mate ... didn't see you ... won't happen again ... Oops, there I go again ..."

"What the *fuck* are you doing?" (This last from the enraged owner, clambering over stalled dodgems to get at me.) But I learned.

Stunt men specialise in various skills. Very few of us are all-rounders. But fights and falls are the two basics behind every stunt you see on screen. You can learn to fall off a horse at full gallop, fall out of a car during a chase, or even out of a plane — I've done all three.

At which point I should add that the old saying "It's as easy as falling off a horse" doesn't apply to us, because we actually do it. There's no such thing as an easy way to fall off a horse. You're coming down six feet, and it fucking hurts when you hit the ground!

You want to be a stunt man? First off, if you want to get on the Stunt Register you must hold at least six grades of athletic pursuits: car racing, motor-bike racing, maybe gymnastics or canoeing, hang-gliding, judo, acrobatics, parachuting, even ballet dancing! If one man is not properly qualified, he can put another's life at risk.

It doesn't make you a stunt man on the spot, but it gives you a start in the business by putting you on the provisional list as a novice.

Once you get working on a film, the stunt co-ordinator — the guy who really calls the shots — marks you off on a work sheet: you did so many falls, you acted throughout in a professional manner, always on time, and so on. It takes two years minimum, and you're under the instruction of an experienced stunt expert.

When you've got enough work sheets under your belt, you come up before our committee. A dozen of us sit around a table at our head office in the West End, usually on a Saturday, and we'll go through them.

If you pass, that makes you an intermediate, and you'll be doing more difficult stunts for at least another four years. The final hurdle qualifies you as a fully fledged stunt man who can work without supervision.

It's a long hard slog, but the rewards can be immense. The bottom rung is fifteen hundred pounds a week, but a stunt man can negotiate his own money — and that goes for the girls too, of course. If they want you to hang from an aeroplane a thousand feet in the air, then you work out your own fee with them.

For instance: the opening sequence to *The Spy Who Loved Me*, the James Bond movie where Roger Moore skied off the edge of a precipice on skis. The stunt man was Rick Sylvester, and they had five cameras to record that incredible jump, with the Union Jack emblazoned on our indestructible hero's parachute at the end. They paid him a cool twenty-five thousand pounds to do that one leap of faith — twice. But no one will ever forget it, so it was worth every penny.

In fact, I'd already had my first taste of stunt work on a movie before I even did my National Service. I was seventeen, and it was a *very* good year. I was a husky lad shifting crates at Covent Garden, and learned through the grapevine (no pun intended) that they were looking for extras to fight the battle of Agincourt. The movie, of course, was *Henry V*, directed by and starring Laurence Olivier. They needed two hundred riders, and they were short of experienced horsemen.

That's for me! I thought, and headed off on the train — bound not for France, but for Salisbury Plain, doubling as Agincourt.

The result was that the first time I ever faced a camera I was wearing a suit of armour. From then on, I must have clanked around in chainmail in more movies than anyone alive. I was at it again not long ago in *First Knight*, with Sean Connery and Richard Gere, and I'd lay a bet I was the most experienced "Sir Knight" on the field of battle.

Back to square one. Apart from horsemen, the other problem was that horses immediately after the war were not too plentiful either. They solved the riders without trouble: since they were paying five pounds a day and only a quid for foot soldiers, everyone wanted to get into the saddle — even if their only previous experience had been a donkey on Blackpool sands.

The call went out. They rounded up nags from Express Dairies and United Dairies, raided any milk cart they could find, along with costermongers, drays, rag-and-bone merchants, buying up anything with ears and a tail on four legs that went clip-clop. Since most of the beasts had docked tails, the film company actually tied on false hairpieces above their arses!

Some of the poor creatures had never experienced anyone sitting on them before. Moreover, when you're a knight of old you had to control your steed with one hand, the other left free to point your lance or wave a sword.

Remember the hiss of arrows whistling through the air in that unforgettable battle? That was another hazard to face. We had never seen anything like it, and neither had the horses. I can still hear them now. But do you know how it was done? By a feller running his finger along a thread, that's how!

It happened like this. The BBC Sound Effects department had a reputation bar none, and they were hired for their expertise. Three guys — Freddie Bell, Harry Morris and 'Laddie Ladbroke', legendary sound men all — huddled together around the Gramophone Deck in Broadcasting House (actually Room TD7) and got to work. Finally they cracked it.

They strung up a thread about five-foot long, attached to a needle on the turntable that would echo through the loudspeaker. Then one of the lads pulled the thread taut, while another simply ran his finger up and down it to make that eerie whooshing sound as the horses came charging in and the arrows filled the sky.

The boys repeated it over and over again on the same tape until it sounded like hundreds of arrows — and what an amazing effect that was. It still gives me goose-pimples when I think about it.

When I learned what was about to happen, I thought they'd bolt. The reason they didn't became clear to me soon after I reported for duty on the fringe of Salisbury Plain, where a line of colourful tents stretched to the skyline, banners waving in the breeze.

For the past two weeks it seemed they had stabled the animals under huge marquees, kept them warm, cosy and happy, and fed them like royalty before their date with the cameras. The result should have been anticipated, but wasn't. Those horses had never had it so good, so the inevitable result was that they just grew plump and lazy.

I was there soon after dawn, had my name ticked off on a long list, and mingled with the other extras. There were no organised stunt men in those days, just guys who were prepared to throw themselves off horses or buildings and hope to survive. Personally I had no intention of falling off my steed. But I strode around in the mud with the rest, all of us in chainmail acting the part with gruff voices and an occasional slap on the thigh to get into the mood.

John Paddy Carstairs, later to direct several Norman Wisdom comedies, was the first assistant, and a very gentlemanly type he was, too. We lined up on the edge of a ploughed field to await the command. Through a megaphone, Paddy called out instructions the way Sergeant Wilson would assemble his troops in *Dad's Army*. "All right, chaps. All your horses are over there. Go and select your mount, and that horse will be yours for the remainder of the filming."

He blew a whistle, and there was a mad rush of clanking knights to get to the best horses. I let them get on with it, eventually strolling over to see what remained of the leftovers.

I got myself a right knacker. The wretched thing needed a hot potato up its arse to make it even move. But that suited me, because I wasn't out to make a hero of myself.

Now they handed out the weaponry. I found myself clutching a lance and shield as we were summoned for the big charge sequence, with Olivier out front on his white stallion, an imposing figure bellowing: "God for Harry, England and St George!" at the top of his lungs.

I had to kick my horse a bit to get it into line, and I was afraid it would fall down dead at any minute with my then thirteen stone on it. As it was, my boots almost touched the ground on either side. But eventually we were ready.

Another extra, a little guy named Jack "Kid" Berg, who in another life had been a legendary lightweight champion, had somehow got himself the biggest horse of the lot, and he looked like a pimple on a fucking dumpling. The monster was breathing fire and brimstone, and we kept well clear of it as it snorted and kicked mud and horse dung into our faces.

Paddy Carstairs, small and dapper, appeared at the front armed with a large bullhorn. "Now, chaps," he called tinnily, "keep your eyes on Larry. When he raises his sword on high, you start forward at the walk.

"Try to keep in as straight a line as they did at Agincourt. When he circles his sword around his head, that means breaking into a trot. When he circles it twice, go into the canter. Please, *please*, keep in line. And when he points his sword for the charge, you go hell for leather!"

Our motley assortment of overweight nags and ill-equipped knights lined up obediently. What we lacked in expertise we made up for in enthusiasm. Filming gets to you like that. Suddenly play-acting becomes the real thing. But I couldn't help thinking: If this *was* the real thing, the French would have a field day!

Someone bellowed: "Action!" We trotted, we cantered. Everything went all right until Olivier pointed his sword in the direction of the enemy. We heard his faint bellow up front: *"Charge!"* And then we were off like the Light Brigade itself.

Well, it was an absolute shambles. We agreed later that we had all learned something that day: when horses run, they run like a herd, and nothing's going to stop them short of a brick wall. Even my nag got the whiff of it, and I just let him go.

We finally pulled them up, by which time two hundred knights were scattered all over Salisbury Plain. But the shot was in the can, and we were allowed to relax at base camp while they set up a new angle.

A group of us were still sitting around two hours later playing cards outside the tents when we heard a snorting sound. And there was little Jack Berg, still perched high in the saddle, picking his way gingerly through the ploughed field as if he was sitting on a thistle.

His great steed was one mass of white lather, and looked equally exhausted. The Kid stared down at us from beneath his mud-spattered helmet. "Deal me out of this one, boys," he said. "We've just done the Grand National, and we're fucked!"

Years later the charge scene was shown when I was the subject of *This Is Your Life*. Laurence Olivier declined to take part, but I just wish we could have shown it as it really was.

Two months before enlisting to do my bit for King and country in Egypt I found myself in another historical epic: *Caesar and Cleopatra*, George Bernard Shaw's version of Caesar's years in Alexandria around 50 BC. At £1.25 million it was the most expensive British film ever made. I don't know how much went into the pay cheque of Vivien Leigh, Claude Rains and Stewart Granger, but I do know they brought a boatload of sand from Egypt to Denham Studios because the director Gabriel Pascal wanted to get the colour right! It didn't make a grain of sense to me, but as a lad of seventeen being paid a fiver a day, who was I to argue with the excesses of the movie business?

I played several roles. A Roman centurion guarding the gates of Rome, then demoted to a lowly spear carrier in a loincloth. Finally I was chained below decks as a galley slave straining at the oars with an awful lot of splashing and shouting going on upstairs.

For the costliest film they had built the costliest set in the world at Denham Studios, a vast pantheon of towering white columns and marble steps. Pascal was one of the early moguls, actually born in Transylvania, and with *Pygmalion* (which starred Leslie Howard and Wendy Hiller) under his belt, he was in the mood for a spot of spectacle.

Unfortunately the weather turned. For his triumphal entry into Alexandria, I spent five weeks along with three hundred other extras shouting, "Hail Caesar!" until I was hoarse. After more than a month greeting the emperor, one's enthusiasm tends to fade a bit. But we did keep the humour going with comments like: "Hail, Caesar? Well, at least it's not snowing!"

The bad news for the director was that the film was a flop at the box office, and virtually brought Pascal's career to an end.

Those two films gave me my first taste for movie-making. I remember thinking: This is the fucking game for me! And two years later I started to make it happen.

# 29: MAKING A SPLASH

My old friend Lewis Gilbert hired me for two more of his films. *Emergency Call*, with Anthony Steel and Freddie Mills, saw me in another spot of type-casting — as a boxer, what else? It wasn't brilliant — one critic simply wrote: "Don't bother to dial!" Oh dear.

But Tony Steel was Britain's own heart-throb, hero of countless war films, a dashingly handsome devil with a chiselled jaw, stiff upper lip — and an alcohol problem. His upper lip couldn't have been the only thing that was stiff because he managed to woo and win the statuesque Swedish sex bomb Anita Ekberg, who had a bust like a battleship. He was the envy of the entire crew, especially when he married her, lucky sod. But it didn't last, and when I met Anita in Rome, when she was making *La Dolce Vita*, she told me why in one pithy sentence. "I married a bottle!" Sad, really.

In *Cosh Boy*, scowling and growling in the shadows as a moronic thug, I renewed acquaintance with a young Joan Collins, the sexiest teenager in the country and soon to challenge Diana Dors as Britain's number one pin-up.

The first real stunt I did came about by accident — somebody else's. *Those Magnificent Men In Their Flying Machines* was a rip-roaring knockabout comedy set in 1910, all about a newspaper magnate (played by a quivering-jowled Robert Morley) sponsoring the London–Paris air race.

They had amassed an impressive comic array of Britain's finest, led by Terry-Thomas, Eric Sykes, Benny Hill, Tony Hancock and Willy Rushton. Sarah Miles provided the glamour, and Stuart Whitman was America's entry as leading man. Germany was represented by Gert Frobe, still basking in the accolades from his triumph as Goldfinger the previous year. Alberto Sordi (Italy) and Jean-Pierre Cassel (France) completed the international line-up.

The film received mixed reviews. In the script, the winning time of the race was twenty-five hours and eleven minutes, handing the critics a gift for their poison pens. "The film seems to last just as long," said one. At least the public didn't agree — they queued round the block.

For me, it was a milestone. On the off-chance of a spot of work, I drove my old banger estate down to Pinewood and wandered into the bar. It was lunchtime, and crowded, and I couldn't help noticing that people were looking at me in a knowing way, with nudges and nods. Finally a guy came over and said: "You're in the business, aren't you?"

I said: "Yes."

"I'm Jack Davies." I knew the name. He was a prolific comedy writer, and had written the script for *Mag Men*, as it became known in movie shorthand. "Will you come with me, please."

He led me over to an amiable-looking cove in the far corner, and muttered a few words in his ear. Then he gestured for me to sit down.

The other bloke introduced himself as Ken Annakin, the director and co-writer. "We've run into a spot of bother," he said, without wasting words. "There's been an unfortunate accident."

I said blankly: "Oh?" I had no idea what he was on about.

"Yes. One of our stunt men was doubling for Gert Frobe this morning. Chap named Kenny Buckle. He was in the side-car of a motor-bike."

I knew of Kenny, a very experienced operator.

Annakin went on: "The bike has to go up the wall of a track, hurtle over the top and splash into a reservoir on the other side. It's a hilarious sequence."

I nodded politely. "Sounds like it."

"I should mention there was no driver, just the Gert Frobe character in a German uniform in the side-car." I'd lost the plot, but Ken plunged on. "Being such a big feller and such a tight fit, Kenny couldn't get out! He's in hospital with a cricked neck and a broken arm."

"Sorry to hear it, but —"

Annakin said abruptly: "You could pass for Gert Frobe. You're the same size and build. You've even got the same colour hair. Will you do it?"

I suppose I must have nodded and muttered something, because next thing they were both shaking my hand and saying: "Thanks, thanks a lot!" And then I was being bundled down to Wardrobe and kitted out in a German officer's uniform, pre-First World War, all blue and gold, with a stiff collar and a peaked cap to round off the image.

"Do you mind if we crop your hair?" They were very polite. I got a haircut on the spot. "Oh — and a moustache." A ginger one was glued above my upper lip.

At last I looked in the mirror, and saw Gert Frobe staring back at me.

I was still trying to catch my breath when they led me to the set. Annakin's eyes widened. "My God, it's you. I thought it was him." Which I suppose made some sort of sense. "Incredible!"

From that moment I became Gert Frobe's double. They got the earlier shot safely in the can, and I didn't go down with pneumonia. Then they lined up something even more hazardous.

"Will you do it, Nosher?" asked Annakin. By now, at least, he had asked my name.

"Yessir," I replied promptly, anxious to make an impression — before I realised I didn't even know what they were asking me to do. Served me right for being a brown-nose.

They were using the big water tank on the back lot, a huge area a hundred yards square and five foot deep. Somehow the set designer magicians had concocted an old Blériot biplane, suspended on wires forty feet in the air — upside down.

"What we want you to do, Nosher," said Annakin, taking my elbow in a fatherly grip and leading me to the side of the tank, "is to hang from the steering column. We're going to release the plane, and it will go whooshing across above the water."

"Oh?" I said, suddenly apprehensive. In all the excitement I'd forgotten that I can't stand heights! But ... *think of the pound notes!*

"You'll be just above the surface, and we want you to run on the water, as if you're cycling. It will look fantastic! And whatever happens, don't get the uniform wet! We'll be dropping you in the water later on."

I didn't like the sound of "whatever happens". But I climbed the rigging. And now — a lesson in heights. When you're looking *up* at forty feet, it doesn't look much. When you're looking *down* from forty feet, it's a fucking long way to fall!

So I spent the next three days running on water, and heard all the jokes about the Second Coming. Finally came the drop. "Straight down and right under, Nosher, with no splashing around on the surface. Okay?"

Okay.

It worked a treat. Jackboots and a heavy officer's overcoat made the scene even more outlandish. The entire crew applauded as I came up, breathed in good fresh air, and gave them the Heil Hitler salute. Why not? It was that kind of film. Midsummer, lovely warm weather, and everyone having a ball.

Now the calendar moves on.

November. Freezing cold, brass-monkey weather, and the phone rings. It's George, an assistant on *Mag Men*, a pleasant young feller I hadn't seen in months. I'd been paid off handsomely, and gone on to other things. *Mag Men* was just a memory.

"That scene, Nosher, the one you did with the plane. Remember it?"

I cast my mind back five months. "Oh, yeah."

"Well, it worked out so well that they want to carry on with it."

"Carry on with it? How can they? I finished up in the water, and that's the end of it."

"Er — not quite." George's voice was hesitant. "It looks so good that they want to see you do the whole thing against the real background."

I suddenly twigged what he was getting at. "And that means?"

"The English Channel," he said. "Near Eastbourne. Like, next Wednesday?"

"Christ," I said. I thought I'd seen the last of that German uniform.

We were to take off from a small airfield ten miles or so from the coast. Sure enough, there stood a vintage biplane at Roxford Aerodrome, painted black, red and yellow. And it could fly!

More than that, it had been specially built so that it looked as if it was flying upside down, which was going to be an eye-opener for anyone seeing us from the ground. They say you can do anything in the film business.

It was an amazing flying machine. We took off from the airfield with me crouched in the cockpit beside Jeff the pilot, ready to clamber out on the struts. I thought we would hedge-hop to the location. Instead Jeff swung up high into the air over the coast before I spotted a fleet of small boats lined half a mile out with cameras trained on the sky.

Jeff's earphones crackled. He raised a thumb. *Time to go!* There was no door, just an open space so that I wouldn't get snagged. *Out!* The slipstream tore at me as I crawled out, fumbled for the struts. Then I was dangling like a puppet on a string for a mile along the coastline while Jeff made two dummy runs. Finally the order came through: "Okay, we're going for it!"

I said seven fervent Hail Marys and four Our Fathers, and went for it.

The dummy wheels were sticking up above my head, while the real ones were camouflaged by the fuselage — not that anyone would be looking too closely, anyway. We came in from five hundred feet, dropping down close to sea level. Stalling speed on that plane was fifty miles an hour, so we daren't go less.

To add to my discomfiture they had a large wind machine on one of the boats, whipping up the waves.

Scared? I shit coloured lights, I don't mind admitting it. But I've always said that any stunt man who tells you he's not frightened is a liar. If you haven't got fear, you haven't got safety.

The thought briefly crossed my mind that I could have been in Covent Garden now, humping boxes of apples around. Instead here I was dangling from a pre-First World War plane flying upside down over the English Channel. Well, it's different.

Below me, the cameras were whirring. Capturing the plane thundering in upside down with yours truly dangling by one hand ... "walking" frantically on the surface ... finally letting go of the strut and plunging in. They wanted the splash entry, and they got it. But, Christ, it was cold! Brass monkey temperature ten times over. I had a wetsuit on under the uniform, but I was more worried about the jackboots and heavy overcoat dragging me under than getting a chill.

The impact and the freezing Channel knocked the stuffing out of me, and I probably spoke in a high voice for weeks. But I kicked my way to the surface, and gulped in lungfuls of fresh sea air. Following instructions, I went on waving my arms realistically and thrashing around in the water, as per the script, until a rescue tug came along.

It was all on film, and six months later it was all there on the screen. Wonderful début performance!

Overnight I became a celebrity. That action shot was my first individual stunt — and it got me into the Hollywood Hall of Fame. To my immense pride I was also immortalised in the corridor leading to the studio restaurant at Pinewood: you'll find me there in a large framed photograph on the panelled wall, plummeting into the sea.

I told you it was a milestone!

I had another memorable underwater escapade when I was working on the crazy Michael Bentine TV series *It's a Square World*, only this one didn't go quite so smoothly.

They put a grand piano on the deck of a Trident submarine. Real piano. Real submarine, used by the Royal Navy as a training vessel. The piano was clamped down on the deck. They had me dressed in white tie and tails playing the piano half a mile out in the English Channel, filmed from a boat a hundred yards away.

And suddenly the klaxon went *Dive! Dive! Dive!*

I was just getting stuck into the Warsaw Concerto when, sure enough, the submarine started to slide forward under the waves. I saw the sea washing over the deck. The plan was that they would go under until the conning tower was submerged, then come up again.

I was holding on to the underneath of the piano as we went down, but with the rush of water swirling over me I couldn't stop myself floating to the surface. The director, nice and dry in oilskins, came up in his boat as I was dragged back aboard. He greeted me pleasantly enough. "That was no fucking good, Nosher. Try it again!"

Okay, he's the boss. So this time I got some webbing, and tied it round the stool and over my legs. "Let's get it right this time," he added.

Down we went. But, as so often happens, they'd overlooked something rather crucial. By the time the conning tower was under, I was thirty feet down — and I couldn't hold my breath any more. No snorkel, no bottles for the concert pianist. I went to release the belt — and the webbing twisted. I was trapped.

But safety first: I had a knife in my belt. I fumbled for it, sawed through the belt, and managed to cut it free. WHOOSH! I shot up to the surface and out into blessed fresh air like a guided missile in full white tie and tails.

Or, more accurately as someone suggested later, like a misguided muscle.

When I saw the final result, they'd put a full orchestra behind me with that wonderful *Bam Bam Bam BAM!* introduction. It looked wonderful, even if could have been my own lost chord!

## 30: FALL GUYS

We have a saying in the stunt business: 'Make it real. Make it believable.' But sometimes it can get too real. When I hear it, my mind goes back to *Ben Hur*, and the chariot race that must be one of the greatest sequences ever filmed. Did you know there is a cinema in Munich that plays just the race — sixteen minutes of it, including the build-up — over and over again? I was part of it, and I feel privileged to have been in that great arena built near the Cinecittà Studios.

It took six weeks, and everyone in Rome seemed to be an extra. They were paid a fiver a day, and six thousand of them were milling around in togas and sandals. And, yes, there really was one idiot in a cloth cap — you can spot him up in the left hand corner of one of the crowd scenes if you look carefully.

I met Mr Epic himself, Charlton Heston, a true gentleman of the screen. For this, the role of his life, we discussed horses in general and chariots in particular.

"They're actually quite easy to handle," I reassured him. "I've driven chariots at Elstree Studios, just for the fun of it. They've got a few stashed away for films like this, in case they're ever needed. And you've even had hydraulic brakes fitted, so you'll be okay!"

"I sure hope so," Heston drawled, with an uncertain grin. "Brakes, huh? I think I'm going to need them." In the old days, of course, there weren't any.

The second unit director was the legendary Yakima Canutt, a giant of a man in every way. He'd won his spurs back on the classic John Ford Western *Stagecoach* when he jumped from horse to horse to stop the runaway coach. I had idolised that man ever since.

He hailed from Washington, actually born Enos Edward Canutt, grew up as a ranch hand and joined a Wild West show at seventeen. People thought he might be part-Indian. In fact, he took his unusual name from a newspaper caption he saw of himself after a rodeo: "The Cowboy from Yakima".

He was tall and rangy, and had a small scar on his cheek. When he caught me inadvertently looking at it, he stroked his face with a reminiscent grin. "I got a spear through it in a movie fight," he explained. "There was quite a hole there, so I stuffed it with the nearest thing to hand, which happened to be gunpowder wadding for blank cartridges. Then I forgot about it, lit a cigar a few minutes later — and bang! I guess I was lucky I didn't blow my head off!"

*Ben Hur.* We all knew we were part of a monumental epic, and maybe some of the guys took chances to make it happen. I hoped I would be a charioteer, but after a few try-outs round the track, in the end I was given another job: to stop any runaway horses!

There was always the fear that the centre pole of a chariot might snap, in which case the horses, freed of the weight behind, would take off like the clappers. Trying to stop them on the straight would be hopeless. But at one end of the arena stood an enormous lion that had been carved out of real stone, and will be at Cinecittà Studios for ever.

I talked the situation over with Yakima. Finally he positioned me by the lion, at a point where the horses would slow down to ten miles an hour or so as they rounded the bend. Then I would have to dash out and grab the nearest harness.

Nobody could have foretold what happened, though it could have been prevented. Brakes or not, we had a stunt man killed in the third week, and it happened right in front of me. You saw it, too, because the cameras kept turning and it's in the movie. The poor guy was pulled clean out of the chariot, and dragged for two hundred yards, just like Stephen Boyd in the film. But this was for real. That really is a man being killed.

And the reason? He had made the mistake of wrapping the reins round his fist for balance, something he should never have done. If he had been holding the reins normally, he could have let go and probably suffered no more than a few bruises. When the horses finally stopped, I was one of the first to get over to him — but there was nothing we could do.

When a shocking thing like this happens, there is only one thing for it. Keep going. But it's only human nature to think: *That could have been me.*

The most feared elements in stunt work are fire and water. You never know when they're going to get out of control. One of our best guys, Rocky Taylor, was voted Stunt King of 1982. Three years later he was in hospital with the most horrific injuries after a fall through flames that made headlines round the world.

It happened on the Michael Winner film *Death Wish 3*, with Charles Bronson playing vigilante Paul Kersey yet again, this time bringing mayhem to the streets of London in his quest for rough justice. They'd taken over a derelict building south of the river, which they were going to set ablaze. The idea was that three younger stunt men would jump out of the lower windows, while Rocky took off from the roof, around fifty feet up.

I was on the Stunt Committee, and helping on the film if I was wanted. Watching this crucial scene from the yard below beside the cameras, I knew better than most that, however many times you've done it, something can always happen. Rocky was a seasoned veteran at forty, with a career that went all the way back to the first James Bond film, *Dr No*. But he knew it too.

In a high fall, you can do the same stunt ninety-nine times, exactly the same speed, same height, same angle of descent — but on the hundredth it all goes to fuck. Don't ask me why, but it happens.

You only need a gust of wind, and you're in trouble. You think you're going to plummet straight into that airbag that looks like a tiny rectangle far below — but say it's cool in the evening after a hot day, that's when a sudden breeze can spring up from nowhere. Just look at a sky-diver to see how the wind affects you.

I once saw Dickie Graydon, one of our best high-wire men, taking a fall off scaffolding at Pinewood. A gust of wind hit him and took him right back into it. He crashed his way through 180 feet of scaffolding, and wound up with breaks everywhere: legs, hips, arms, the lot. Yet the last I heard of him he was seventy-five and still working!

Sometimes I wonder if it's really necessary. Let me explain. A falling body has no shape. Provided it's weighted properly, you can put a dummy up there, push it over, and get the arms and legs waving like catherine wheels as it falls. The camera follows it all the way down, and nobody is any the wiser.

But we will do it. People get talked into things, and maybe they're after making a name for themselves. I know. I'm one of them. Though whenever I hear about one of our blokes being killed or maimed, a shiver goes through me. *There but for the grace of God ...*

So here we are, standing around in little groups outside this rotting old tenement, and Michael Winner is striding around with a megaphone shouting instructions. The cameras are next to a couple of cars, pointing upwards. They've lit the gas jets, which are roaring realistically through the building. The air bag's in place like a kid's bouncy castle, and smoke is drifting everywhere.

Everything's going nicely when Winner bellows: "Action!" A little too nicely — because from where I'm standing that fire looks as if it's getting out of control. Now, when you're standing at the top of a building and you hear the director shout, it's entirely up to you when you fall. If the camera packs up, they just yell, "Cut!" and do it again. But you can be half-way through the air, saying to yourself: "What do they mean, *cut*?"

But now the flames are engulfing the building, the kids have jumped, hit the air bag and rolled off — but five storeys up, the smoke is too thick for Rocky to see the ground. Down below, panic stations. Someone bellows: "*Go! Go! Go!*" Rocky's got a choice: either jump or burn. So he jumps.

He comes hurtling out of the smoke — and misses the bag by a foot. *Smack.* An ugly sound. I thought: Christ, he must be dead!

But he wasn't. Rocky was built of strong stuff. He lay there like a puppet until they could get him on a stretcher and race him off to St Thomas's Hospital, fortunately just down the road.

I sat in Casualty for nine hours waiting and praying, because sometimes that's all you can do. Every now and then other stunt men would appear, ask after him, and leave when they realised there was nothing they could do. We're a small club — but we're family, and we look after our own.

Finally they told me to go home. Rocky was in intensive care, and it was touch and go.

Rocky did pull through, but only just. That guy was strong as an ox, but he still suffered permanent scarring and multiple fractures. The surgeons had inserted plates and two foot-long metal rods in his shattered pelvis, and for good measure they added another bolt in his left knee. When he could smile again without it hurting, we dubbed him "Bionic Rocky".

He was finally able to leave hospital after three months, hobbling on two sticks, and he lay on a sofa at home for another twelve. But two years later, I happened to be down in Cobham, Surrey, near where he runs his own club Rocky's Bar. I was playing snooker with a friend at a pub when in walked Rocky, unaided.

"Hi, fellers!" he said. "I've come from the hospital." With that he threw some metallic objects down on the green baize cloth with a clang. We found ourselves staring down at two big nuts and bolts. "Just come out of my stomach," he added cheerfully. "They were holding me together."

It quite put me off my stroke.

But I can tell you that, believe it or not, Rocky is back in action. He was last seen in the film *Plunkett and Macleane* that came out in the spring of 1999. It sounds like a firm of country solicitors, but actually it's a highwayman yarn starring Robert Carlyle and Jonny Lee Miller. More important, it gave Rocky a chance to go galloping around on horseback and prove my old mate was back in the saddle in more ways than one.

It just goes to show that however much you prepare, things can always go wrong. Take my brother Dinny, for example.

He is one of the most experienced stunt men in the world, bar none. He's done the lot. But even he has had his nasty moments.

We were working together on a piece of medieval nonsense called *Krull*, set on some weird planet and starring Lysette Anthony, Francesca Annis, and even Bernard Bresslaw, a mucker from my old TV comedy days. This was a sword-and-sorcery saga directed by Peter Yates, who had made his name with the famous car chase in *Bullitt*, with Steve McQueen, and should have known better.

This time the cast were up to their necks in a yarn about a prince whose bride was abducted by the "Beast of the Black Fortress". Dinny and me, we were up to our necks in jelly beans. I promise you, jelly beans. That was what they'd used to fill up a lake to make it look like a swamp, along with flour and sand to turn it into a quagmire. Full marks for enterprise!

That lake was nine foot deep, and we were dressed as scaly frogs, which made me suspect someone had lost the plot in more senses than one. I just reported for make-up every day, and an hour later waddled out into the sunshine daring anyone to laugh.

That day four of us were standing on a square wooden platform on the lake, holding air bottles and wearing snorkels over our frog faces. We were loaded with a hundredweight of lead sinkers round our waists to keep us from bobbing up unexpectedly and ruining the shot.

On the call "Ready!" we started breathing, and the frame was lowered into the lake. Then we stood on the bottom, waiting for something to happen. Eventually a jolt on the frame signalled "Action!" We undid the weights, which sank to the ground, removed the masks and rose slowly to the surface to frighten the daylights out of Lysette and Francesca. Well, that was the idea.

Okay, we got the signal. We came up, stared around — and there were only three of us. Dinny was missing! When the frame was jolted, he'd toppled over.

Now he had no breathing apparatus, nothing. The cry went up: "Where's Dinny?"

That was when the frogmen went in — the real frogs, not us, standing by for just such an emergency. They located my brother lying in the mud under water, and found he hadn't been able to release his weights. It must have been fucking murder under there and, worse, he'd swallowed all these jelly beans, so his windpipe was clogged.

Well, they got him out of there in his frog outfit, and laid him on the bank and gave him artificial respiration. He finally came to, and after a lot of gasping and choking looked at me as I knelt anxiously beside him.

"You know what?" he said thickly.

"What's that, Dinny?"

"I nearly croaked down there!" he said.

Dinny was one of the most experienced submariners in the business. He'd done all the underwater stuff in North Sea Hijack, with Roger Moore and Anthony Perkins aboard an oil-rig. And lots more. But suddenly, as he told me later, under all that shit and mud he became claustrophobic.

He has never done another underwater scene since. And he's gone off jelly beans, too.

Now it can be told. Hands up, I have to admit it: I'm really scared of heights! When I say scared, I mean that every time I do a high stunt, I shit a brick! We all have our weak spots, and mine happens to be vertigo, which isn't a very good reference if you're a stunt man. Blokes like Rocky Taylor, Terry Clark, Dickie Graydon, Terry Richards, they could walk on a plank over Niagara and not fall in.

It didn't help that I'd personally known one American guy who did a fall of 320 feet, survived it — and then was killed soon after on another, much lesser fall. He died on the job, as we say. Stunt men have a dark sense of humour, because it's the only way we can get up in the morning and go to work.

I managed to get away with it for ten good years without anyone sussing a whiff of the truth. Somehow I steeled myself to peer over thirty-foot balconies before somersaulting on to a mattress and rolling safely off.

The highest stunt I'd done was to double for Tommy Cooper in one of his comedy shows. We were about the same size, both of us as big as brick shithouses, as someone once observed.

Tommy had been useful with his gloves in his time, too, and loved to fool around, so the two of us had a lot in common. What a man that guy was — and what a way he finally went, keeling over on stage in front of an audience that loved him. If it's got to happen, could you ask for anything better?

For this particular show I had to climb a staircase wearing a wig and a fez, overbalance at the top, and come hurtling down like a sack of potatoes. There was a grand piano made of balsawood waiting for me below, and I crashed right through it on to a couple of mattresses thoughtfully provided by the BBC. Then I got up and walked away unscathed. No problem with the fall: it was looking down on the piano from forty feet up that made my bottle quiver.

Then, in 1967, I signed on for the James Bond thriller *You Only Live Twice* — and finally had to face up to the inevitable. You'll remember the movie, of course. One of the classic Bonds, with Sean Connery. This one took our hero all the way to Japan to sort out a spot of bother among the locals, with Donald Pleasence as a wonderfully spooky Blofeld, stroking the white cat on his lap and uttering the immortal line: "I shall look forward to exterminating you personally, Mr Bond!" Ah, they don't write dialogue like that nowadays.

Sean and me, we go back a long way. We've even posed stark bollock naked together on stage, honest God's truth!

Early on, Sean had stimulated his brain cells with jobs such as a brickie, lifeguard and a coffin polisher before taking part in the 1950 Mr Universe contest as Mr Scotland. A year later he was singing and dancing in the chorus line in *South Pacific*, and starting a career for himself as an actor.

I was getting fifty quid a week in Covent Garden, and augmenting my income, as they say, with as much stage work as my agent Gabbie Howard could pick up for me. So I found myself in a holiday show called *Wish You Were Here* — no, nothing to do with the TV series, because they don't use too many nude male models as far as I can see. But that's what I played, flexing my muscles on a white plinth, for twenty-five smackers a week.

And guess who was standing on the next slab, starkers? Sean Connery, that's who!

In those days you weren't allowed to move until the curtain swished down, and then you could adopt a different pose. But each night Sean and me would wind each other up, whispering gags and insults, trying to make the other laugh in public. Or pubic, in this case.

We all called him "the Outsider" because he spoke broad Scots in an accent as thick as porridge, and we couldn't understand a lot of what he was saying.

Next thing I know, Sean is being cast as James Bond in *Dr No*, and his life changes for ever. I was offered a role in that film as one of the doctor's henchmen, but somehow I got my wires crossed and thought they said *Dr Who*. Since I didn't want to be stuck inside a Dalek shouting: "Exterminate!" I turned it down.

Never mind. I got hired for the next one, *From Russia With Love*, and from then on I became part of the Bond scenery. They were great films, although I have to say that there was only one James Bond for me, and that was Sean Connery. I either worked on, or was on the set of all the 007 films apart from Dr No — including the spoof Casino Royale — so I had a chance to see the actors first-hand.

Sean was the heavyweight, the definitive Bond. Timothy Dalton was featherweight. George Lazenby could have been a superb Bond, but he fell out with Cubby Broccoli. Pierce Brosnan has a certain boyish charm, so I'll rate him a welter.

Roger Moore was lightweight, in the sense of lighthearted. As my old mate Lewis Gilbert, who directed both Sean and Roger, said: "I made him tongue-in-cheek, with fun in it. When Sean killed someone, you felt they were dead. Whereas when Roger did it, you thought: Well, the guy's going to get up and walk away."

Roger can lift any set out of the doldrums the moment he walks on. He once greeted me: "Hey, Nosher. Do you know what they call an Italian suppository?" I shook my head. "An innuendo!" said Roger, going blithely on his way. And he once surprised a BBC TV crew on location down a South African mine on the movie *Gold* — which he hated — by asking: "Who do I have to fuck to get *out* of this film?"

But behind the jokey manner and the arched eyebrow lies a serious man — with principles.

On location in Rio for *Moonraker*, a junket was laid on for the press from around the world to meet the stars, including the seven-foot-two Richard Kiel, who played Jaws. I should mention that once he takes out the steel teeth, Richard is the gentlest giant you could ever wish to meet.

Two of the shrewder scribes went after Ronald Biggs, languishing in enforced exile from the Great Train Robbery and doing very well, thank you, on his notoriety by charging Japanese TV crews two thousand dollars for an interview — and getting it. This pair tracked him down, and had the bright idea of smuggling him into a crowd scene to stand behind Bond, a picture that would certainly have gone round the world.

Biggsy agreed to be a face in the crowd. But when the pair approached Roger to ask if he'd pose with Ron, he shook his head. "Sorry, fellers, it's a nice idea. But my father was a policeman, and I don't think he'd have liked it."

That surprised Fleet Street's finest, but it earned their respect. Biggsy stayed out of shot, and never made it to the big screen.

Anyway, I'm getting off the point here. In *From Russia with Love* you can spot me in the fight in the gypsy encampment, starting with two gypsy girls in a grudge match (one of them being that sexy lady Martine Beswick) and ending in an all-out brawl.

We filmed it at night on an open-air lot at Pinewood. There's a lot of hanging around on film sets, and I found Sean standing next to me. Out of the corner of my mouth I muttered: "Just like waiting for the curtain to drop, ain't it, Sean?"

Puzzled, he asked: "What do you mean?"

"*Wish You Were Here?*" I said.

"Christ!" he exclaimed. "Don't remind me. And whatever you do, don't tell anybody!"

Sorry, Sean, I can't resist it.

*You Only Live Twice* was Sean's fifth appearance as Bond. His arch-enemy Blofeld is operating inside an extinct volcano, screwing up our satellites and threatening to start the Third World War. I never made it to Japan, but I was hired for the grand-slam action finale in the huge 007 set on the back lot at Pinewood, which is so big I sometimes wonder if you can see it from the moon.

The "lake" of the crater was, in fact, a hard blue-mirrored casing that hid a complete laboratory underneath. It slid open to allow Blofeld to fire his own space rockets. Very ingenious — but isn't every Bond?

I was one of the good guys, part of the attacking force sent in to back up Bond and destroy the lab. Wearing a grey balaclava and grey combat suit, I was one of fifty stunt men who had to abseil into the crater and wreak havoc on Blofeld's underground fortress.

Remember this yellow streak between my shoulder blades when it came to heights? Listen to this. Our mob had to clamber across girders 160 feet in the air, sit astride them, drop ropes into the volcano, then abseil all the way to the ground ...

By now Pinewood was like a second home to me. After all, I'd known the place since the days of Laurence Harvey, and the studios had come on a treat since then. There was even a Stunt Room, where we had lockers and showers, and an area where we could relax with armchairs and a sofa. There was a security guard to look after our gear, and we could stow away our padding and protective clothing, and know it would be safe.

To be frank, it was better to lay our stuff out on seats or benches, because when you're working as we did, you didn't half get up a muck sweat. If we'd left that lot in a locker overnight ... next morning — Phew! No one would come near you!

Dickie Graydon and I strolled up to the set, a ten minute walk from the main building. It was enormous, another miracle of engineering and inspiration from production designer Ken Adam, who once again had let his imagination run riot.

A few scene shifters were banging nails in various walls, and a group of riggers were moving a small train on to the miniature rail track that ran round the entire set. This was Blofeld's Command Centre, with a glass control booth, laboratory equipment, computers, screens, the lot.

I looked up, and blanched. Two hundred feet above, the roof was a mass of criss-crossing girders and scaffolding, with small landing-stages at different levels. A slim ladder with steel rings around it went up the whole of one wall, connecting the platforms.

Sooner or later I was going to have to climb that ladder. I was just getting my bearings when there was a terrible scream from high up in the rafters. I looked up to see a figure plummeting down, bouncing through the girders like a ping-pong ball, hitting each one with a jarring thud and cannoning off to the next.

"Christ!" Dickie shouted, as we ducked away. It was a rigger who had slipped from the top platform. The poor bastard landed just six feet away, splattering like a ripe fucking tomato. By the time he hit the ground he must have broken most of the bones in his body.

We put a blanket over him while they called the ambulance, and he was taken away within minutes. Miraculously, he survived, though Christ knows if he ever walked properly again.

Dickie grabbed my arm, and gestured to the ladder. "Up we go!" he said firmly.

I was shaking like a leaf. "I can't!"

"Let's do it," he said. "That's what we're here for."

I knew what I had to do, and I'd brought a two-foot length of hosepipe with me for the descent, stuffed inside my shirt. But when I looked up again I nearly shit myself. First, there was the sixty-foot ladder, and beyond it another one soaring to a hundred feet. I actually broke out in a cold sweat.

"Come on, Nosh!" Dickie scurried up the first ladder like a squirrel up a drainpipe. I followed reluctantly, hand over hand. At least the ladder had steel rings all round it to stop you toppling into space. Now we're on the first safety platform. "Okay?" says Dickie — and he's away again, up to the next level. It's not okay, but I go after him because I have no choice. Now it's a hundred feet, and I'm on my hands and knees on the small platform up among the girders as he calmly walks off, grips the rungs, and hoists himself up, up and away. I'm left, shouting: "Dicki-eee!"

Somehow I make the next stage, climbing the ladder with sweaty palms that slip on each rung. And now we're up on the 160-foot level, with three eighteen-inch girders stretching out across the volcano.

I make the mistake of looking down — to see small groups far below, all staring up, the size of dolls. The set starts to swim and blur.

That's it, I'm gone. There's not a lot you can do about vertigo. Your knees turn to water. You get the shakes. The earth moves, but for all the wrong reasons.

Quietly Dickie says: "You'll be all right." Oh, yeah? After what I'd just witnessed? And pigs might fly.

Several ropes were already hanging from the girder, ready for rehearsals when the main team came back. "This way," Dickie said briskly — and *walked* out along the girder. Over his shoulder he added: "Don't look down!"

A bit late for that. I sat astride the cold steel girder, inching my way forward. Dickie called: "Right, hang on to the rope. Get your hosepipe. You know what to do."

The hosepipe is an old stunt man's trick. If you leave it wrapped tight around a rope, it will stay here like glue, without slipping. It will support your entire weight. So you wrap it round, and when you're ready you shift your hand to the middle of the hose, and gently release it. This way you can control the speed of your descent. Tighten your grip, you slow up. Open it, and you accelerate.

I was frozen to the girder, with no safety net. But I managed to extract the hose from my shirt, and wound it round the first rope. Dickie crouched down beside me, cool as ice on eighteen inches of steel.

"Now ... lower yourself off, and hang on to the rope!"

Well, it must have taken half an hour. In that time Dickie cajoled me, cursed me, poked fun at me, taunted me. Finally he threw out the ultimate insult. "Come on, you ginger c--t! You've got no fucking guts!"

That did it. The hose was ready. I bellowed back: "I've got guts all right!" And I flung myself off into space. As I dangled like a large spider on a single thread, Dickie looked down at me with a beaming smile. "That's all I wanted you to do, Nosh!" he said.

I tell you, if I'd gripped anyone by the throat the way I gripped that hosepipe, they'd be dead! I inched my way down 160 feet, a foot at a time. Stop, start. Stop, start. Every time I eased off the hose and dropped a foot, I cried out: "Ooh — ah!" What a baby!

I don't know how long it took, but when I got to the ground there was a huge burst of applause. And a swishing sound as Dickie came down one-handed — just like that, as Tommy Cooper would say. It probably took him eight seconds.

He put an arm round my shoulder. "You need a drink, Nosher," he said. "And I'm buying."

For the first and last time in my life I got as drunk as a skunk. Dickie, God bless him, got one of the boys to drive me home.

That was fear, and I had reached the apex. I won't say I haven't been afraid again. But after that episode, my own personal Room 101, I could never be more frightened if I was turned loose in a room full of ravenous tigers.

Before the boys came back from Japan, I did that slide a dozen times, not knowing that when the cameras finally rolled on the big action sequence the fickle finger of fate had something else lined up for me.

## 31: BOND

Now came an ugly incident of which I'm not particularly proud, but which I deemed necessary at the time. The team on *You Only Live Twice* finally came back from Japan, with a bunch of Japanese actors and stunt guys in tow.

The crew sported a nice tan, and had all sorts of stories, including one I perhaps shouldn't repeat about an outing to a massage parlour where they were greeted by an old hag, the madam, sitting on a block of ice — naked! How she managed that without getting her assets frozen no one could ever work out.

The Japanese stars had names like Tetsuro Tamba, Akiko Wakayabashi and Mie Hama, and while they were big in their country and wonderfully courteous, I couldn't even be sure I could spell their names right.

Anyway, I was more interested in their stunt boys and girls, all of them martial-arts experts. These are tough cookies, and you mess with them at your peril. Not a lot of them spoke English, but with a smattering of Japanese, complete with sing-song voice, I finally got through to them.

They had been recruited from the elite Toshido Martial Arts School in Tokyo. After their stint on the film, they would go back to what they did best, guarding millionaire businessmen, politicians and industrialists, and be ready to take the bullet if necessary. They were extraordinary guys, brought in specially to show us the moves — we were part of security chief Tiger Tanaka's elite rescue force, after all, and they had a special way of fighting.

I spent hours with them on and off the set, and learned to respect a different culture and a different attitude to the martial arts. It did occur to me that even in my grey hood and boiler suit, I would stand out as the biggest Japanese in the whole movie, but since no one else mentioned it I kept my mouth shut.

One day I had a sharp lesson in the art of respect. "Misser Nosser?" It was the top guy, Sen. Sorry, make that *Mr* Sen. I'm forgetting my manners.

There were fifty of the Toshido. Yes, fifty. A Bond budget is bottomless when they need something important. I had been accepted into the ranks, and allowed to work out with our Oriental guests in their daily ritual exercise sessions held on an empty lot at the back of Pinewood, far away from prying eyes.

"I have the honour to present my daughter, Misser Nosser." Mr Sen bowed deeply, and ushered a waif-like young girl forward into my presence. She was tiny, under five feet, with porcelain skin and dark almond eyes.

"How old are you, my dear?" I inquired, taking the small hand gently in mine.

"She twelve years old," said Mister Sen proudly. "Her name Yoko. Means 'Little Flower'. Will you care to exercise with her, please?"

Anything to keep our guests happy. In front of the fifty black belts, I squared up to Little Flower, feinted with my famous left jab — and *bonk*! I was flat on my back, all seventeen stone of me, after the little petal had smacked me in the chest with her right hand, fingers extended, not even a fist!

There was a polite ripple of applause. "How did she do that?" I asked, astounded, climbing slowly to my feet.

Mr Sen beamed with paternal pride. "Taught from age of three," he said. "If she had struck you in throat, you be dead now!"

Like I say, one must respect other cultures.

The big day arrived. They would be shooting the attack from all directions. I had no idea of the script, and just did what they wanted. "Big scene, Nosher," said Bob Simmons, the stunt co-ordinator, who had also been Sean Connery's double in every Bond film.

Bob was a veteran of action movies, and had more scalps under his belt than most. My instructions on that first day were to run down into the volcano, where the launching pad of the rocket was housed, stop at the bottom of a staircase, and wait for three explosions. *Bang! Bang! Bang!*

"On the third blast you run across as if you're heading for the rocket to put it out of action, then veer off to your right." Bob was meticulous in his timing. "A fourth explosion will show you running off through the smoke, and out of camera shot. Okay?"

"Okay, fine." I had no problem with it. We'd rehearsed it a dozen times, but without the explosives.

"Good. Get ready, everyone!"

Behind the camera, Lewis Gilbert's voice crackled through the loudhailer. *"Action!"* The explosions were tremendous. *Bang! Bang! Bang!* On the third detonation I took off — and ran right into another one! The fourth bomb went off straight into my face. They were using bucket bombs, which are shaped like they say — a bucket, and the force can be directed to one side or another. I ran full tilt into the blast, which never should have happened.

They said afterwards that I was thrown twenty feet into the air. All I know is that when I came down on hard concrete I thought I'd broken every fucking bone in my body.

My head was ringing, I was winded, and I lay on the floor wondering what the hell had gone wrong.

Dimly I heard shouts. *"Cut! Cut! Cut!"* People were screaming. The cameras stopped running. Panic all round. Then through the smoke strolled Bob Simmons, grinning from ear to ear like a Cheshire Cat.

"Great," he said. "Fucking fantastic!"

I heard my own voice from a long way away. "But, Bob, you told me that fourth one wouldn't go off until I was running away from the bucket. Instead I run straight into it."

He had to speak loudly for me to hear him. "If I'd told you that, you wouldn't have run into it!"

I held my temper then, but only just. *Not in front of the crew.* But three days later I went back to complete unfinished business, and I nearly broke his jaw.

Those were three bad days. I was deaf in one ear for a start, no sound at all. I was bruised and battered. I should also mention here that as stunt co-ordinator, Bob Simmons was in charge of hiring and firing the fall guys.

On the day after my accident, the British stunt men held a weekend meet at a pub in West London. I could only hear out of one ear, but it was enough to know what was going on after I limped in and sat down with them. There'd been problems over money.

I told them: "Fuck this for a barrowload of monkeys." Next thing, I'd got the elbow, along with several other stunt men who had been wanting more danger money. Suddenly I was both hard of hearing and likely to be hard up with it.

I went home, and all that weekend I brooded. And when Nosher Powell broods, he broods!

Come Monday morning, I was in the mood. I went out to the car, and passed Dinny watching TV in the front room. He had been cut from the film as well. "Where you off to?" he inquired.

"Down to the studio," I said.

"What, you working?" he asked in surprise.

I said: "No, I'm going down to fucking give that bastard Bob Simmons one."

Dinny was on his feet in a flash. "Wait for me!" he said. "I'm with you. This is family."

We drove down to Pinewood Studios in a grim silence, parked the car, and walked side by side up the slope towards the 007 stage like Wyatt Earp and Doc Holliday in *Gunfight at the O.K. Corral*. They'd just broken for lunch, and we met a load of other stunt men approaching us. And did they give us a wide berth!

Up on the 007 stage a few technicians were hammering and sawing — and there was Bob standing in the middle of the volcano with one of the extras.

He had his arm round the geezer's shoulder, and a couple of pages of the script, and was talking to him earnestly, when he suddenly looked up and saw Dinny and me standing there like Montezuma's revenge — except he was the one who'd be shitting himself.

Dinny said: "I'll have him, Nosher."

Bob knew the SP, knew what was going to happen to him, and he held on to this guy like a drowning man clutching a lifebelt. We stood there staring at him for what must have been five or six minutes, just waiting. Every time the extra turned to break away, Simmons pulled him back, and kept talking. But eventually he ran out of dialogue.

He turned to us, forcing a smile. "Why, hello, Nosher! Hello, Dinny!"

He went to put an arm around Dinny's shoulder — and whack! That was when Dinny hit him with a massive haymaker, and Simmons went down like a fucking tree.

The other geezer gave a startled squawk, and ran for it. There was blood all down Dinny's shirt — but it was Dinny's blood. He had hit Bob so hard he had split his knuckle all the way down to the nail, and his whole forefinger was hanging open to the bone. But he hadn't quite caught Simmons right. Bob was groggy, but trying to get up.

I said, "Dinny, that looks bad," and I wasn't talking about Bob. "Go down to First Aid straight away and get it seen to."

He said: "Okay, see you down there."

There were three or four stunt boys standing around, open-mouthed. I said to them: "Right, you lot. Pick him up and take him down to the stunt room." They jumped to it, lifted Simmons on to a plank of wood, and carried him down the slope to the main studio. Half way along, they started singing the funeral march: *Dum dum de-dum ...*

All the boys, about thirty of them, were in the stunt room. We brought Bob in on the board, and laid him on the floor. I looked around. "Anybody here got anything to fucking say?"

They all chorused: "No, Nosh. No ... no ..."

Simmons tried to get to his feet. I said: "If I were you, Bob, I'd stay lying down. Delayed action. Know what I mean?"

He mumbled: "I'm all right. Piss off —"

So then, okay, my turn. *WHACK!* My fist of numbness, full strength, straight on his jaw. I thought I might have broken it. This time he was spark out. I said to the prone figure: "I told you, *lie down!*"

I made my exit in total silence, though I wasn't actually expecting any applause, and headed for the canteen to get myself a coffee. I hadn't finished yet. Eventually Bob walked in, rubbing his jaw. I'll give him this: he was a tough cookie.

I went over to his table, and sat down. "Listen," I said, "you're a no-good c--t. You nearly got me killed. I could have accepted that — but I can't accept the way you did it. If you'd said to me: 'Nosher, I want you to run into that explosion,' okay, we could talk about it. But you never said nothing. Now, don't ever do that to me again." And I walked out.

But I didn't leave the studio. That day there were scores to be settled. Instead I made for the restaurant, where people were finishing their lunch. The restaurant at Pinewood Studios is a byword for elegance — chandeliers, oak-panelled walls, wonderful views of the garden through the picture windows, waitress service, classy wine list, the lot. Ask anyone from Hollywood or Cinecittà or the Paris studios. They'll all sing its praises, and rightly so.

Every big star I've ever met loves to eat there, and this day was no exception. The restaurant is split level, with a stage at one end as you walk in. You can look down on about thirty tables stretching away in four rows to the far end to another door leading to the bar.

I walked through, and took up a position on the stage, surveying the room. That month, Pinewood was buzzing. I spotted Sean Connery, Donald Pleasence and Bernard Lee, who played M in the Bond film. Michael Caine was over by the window, taking his lunch break during *Billion Dollar Brain* with the director, Ken Russell. Their co-stars Karl Malden and Ed Begley were at a neighbouring table.

Dick Van Dyke and Sally Ann Howes were there, from *Chitty Chitty Bang Bang*, and to make up numbers the *Carry On* team of Sid James, Joan Sims and Kenneth Williams huddled in a cluster in the far corner. The stars were out in force to witness my own Oscar-winning performance.

I spotted the geezer I wanted — another stunt man who had been at the meet two days previously, and given me a lot of grief. I beckoned with a finger. Loudly I said: "Oi, you! Up 'ere!"

Reluctantly he got to his feet. I led the way into the gents' toilet along the passage, then I turned on him. "Now, have you got anything to say, you bastard? Say it now!"

"No, Nosh, no," he mumbled. "Nothing."

"That's all right, then," I told him. "Just don't say nothing against me ever, or even mouth a little bit of gossip, or I'll have you." And I gave him a kick up the arse as he left in a hurry.

Back to the restaurant, and I found another face. Same dialogue. "Oi, you! Up 'ere!" Back to the loo. Now everybody knows it's off and running, and the word is out. *Nosher's on the rampage! Get ready to duck!*

I do the business, pulling every stunt man in that room off into the toilet, one by one.

"You got anything to say to me?"

"No, Nosh, no ..."

"Right, out you go!" Kick up the arse. And back to the restaurant for the next one. Much later, when I was back on the film, Connery said to me: "That was quite a cabaret you put on, Nosher. What was it all about?"

"Just a few things to get sorted, Sean," I told him, and he nodded. But he was no fool. He knew the SP, too.

I got through half a dozen of them, then headed for the other gaffe, back into the canteen. There was one guy I had to see, Morrie, who was actually a pretty fair heavyweight in his own right, and acting as Bob's lieutenant. I'd beaten him twice in the ring, first on points, second time a KO.

He was standing up at the bar waiting to be served with his food. I came up behind him.

"I want you," I said, not wasting words.

He looked startled, then apprehensive. I said: "I've just fucking knocked your guv'nor spark out. Do you want to take it up where he couldn't finish?"

Wisely, Morrie raised both hands. "It's nothing to do with me, Nosher!"

But at that moment Dinny walked in, and he had his bandaged hand in a kind of medical glove, with his forefinger sticking out. He had gone to First Aid for attention, and they'd patched him up. But someone shouted: "Look out! He's got one!" And people actually dived under tables for cover, thinking Dinny was waving a shooter!

That's when Security turned up to escort us off the premises, in the shape of a nice old boy named Dickie Prince. I'd known him for years. He said: "Okay, son, whatever your argument, that's up to you. But I've got a job to do."

I told him: "That's all right, Dickie. We're leaving." I looked around at the canteen, and all the guys in it. "If I hear one word out of line, buy yourselves a wreath!" And Dinny and I walked out.

Looking back, it wasn't a bad exit line.

We all have our rucks in the business. But I have to say this for Bob Simmons. He made the stunt men of Great Britain what they are today. He was a good stunt man himself, and the last time I saw him, I shook his hand and said: "Son, you was one of the best. No hard feelings. What went between you and me was something personal. Come and have a drink."

But in his later years Bob became a recluse, and finally died alone in his terraced house in Ealing. Very sad. Dinny and I went to a massive funeral for him. Sean Connery was there, and other stars he'd worked with.

Dinny and I sent a wreath, and we put on it: *Simply the Best*! Well, the poor bastard earned it.

## 32: BING AND BOB

Chicks, horses — and golf. The only reason Bob Hope and Bing Crosby came over here for their last *Road* movie was to play the best golf courses, lose their money at the races, and chase the birds. Well, Bing certainly devoted his energy to this last goal. The film was *Road to Hong Kong*, the seventh in the incredibly successful series that stretched over twenty years. They filmed it at Shepperton Studios by the Thames, with director Norman Panama in charge, a funny, energetic guy who could wring a laugh out of a boiled egg.

I was brought in to show this prize pair how to fight, which was rather like trying to persuade the Pope to join the National Front. They were two peaceful, relaxed fellers who were so laid back that an inch further and they would have fallen flat. The only time they balled their fists was when they wrapped them round a number five iron.

My first meeting with Bob Hope set the tone for the six weeks of hilarity that followed. The director got us all together in the studio restaurant behind the Bulldog pub for a get-to-know-you party, and I found myself facing the great comic.

"This is Nosher Powell, your fight co-ordinator," said Panama.

Hope took my hand. "Mr Powell, it's an honour and a privilege," he intoned gravely.

Such modesty. "Oh, no, Mr Hope. It's an honour and privilege for *me*," I responded.

"That's what I meant," said Hope, deadpan.

From that moment we were pals.

In the *Road* comedies, Hope played the complete idiot. In real life, forget it! He was one of the most astute businessmen I ever met. I heard him on the set making deals over the phone, discussing percentages with his agent, working out his fees and first-class travel perks for promotional appearances. His mind was a human calculating machine.

As for Bing, he was strictly for the birds. He was never blatant about it, but he couldn't resist a skirt. It was common knowledge among the unit that he was having flings right, left and centre but, wisely, he kept his own doorstep clean, and whatever went on happened away from the studio. Only when it came to racing did he lose his shirt in public. On the set we used to say he would back the slowest horse on any racetrack in the country.

But for both of them, golf was the game. I've seen it before with actors, from Sean Connery to Christopher Lee — who, incidentally, played off a two handicap — and many others. For some what started out as relaxation became a religion, and it was so with Hope and Crosby.

I remember once seeing Dean Martin arrive on the set at Universal Studios, strolling on with a number nine iron swinging languidly from one hand and a lackey trotting behind with a bucket of golf balls. They'd rigged up a net across one wall, and Dino spent his time between takes thumping the balls against the net, practising his swing.

Bob and Bing went one better. Outside H Stage they had a miniature putting green set up. They would emerge from their star trailers, moored next to each other, armed with a putter each, toss a coin, and go to war.

I would stand by as Bing started off the wager. "Okay, five bucks!"

"No," said Bob. "Make it twenty!"

And that was per hole.

Norman Panama assigned me to ensure the pair of them were on the set in time for the next shot. "When you hear the word, get those two in, Nosh!" Believe me, it wasn't easy, with Hope squaring up for a putt and all of twenty dollars riding on it.

They tried all manner of dirty tricks to put each other off. Bob would be shaping up, when Bing suddenly started humming, "Ba-ba-ba-ba-ba-bum!" in that inimitable voice. But they were pretty evenly matched, and came out just about even.

At the end of the day a car was waiting outside the huge double doors of the sound stage. Two sets of clubs would be in the boot. When the bell finally jangled to indicate the end of shooting, they'd be out like greased porkers, into the car, and off down to Wentworth to get a round in before dark. As Bob confided on the last day: "Don't tell the producers, Nosher. But the only reason we insisted on making the movie here was so that we could swing a club where they play the Royal Open!"

They also played it for laughs off the set. One scene called for the pair to walk backwards, manacled together, out of an underground fortress, leaving Dorothy Lamour, Joan Collins — yes, I was with her again — and arch-villain Robert Morley inside.

Don't ask me why they were going backwards, but they were. I think the idea was to confuse the opposition that they were actually going in rather than out. But they'd shot the scene, filming was over for the day — and out came Bob and Bing, marching backwards, arm in arm all the way to the car. Even the chauffeur cracked up.

Oh, I had a brilliant time with that prize pair.

But the moment I'll never forget came when I arrived to direct their fight sequence, scheduled for noon.

In the plot, such as it was, they had collared a formula, something to do with a bomb that would destroy the world. The boys never knew what the formula was, and as far as I could make out it was all one big chase. Me and my brother Dinny were cast as villains working for the mastermind (Morley), both of us dressed in black roll-neck sweaters like evil twins.

After the fight we would link arms and yank Bob and Bing bodily off the ground so their feet were dangling in the air, then march them away. They were fucking heavy, I can tell you — both over twelve stone apiece, which meant that between the pair of them, me and Dinny had to lift up twenty-five stone.

To make life easier, I said: "Hey, fellers. You're supposed to be cowards. Hang on to one another, and that'll help us get you off the ground." We were able to pick them up, and it looked hilarious with the four of us belting around like madmen.

For the rehearsals, I figured it would take no more than half an hour to get it right, and I was on the set in plenty of time to meet the boys and run it through.

The place was full of hammering and shouting and sawing, the usual cacophony that goes with a film set. Bing wandered in with the *Sporting Life* tucked under one arm, made for the green canvas chair with his name on the back, sat down and started turning over the pages. He was wearing his usual pork-pie hat, tipped jauntily over one eye, because he always hated wearing a toupee to cover his baldness.

Suddenly I became aware of a familiar sound, discernible despite the racket going on around us. "Ba-ba-ba-ba-ba-ba ..." Bing was humming. The hum became a warble, "When the blue of the night ..." which, you may know, was actually the theme song of the radio show that made his name. And slowly the hammering stopped, the sawing stopped, and from a hive of activity a complete silence descended on the set, with all the stillness of an empty cathedral.

Bing, seemingly oblivious to the effect he was having, kept on turning the pages, marking down a potential winner with a pencil here and there. But now his voice was gaining strength. "... Meets the gold of the day ... ba-ba-ba-ba-bummm!" And he went right through the song to the last line. "Someone ... waits for ... me ..."

That's when he looked up, gave a broad grin, and said: "Not bad for an old 'un, eh, Nosh?" The old ham had known what he was doing all the time, holding us in thrall.

Magic! The gaffers led the applause, and we all joined in. After all, it isn't often you get a free show from one of the world's greatest entertainers.

As an encore, Bing gave us 'The Waiter And The Porter And The Upstairs Maid' before the first assistant called us to the cameras for our rehearsal. "Places, please!" After that, we never heard Bing Crosby sing again.

It's not generally realised that those two were actually born in the same month of the same year, May 1903, with Crosby older by twenty-seven days. Hope never smoked or drank, stayed married to the same woman all his life, and would outlast his old sparring partner by more than twenty years. Bing ran out of road in 1977.

Bob, meanwhile, had a bizarre bet with George Burns. "Whichever of us dies first, the other one has to pay for his funeral," he told me one day, as we were chatting in his caravan.

Of course, dear old George — who was never without a cigar or a piece of jail-bait close to hand — died just before reaching his century. So Bob had to put his hand in his pocket.

## 33: JOHN WAYNE

John Wayne would have made a good fighter, and I'm talking the real world. Believe me, the big guy was tasty with his fists. I should know, because I've been on the receiving end. Now here was one big man, in every sense.

He could swing a blinder. We used to call it the "John Wayne Bluffer". He'd sling a punch that came all the way round the mulberry bush before it landed — but when it did, surprise! He'd perfected the camera angle so the whole world saw it on the screen.

Wayne — "Call me Duke, everyone does!" — also mastered that swivel-eyed look when he took one on the jaw. Which proved that even if he wasn't the world's greatest classical actor he knew how to take a joke.

John Wayne had been my boyhood hero ever since I first saw him from the stalls in South London with my kid brother. How could I know then that one day I would work with this hero of two hundred sagebrush sagas?

But I did.

Wayne was a genuine hard man in his own right. Tough as teak, an ex-footballer, stunt man and horse handler, he got his first chance in a film called *Salute*, made by the legendary director John Ford who took him on to glory with *Stagecoach*.

You could say we talked the same language. Horses and fists. And finally the time came when I got the chance.

*Brannigan* was the film, the name of a Chicago cop who comes to London to arrest a gangster (John Vernon, who looked as if he ate nails for breakfast) and take him back to the States for trial.

I was hired for various fight scenes, notably a pub brawl they filmed close to the old Smithfield meat market in the City. We'd be punching our weight, the Duke and I, with the place reduced to matchwood, so I felt I should at least attempt more than a friendly hello to the main man before taking it on the chin.

The problem was that the Duke, amiable and smiling as he was and ready with the occasional quip, *was* a huge star, possibly the biggest I would ever meet. So I wasn't sure how to approach him and have more than just a "Hi, how are you?" conversation.

Then someone told me he liked chess. He liked it so much that he played it every day on his own board in his trailer. Right, I thought. This is the way in. I got myself a copy of the *Evening Standard* and located their daily chess problem, with the solution on the next page, and memorised it.

I only play a little, maybe a couple of times a year, and I'm not that good. But I had my own pocket set. So I sat down just inside the door of the pub where the Duke would have to pass, laying out the pieces on an upturned beer barrel.

Sure enough, Wayne spotted me as he came through the doors. He was over faster than a ferret up a trouser leg, and towered above me, peering over my shoulder. Naturally, as any chess aficionado would, I ignored him.

After a few moments, the Duke's distinctive deep voice drawled: "What's the problem?"

"White to mate in three," I replied briefly, not looking round or up. We studied the board intently. Then a big hand came past my ear, and moved a pawn.

"How about that?"

I waggled an admonishing finger. "Uh-uh. The knight takes it in two ..."

"Oh ..." The Duke's voice grew doubtful.

At last I looked up. "I've been here an hour, Duke, and I'm darned if I can do it."

A frown added to the creases on his leathery features. The Duke didn't like to be beaten. "We'll lick it, feller. By the way, what's your name?"

I introduced myself. We shook hands. He was called away for a rehearsal — but when the lunch break came, there he was, pulling up a stool opposite me. He beckoned the third assistant. "Two steak sandwiches and two beers for me and my friend!"

"Yessir, Mr Wayne!" The assistant raced off.

I gave the Duke the full hour, sharing his grunts of frustration as each move was thwarted. Five minutes before we were due back to face the cameras my face lightened.

"*Got it*!" And I moved the pieces with blinding expertise to mate the black king.

The Duke eyed me with considerable respect. "Well, Nosher, I guess you and I are going to have to have a game."

Wisely, I made sure we never did. He would have crucified me. Instead, we chatted every day on that movie, talking horses, talking stunts, talking the fight game. And I got to know the man behind the image.

The fight scene, when it was filmed, was thoroughly satisfying. The brilliant stunt director Peter Brayham, who had cut his teeth on TV series like *The Sweeney* and *The Professionals*, saw to it that the place was reduced to a shambles of splintered wood and broken glass.

Wayne and Richard Attenborough, playing a toffee-nosed Yard chief, ended standing back to back trading punches with a line-up of willing sacrificial stunt boys, including me, and I was reminded of the classic fight scene in *Shane*, with Alan Ladd and Van Heflin doing much the same thing.

John Wayne was all I hoped he'd be, and more. He also had a sense of humour — and he needed it after one gag we played on him at the end of the film. It's known as the Stunt Man Special, and we do it both as a tribute and a joke to a star, or a director, or anyone we think deserves it — for whatever reason.

It goes like this. On a quietish day at Shepperton Studios when we were all standing around waiting for something to happen, one of us said to the big man: "You know, Duke, I can lift two grown men up with one hand!"

Wayne stared at him in disbelief. "What do you mean?"

The rest of us nodded in confirmation. "It's true, Duke. He can."

"Never!" said Wayne.

"I'll show you," said the first guy. He lay down on the ground, face up, and a second stunt man stretched out flat on top of him, face down, with his head between the other guy's boots. "Okay, lie on top of us!"

Looking dubious, but not wishing to be a spoilsport, the Duke gingerly stretched his full six foot four frame out on top of the pair, face up. At which point both stunt men's arms came up to clamp around him, front and back, holding him helpless in a vice-like grip.

That was when I stepped in. With a handful of gooey mud.

"Hold him steady, lads!" I undid the Duke's zip, and slapped the dollop of mud down inside. Then I zipped him up again.

"Yikes!" roared the Duke.

"Okay, let him go!"

Well, the bellows went round the studio like those of a trumpeting elephant on heat. The boys rolled him off, and we scattered to the four winds.

But the Duke had a great sense of humour. He liked a practical joke as much as the next feller, and took it well. Later that night in the bar he bought us all a round of beers to show there were no hard feelings. Like I say — a real man.

Back to the chessboard. Wayne had the same need to win as another screen legend, Anthony Quinn, who also fancied himself at the game. I know because I once met a guy on another film set who was hot stuff with the moves, and he told me how he was hired for *Zorba the Greek*, paid to play Tony — and *lose*. Can you believe it?

This guy was an American–Greek named Soloyanis. He'd spent ten weeks in Chania, on Crete where they filmed it, keeping the star happy. Solly told me as much. "I hung around the chessboard all day, and when Tony felt like a game I was there to accommodate him. But I'm under strict orders. 'You lose nine games out of ten, but win the tenth to retain his interest.' So that's what I did."

The film won two Oscars and Tony got a nomination, so something must have been right.

Meantime, John Wayne would invite me into his trailer to share a few beers. The unit had moved south of the river, to a derelict area of abandoned buildings that Stanley Kubrick would eventually use as his location to fight the Vietnam war with *Full Metal Jacket*. All of a sudden the Duke asks: "How did you get into the business, Nosher?"

Without going into my life story, I start with *Wall of Death* and Laurence Harvey.

"Harvey?" He looked up suddenly, and squinted at me. "That bit of spunk! Good actor, but a stuck-up bastard. When we made *The Alamo* he wanted everything. He even sent a car back because it wasn't big enough. But he did a damn good job on the movie."

Wayne was talking about the 1960 epic charting the fate of a few brave souls defending a fort against the overwhelming forces of General Santa Anna.

I had to ask him. Was that story really true about the bar and the gents' loo?

If you don't know it, the tale goes like this. They shot the movie on location around Santa Fe, making full use of the wonderful red earth and New Mexican scenery. Wayne starred as Davy Crockett, and also directed the stirring saga that would be nominated for no fewer than six Oscars. At the end of each day the crew would repair to the nearest bar, and knock back copious quantities of beer and tequila to get the dust out of their throats.

On one particular evening, with some great footage in the can, everyone was celebrating. After a few beers, Wayne announced loudly: "Gotta take a leak!" And off he headed in the direction of the rest room. Moments later he came storming back, wet down the side of one leg, brushing his trousers and muttering: "Son-of-a-bitch! Son-of-a-*bitch*!"

The acolytes crowded around him anxiously. "What's the matter, Duke? When you left here, you were fine. We've had a great day. What happened in there?"

And Wayne, still brushing away furiously, growled: "It's always the same. I'm standing there minding my own business, and the guy next to me swings round exclaiming: '*It's John Wayne!*'"

That story, I was always led to believe, was true! So now I had to ask. *Well, Duke. Was it?*

He squinted at me with that quizzical look I'd seen so often on the big screen. "Sure it was. If it makes you happy."

I always had a soft spot for Julie Andrews. So when my agent Gabbie asked me if I'd like a role in *Victor, Victoria*, I jumped at the chance. And meeting Julie — I was right. She was a cracker. No side. A warm word for everyone. And no Mary Poppins, either.

Behind the sugar-and-spice image is a mischievous lady with a wicked sense of humour. I mean, she even dresses up as a French maid to titillate her husband Blake Edwards when they're in the mood. She told me as much! Thinking about it now, I'm sure she was just teasing me, but still, there's a thought to make strong men go weak at the knees.

Perhaps that's why Blake was directing this ooh-la-la comedy set in 1934 Paris, with Julie as a singer who poses as a female impersonator. In other words, both Victor and Victoria, with all the innuendos thrown in. James Garner was the male lead.

Naturally, I was curious about my role, though I imagined I'd probably have to hit someone . "What do I have to do?"

"Sing," said Gabbie. "Get pissed. Then you hit James Garner." Was I right, or was I right?

My voice is more foghorn than Mozart. But I took off down to

Shepperton, where I joined a queue of sturdy types outside a recording studio. Inside, Blake Edwards sat with two aides by a turntable.

"Okay, Nosher. In your own time. There's no music, so sing us anything you like."

I took a deep breath, then gave my lungs an outing with "Any Old Iron". After two bars Blake held up a hand with a pained expression. "That'll do. That's just what we want. You're in!" Meaning I'd got the job.

The job was a comedy fight sequence in a bar full of French stevedores, drunks, and odds and sods from the street. We would all start out in a drunken song, then someone would throw a punch, and the place would disintegrate into a massive bar-room brawl. I had to try to lay one on Jim Garner, and take one on the jaw in return. Afterwards we'd all end up against the bar singing again.

As we rehearsed, Jim gave me his quirky grin. "I used to hit people, usually the *paparazzi*," he said, in his friendly way. "They always gave me a bad time in Rome, following me everywhere, hanging around outside restaurants, trying to get me mad so they could get a picture. But I had a way of dealing with it. I just kept smiling, even while I was saying: 'Listen, you sons-of-bitches, I'm gonna throw you through that window if you don't leave me alone!' Because I was always smiling, it never made the picture they wanted." Good tip to remember.

Now came the problem. The song had to be in French. Why not hire French actors? That would be too easy, and this is the movie business. So we lusty costermongers sang some ditty we all knew in English — and later they dubbed it with our lips synchronised into French!

.      How they did it, I'll never know. But we sang away like an unholy choir, and when I saw the finished result, we all sounded like Frogs, and everything matched up. Amazing!

I saw *Victor, Victoria* on TV again the other night, and there I was singing away and destroying the furniture. The good news is that with the right contract I get repeat fees: the first repeat on TV is worth 75 per cent of your original fee. Then 50 per cent. On the third viewing: 25 per cent. Then you get down to the minimum: 17.5 per cent.

My lowest repeat fee? Don't hold your breath. It's sixty-five pence for *Lorna Doone*!

# 34: TALKING TURKEY

Turkey, 1970. Magic-carpet time. Ali Baba. A fez or two, perhaps, reminding me of my days with Tommy Cooper. I was called in to do some stunts on *You Can't Win 'Em All*, an adventure yarn which my old mate Peter Collinson was directing on far-flung locations somewhere in the mountains. I had no idea what I was in for.

The movie starred Charles Bronson and Tony Curtis as rival mercenaries chasing a fortune in jewels in the days of the Ottoman Empire, *circa* 1920. Overgrown kids' stuff. I'd had a quick glance at the script, and it looked like there was nothing but fights and horseback chases and more fights.

But armed with a pocket phrase book optimistically titled *Let's Talk Turkey*, I headed out into the unknown, with Dinny along to keep me company.

I'd heard there'd been trouble on what had become known as "the Collinson film", with all sorts of rumours reaching us. Deaths ... drugs ... fights ... "So what else is new?" I said to Dinny, as our plane touched down at Izmir airport.

But Pete had called me up to get it sorted, and I was glad to do him a favour. He had directed *The Italian Job* the year before, and had a reputation as a tough, no-nonsense action man who drove his guys hard.

Sometimes a little too hard.

On the phone, he had said: "I can guess what they're all saying about us back there. 'That bastard Collinson is at it again!' Am I right?"

"Something like that," I said. "I'm on my way."

All I knew was that we'd be filming in the desert, it would be hot, and it would be what we call "a tough location". We got an inkling of how tough when we saw that the battered old taxi they'd sent to meet us at the airport was riddled with bullet holes.

I asked the turbaned driver: "What happened here?"

He replied: "I'm new. The last driver didn't show up."

Welcome to Turkey!

The location was three hours away up in the mountains. The heat was stultifying. As our rattle-trap bounced over potholes in tracks that were more like dried-up riverbeds, past the occasional donkey that had expired by the roadside and been left for the flies, Dinny leafed through a guidebook. "Where we're going," he announced, "is, I quote, 'some of the most inaccessible terrain in the world'. How about that?"

"Nice," I said. "Trust Pete!"

First, to our hotel. Somehow they'd found rooms for the unit, all 130 of us, in local villages that clung to the slopes like leeches amid the parched rocks and scrub.

We were about as far off the tourist map as it was possible to get, but that was the way Pete wanted it. As we unpacked, I heard someone clear his throat through a loudspeaker outside the window. Then, startlingly, the voice of a muezzin floated tinnily out over the rooftops, calling the faithful to prayer.

I didn't notice a mad rush, in fact the streets were totally deserted. An hour later, as our taxi pulled up by a line of trailers and camera equipment, it became apparent why. The faithful were somewhere else, squatting ten deep along an entire hillside above us, their dark eyes fixed in fascination on what was going on below.

"Hello, Nosher. Welcome to this great big brute of a picture!" Collinson, a rangy, bearded figure in a battered straw hat, shook our hands. "This is one wild location." It was certainly a long way from the family hearth in Chertsey.

From the moment I set foot in that heat-hazy wilderness, the action never let up. I had thirty stunt men working with me, wild figures cast as mercenaries who entered into the spirit of the thing as if they had been given the keys to the kingdom.

Somehow Peter had managed to beg, borrow or steal an entire cavalry division of the Turkish Army, superb horsemen every one of them. For today's scene, they were called on to dress as fierce tribesmen ambushing a dozen of our chaps in a narrow ravine, and that first day gave me a taste of things to come.

On Peter's shout of "*Action!*" through a loudhailer, the carnage began. It was a sight to chill the blood as two hundred of them came charging over the brow of a hill and down into the scrub with the dust churning up under flying hoofs, yelling their lungs out. I was just glad I hadn't been around fifty years ago, if this was what it was like.

Guns clamoured. Horses and men toppled into the sand. The local Turkish doctor in the medical tent had his work cut out.

A whistle blew. "*Hold it! Stop!*" Two of the riders had collided. They were brought down on stretchers, and rushed into the tent. "Christ!" Collinson muttered to me. "Here we go again."

"Yeah?" I raised an eyebrow. "Like what?"

"I know what will happen. Our two injured stunt men will become: 'He's killed two of them!' A year later I'll have killed twelve. Then someone will meet me in a bar and shout: 'What's this about the slaughter of forty people in Turkey?' That's how the stories grow."

He was right, of course. They do, and they did. That's the movie business for you.

A major part of my job was to make sure the horses weren't injured. A dozen had been trained to fall, and shipped specially from England. Only my stunt men rode them. The Turkish cavalry stayed up in the saddle, and if they came off it wasn't intentional.

How do you train a horse to fall? First of all, you become friends with it, winning its trust. A horse is a noble beast, one of the great symbols of strength and speed. They have long memories, and if you hurt one, he'll never forget or forgive.

Starting from scratch, we find an area that is well dug up, with loose earth, dirt or sand to soften the fall. You tie the left front leg up, bending it underneath to the girth so that it's standing on three legs. Now you stand beside it and put your arm over its neck, talking quietly, persuasively, all the time as you would to your best friend.

Then you lean on him. A horse has only got a brain as big as a walnut, and he keels over — but you're holding him, letting him down gently into the soft sand. "Easy, boy, easy ..."

You hold his head, and make a fuss of him. Then you release his hoof, and stand him up. And tie the leg back again. This goes on for two weeks, four hours a day.

If it fights you, and gets hurt, that horse will never fall deliberately again. As we say in the business: "*He's got the pox of it!*" You can slide him over ice, and he'll keep his feet.

You don't touch the other legs, because he's only going to fall one way. Slowly you pull harder, snapping the rein at the same time until he gets used to the fall. Finally, when that *snap* comes, he just goes.

Then comes the crucial day when you climb up in the saddle, and just sit there for a while, talking, talking. But one stirrup is higher than the other — and you suddenly push with your right foot, snap the rein. And he's down. "Good boy. Easy, feller ..."

You stay down with him, holding his head. Unlike a cow, which gets up with its arse in the air, a horse gets up head first. Just the weight of your hand on his head will hold him down, that's all it takes.

Then you move into the walk — *snatch*, *snap*, and he's down. Now a trot. Eventually a canter. And finally, the full gallop. The slightest pressure on the rein is all it takes, and I've never had to whip a horse in my life. If a horse needs whipping, there's something wrong with it.

Falling off at full gallop, you must keep one foot in the stirrup until the last moment. That's when you shoot your leg out, and go down with it, with your leg over the horse's neck.

One of my specialities was the "one and a half ganger". This happens when the camera is very close, and you complete a half somersault straight over the horse's head in close-up. It's very dramatic. It also requires perfect timing unless you want to take half the camera crew with you.

Today we've got it all down to a fine art. The Royal Humane Society and other animal welfare groups watch our methods like hawks, and they can't fault us.

Sadly, it wasn't always like that. I'll be truthful with you: I made films in Spain in the early days, when that country wasn't governed by the same humanitarian laws we have here.

They used to use the "Running W". Now, thank God, it's illegal. This was a leather pad fixed around the fetlock, with a cable attached to it that ran around two legs. The wire went from one fetlock, which is like the human shin, to another with a second cable, sixty foot long, stretching back through the rear legs all the way to an anchor buried in the ground. That meant he could go sixty feet any way you wanted.

On "Action!" we'd gallop 120 feet flat out. The wire would spring taut, and the poor bloody horse would go down. The shock was terrible. They had no training for this kind of thing, they weren't prepared for it.

They would be deeply traumatised — can you imagine it? Full gallop, then *bang*! After that they'd refuse to fucking move, and I don't blame them.

Some of those early films I can't see now without wincing. Like the first *Charge of the Light Brigade*, with Errol Flynn and Olivia de Havilland. They actually had a hundred horses destroyed — Flynn told me so himself. I can believe it. If you watch those horses, they go straight down with their noses slamming into the ground because their legs are stretched out underneath them with the impact. Revolting! But now, at least, everyone has cleaned up their act. If not, they'll get clobbered.

So now we come to the two-legged stars. Charles Bronson was a natural in the saddle. After all, he may have been the son of a Lithuanian coal miner, one of fifteen kids, but he was weaned on Westerns. His craggy face always looked to me as if he'd been fed one bare-knuckle sandwich too many.

We all remember *The Magnificent Seven*, where he was the knife thrower. But Charlie earned his stirrups in horse operas like *Riding Shotgun*, *Apache* and *Vera Cruz*, under his own name of Charles Buchinsky, before he took on the macho Bronson moniker for *Drum Beat*, *Run of the Arrow* and *Showdown at Boot Hill*. Usually playing the Indian brave, occasionally the paleface. But always the bad guy.

So Charlie was comfortable in the saddle. And Tony Curtis? Average. Six out of ten. But what can you expect of a guy born Bernie Schwartz, who never forgot his roots in the Bronx?

Charlie did his job, but he never talked to anybody. No "good morning", no "goodnight", nothing. He had a taciturn, almost intimidating air about him that discouraged people from coming over and passing the time of day. I tried to chat with him, but it was always one-way traffic.

Oranges. You'd think that oranges would be hanging off every tree in Turkey. They weren't. All the oranges came from Israel. We felt like oranges. "Let's go scavenging," I said to Dinny one day.

We found a local market, and bought a crate of Israeli oranges, together with an ancient fruit crusher I've still got at home today. Who knows? I might even find it's worth a quid or two on the *Antiques Road Show*. I became the "orange crusher". If anyone wanted a glass of squeezed orange juice, they came to me. The boys put their little whack in, a dollar each every day for the privilege.

On this day Charles Bronson walked over. He'd never put a penny in the kitty. He strolled up with a fucking big jug, and said: "Fill her up, Nosher!" He had the family with him, the lovely Jill Ireland and various kids like a small football team, so I couldn't refuse.

I poured in the precious orange juice, and he was off to his trailer. Soon after, he was back. "Fill her up again, Nosher!"

I said: "Sorry, Charlie. All the boys have paid, and they're working. This is for them. If you want some oranges, I'll have to go and get another case." He gave me a fish-eye stare, paused for a moment as if weighing up whether to take it further, then stomped off with a face like thunder.

Next day he was back with the jug. I said cheerily: "Good morning, you miserable bastard! Where's your money?"

His eyes glazed over. It was the look I would see four years later in *Death Wish* when he was about to waste a few punks. "You talking to me?" The voice was flat and menacing.

I nodded, keeping my smile intact.

Bronson said slowly: "Listen, you! I don't owe anybody a good morning, a good evening, or a kiss-my-fucking-arse! All right?"

I said: "Oh ... all right." Sometimes there's not a lot more to be said. Exit Mr Bronson, scowling.

Now, Charlie only knew me as a stunt man. He didn't know any more about me, and he wanted to keep it that way.

But that afternoon I got my boxing kit out. The boys strung a bag up, and I started. *Flash-dash-Nosher-Powell*, king of the showbiz boxers! All the moves, with a smile attached! You name it, he's got 'em. Joe Louis, Sugar Ray, Archie Moore, Muhammad Ali — I was the greatest impersonator you ever came across.

Out of the corner of my eye, I noticed Bronson come out of his trailer and stand on the step, quietly watching me. The more he watched me, the faster and flashier I became, reliving my reputation of having the best left hand in Great Britain, as if it was on the end of a piece of elastic.

Finally I was through. I stood under a tree in the shade, perspiring like a pig and towelling myself off. At my elbow, a voice: "I never knew you were a fighter," Bronson said.

I looked at him through a film of sweat. "Any time you fancy a workout, Charlie, let me know!"

He said: "I'll do that."

Oh, yeah? I thought.

But next day he was there, in natty shorts and a string vest. "How about that workout?"

We put on the gloves. A few onlookers gathered around, but not many. This was a private performance. Charlie came at me fast. *Pop! Pop!* Throwing his left hand. I countered with my shoulder. The third time, I whipped round, and caught him with my right — a favourite trick I'd perfected years before.

He stepped back in amazement, rubbing his jaw. "Hey, feller, I never saw that coming. How did you do it?"

"I'll show you," I said.

And from that moment onwards, Charlie Bronson and me were twenty-two carat. He only respected a pro, that was his secret. He wasn't a boxer himself, but he was a hard man, working out every day, keeping himself in peak condition.

That night I walked round to his trailer with a jug full of orange juice. "Here," I said. "For the kids."

He gave me a wad of notes. "And here's what I owe you." Back in my trailer when I counted it out, there were two hundred dollars, cash.

It would have kept him in oranges for a month.

## 35: ZORBA THE TURK

The location moved to a town called Nevsehir, which you'll find on the map half-way between the Mediterranean and the Black Sea as the crow flies. That's if you've got a very large map, and if any crow is stupid enough to fly near that dung heap in the desert in the first place.

We were housed in hotels so basic we'd have been more comfortable in an outside loo. Our beds were infested with bugs that seemed particularly large and hungry, and one memorable morning I even discovered shit on the floor of my room when I put my bare foot out of bed and trod in it. It had overflowed from the toilet down the passage and leaked into the bedrooms.

In the end we kicked up such a row they found tents for us, and we camped out like Bedouins for the next month.

The stars and the director stayed in the one decent hotel in town. It was more no-star than five, but at least it had a swimming-pool — which was empty. Tony Curtis had a word with the manager.

Tony was a good guy, one of the gang, hail-fellow-well-met, and as different from Charlie as sugar and salt. Months later he was signed up for *The Persuaders* with Roger Moore — and guess who was slugging him in his first fight scene? Yeah, me.

"Ahmed! Can't you fill the pool so the boys can have a swim at the end of the day?" Tony inquired. "We're all bushed, and that's just what we need."

The manager shook his head. "I keep the pool empty, sir."

"Why?" demanded Tony, his nasal Bronx accent getting thicker with exasperation. "Are you short of water here?"

"Oh, no, sir. Plenty water."

"Then fill her up. I'll pay you personally. In cash. Now!"

And with that, ever generous Tony took out his wallet and handed over a hundred-dollar note. The manager gawped briefly, then trousered the money and made a rapid exit.

Ten minutes later, as our fleet of cars set off for the desert, we were heartened to see half a dozen staff busily scrubbing away at the sides of the pool.

Another long, hot day. At the end of it we were knackered — but we had something to look forward to. Pot of gold at the end of the rainbow. The convoy sped back to the hotel and Tony personally led the charge. Sure enough, there was five feet of water in the pool, and it was almost full. Curtis called for beer all round. "Go get your costumes, fellers. The drinks will be waiting!"

We had our gear with us. We sat around the pool in our costumes downing our beers, savouring the swim ahead. We managed three hearty cheers for the manager. All at once a loudspeaker crackled from the top of the muezzin's tower nearby. I looked at the others questioningly, just as a voice bellowed through the Tannoy.

Quite what the message was, we couldn't tell. But the effect was extraordinary. First a babble of voices, growing louder. Then a rush of figures in sandals, dirty T-shirts and soiled jeans, stampeding past us. And then — *splash*! About fifty of them were in the pool, fully clothed, laughing and shouting and splashing about as if they were having their sins washed away on the banks of the Ganges.

It was when I saw some of them gobbing and spitting happily in the water that I suddenly changed my mind about that swim. Everyone else suddenly seemed to go off the idea, too.

Ahmed appeared, looked at the hubbub, and spread his hands. "That's why I keep the pool empty," he said.

Tony, bless him, never even asked for his money back.

After shooting was over for the day, that's when the real fun started. Back in barracks, I confided to Dinny with my customary wit: "If this film's going to pot, I can smell the cause." You couldn't miss the sweet aroma drifting surreptitiously through the hotel corridors.

The producer, a geezer named Harold Buck, had already issued a warning notice: "The local gendarmerie are under the impression that certain members of the unit are involved in the taking of drugs. It has been pointed out that if proof is forthcoming, the maximum penalty of Turkish law will be enforced." As far as I'm concerned, drugs are for mugs, but he didn't say anything about booze. And, let's face it, stunt men are not exactly known for their temperance. We had thirty-two guys on the film, and we needed to let our hair down after a sweaty day toiling in the heat. To get to the action we used eight black cars for transport, travelling in a convoy that looked like a Turkish version of Al Capone's funeral.

The nearest town was a dump called Ambale, but it was the only place with a decent bar. In the evening it became a nightclub, with earsplitting music, dicey food and a belly dancer at midnight doing her best to keep our minds off the kebab and beans.

On this particular night, most of us were on the local beer, which was surprisingly strong and felt safer than the rot-gut wine. Or maybe the heat had something to do with it. Either way, a guy called Jim got up and started doing Zorba's dance, with an upturned glass full of wine balanced on a handkerchief on his head. It's an old party trick, and the vacuum inside the glass stops the wine pouring out. But, let's face it, Greece's most famous dance isn't the best idea for a Turkish club, especially late at night in a bar full of swarthy locals.

Sure enough, one of the Turks took umbrage and did the obvious thing. He lifted the glass — and as red wine poured down over Jim's face and shirt, the fight was on.

In fact, it was a lovely free-for-all, a thoroughly enjoyable battle. No cops called, despite the damage to the fixtures and fittings, and at the end we all shook hands amid the broken chairs and overturned tables. The locals insisted on buying us drinks while we paid for the breakages.

Nursing black eyes and bloodied noses, the local lads made it clear they thought the world of us. Strange place, Turkey.

For the final two weeks we moved down to Kusadasi, an old seaside port notorious as a drug-smuggling centre, a place where everyone looked the other way when the boats sidled up to the jetty. Today it's a tourist attraction, because the great ruins of Ephesus are nearby, and the place has really taken off.

There was some good swimming further down the coast, and I had brought my son Greg out for a couple of weeks during his school holidays for a spot of sunshine. He was a husky lad just like his dad, and was already set on following me into the stunt business.

A restaurant called Batey's was a favourite hang-out for the crew after hours. Dinny and me were particularly good customers, while Tony Curtis and Charlie Bronson would make an appearance at least once a week.

One evening Dinny, Greg and I went in for dinner, and noticed a group of Arab seamen sitting at a table near the bar with some European women. At that time Dinny had long hair and a big blond handlebar moustache — and in those days, long hair was not in fashion. Not among men, anyway.

We sat down by the window, with a beautiful view of the sunset, and ordered beers all round. There was a lot of noise from the other table, where the men were talking to the ladies, showing off a bit it seemed to me, and glancing over in our direction.

When a ruck starts it can be caused by a careless word or a studied insult. Sometimes you're not sure which. In this case the careless word was "poofter". We heard it more than once, accompanied by roars of heavy laughter and more glances over at our table.

It was a wind-up, and after five minutes of it Dinny couldn't stand it any longer. Suddenly he jumped to his feet, and shouted across the room: "Oi! We're not fucking poofs! So button it."

The guv'nor himself appeared like a rabbit out of a hat. Batey was a retired local official; I never did get to know his full name but he was a good bloke. He hurriedly calmed down the situation, beckoned us into his office and shut the door. Then he opened up a bottle of wine, and said: "Take no notice. Please. They are nasty people."

Dinny and I looked at one another, and shrugged.

So okay, we swallowed it, along with our host's wine. Handshakes all round, forget the meal, we'll come back tomorrow. Smiles of gratitude from Batey. "Thank you, thank you. No trouble, okay?"

So out we go, into the cool night air — and straight into the mob of seamen, six of them waiting. Then they jumped us. No warning shout, no "Do you mind?" Straight in.

Now Dinny can take two men, and so can I. We were slightly outnumbered but, following our usual principle, everything that fucking moved, we hit. I slammed one over the bonnet of a car, and knocked another into the road right in front of a bus. A screech of brakes, shouts, a loud honking, and the bus swerved to avoid him and ran smack into a wall. Young Greg was doing us proud, clinging round one bloke's neck. Good boy!

All of a sudden Dinny called out: "Hold it, Nosh!" I stopped with one fist still in mid-air. There was the law — actually the militia, a posse of them advancing on us with drawn guns. More shouting. Dinny and I were frogmarched up the street to the nick, with the Arabs in tow behind us. In the confusion, Greg nipped into a cab and headed for the unit office.

The cell had bare yellow walls covered in graffiti, and smelt of shit and urine. In the outer office, we could hear the Arabs swearing their life away. A soldier stood guard inside the door with a baseball bat studded with nails, his face impassive, and I didn't like the look of this at all. Luckily *Midnight Express* hadn't come out then, or at that moment I think I'd have needed bicycle clips.

An assistant director arrived from the unit, and a lot of verbals went on outside. I could imagine a fat brown envelope changing hands, which is actually what happened. But finally we were out, with a word of caution from the chief of police. He looked like Lee J. Cobb in a scene from *On the Waterfront*, when he put the frighteners on all and sundry.

Next day we were summoned to the production office. Harold Buck faced us, and he was not happy. "Right," he says. "Any more trouble from you two, and I'm sending you home."

I couldn't help my reply. "That's not a punishment, that's a fucking reward!"

But we had sense enough to keep a low profile after that. Well, let's say we meant to. The movie only had two weeks to run, anyway.

We kept ourselves confined to barracks like good boys, staying in the hotel at night, playing cards by the pool, drinking a beer or two but nothing excessive. I even bought two new sets of cards and instructed Dinny in the finer points of Kaluki. "You know, the last bloke who sat opposite me playing this game was the richest man in the world," I told him.

"I'm impressed," said Dinny, who palpably wasn't.

We lasted a week. Then another stunt man, Peter Brace, came by. Peter was one of our strong-man team, standing six foot five and able to mix it with the best.

"Here," he said, "there's a new place in town called the 007 Club. We're all going down there."

"Nah," I said. "You know what the producer said. If we get involved, we're out — and you never know what's going to happen."

So we sat by the side of the pool playing Kaluki, upping the stakes to reflect our mutual frustration. After an hour we must have owed one another a thousand quid each. All the boys had gone down to this 007 Club. Finally we worked ourselves into a right fucking hump. Why should we be left out? The whole place was deserted, apart from a single barman in a semi-darkened bar.

Dinny broke first. "Let's go down there and have a drink with the boys."

"Dinny ..." I waved a feeble hand of protest.

"Aw, c'mon, Nosh. Nothing's going to happen. Just a little drink ..."

How often have we heard those words? Mug that I am, I nodded. "Okay. Just one." We went on foot down the hill and into town to locate the club, and finally saw the 007 neon sign flickering a welcome. Plus the minder on the door who appeared ready to hand out another kind of welcome if pushed.

He was as wide as he was tall, about twenty stone, and stood with his feet nailed to the floor and his arms folded. "I've seen oak trees that would fall over first," I muttered. But it takes one to know one, so I gave him a friendly nod and we passed the deadpan scrutiny.

Inside, the boys were down at the bottom of the club revelling it up. We ordered the local rot-gut red wine, and were about to join them when, from nowhere, a fight erupted between some Arabs. Four of them to one, which isn't brilliant odds, beating the shit out of a frightened-looking kid.

Peter Brace, being the true blue Englishman that he was, stepped in. "Hold it, fellers." He raised a placatory hand. "One dog, one bone! Okay?"

And bang! He gets his answer: a right-hander straight in the eye. So okay, it's not okay. Different playing-field. Arab rules. The place erupts.

Standing at our end of the bar, Dinny and I stay out of it, panning the scene from long-shot to close-up, as if we're making a film. But the old instincts won't lie down.

"Dinny, time to move in?"

But for once he says: "Fuck 'em. Let 'em fight."

Then all of a sudden this geezer comes staggering back and knocks Dinny's glass of wine over him. Dinny says: "Bastard!" And that's the signal for us to get stuck in.

One of our team came staggering up with his lip swollen and bleeding all down his chin, and I figured it's time to make a dignified retreat. I tucked him under one arm, headed for the door — and found the big minder barring my way. No time to argue. *Pop!* Down he went. We grabbed a passing cab, left our young stunt man propped against a wall, and raced back to the hotel.

The Kaluki game was still set out by the pool, just as we had left it. We sat down, breathing heavily. "Your deal," I said.

Half an hour later they started dribbling in, looking like the leftovers from the battle of Waterloo. Peter Brace passed by, with one eye already bulging out like a boiled egg.

"You missed something, fellers," he said indistinctly as he headed for his room.

"Oh! G'night, Pete!" We heard twenty doors open and twenty doors close on balconies all the way round the pool area as we sat studying our cards in the warm Turkish night.

Then the footsteps came, a lot of them, crunching purposefully over the gravel path. I spoke in a low voice: "Careful, Dinny!"

When I looked up this time, we were surrounded by Military Police, easily a dozen tough blue-chinned figures in khaki, all of them toting rifles. And guess who was in charge?

"Good evening, gentlemen," said Lee J. Cobb. "We meet again!"

"Good evening." We beamed at him in unison.

"May I ask how long you have been playing cards?"

"Ah," I said, thinking about it. "Let me see. Maybe a couple of hours."

"Have you noticed anything unusual in the hotel tonight?"

"Not really. It's been very quiet here." I looked him in the eye, radiating innocence. "We've been too busy trying to win one another's money."

He allowed a long pause. Then: "Be lucky, gentlemen." And away he walked.

Moments later we heard those same twenty doors open again and this time slam shut, as twenty stunt men were frogmarched in handcuffs past us to a line of vans parked close by.

Next morning they sent the usual eight cars to take us to the location, a railway siding in the valley, for another big action scene. Seven stayed behind.

Our lone car pulled up close to where two dozen horses waited under some trees in the shade. We stepped out. Peter Collinson was studying the script with Harold Buck.

Pete called out cheerily: "Morning, chaps. Where are the rest of them?"

I didn't bother with words. I simply lifted my collar with one hand — and I'm afraid that was all it took to wipe the cheeriness out of his day. Peter howled: "But, Nosher, that's why I got you out here, to keep those fellers out of trouble."

I jerked a thumb at the producer. "You tell Pete what happened. You told me to keep out of trouble, or I'd be on the next plane home. I could have stopped it straight away."

Peter rounded on Harold. "You prize dick! Get them out of jail, wherever they are. We need them."

It cost the company several thousand dollars in back-handers, and the scowl never left Buck's face whenever he saw me in his proximity. But we got the film done. And you know what? Despite all the fun and games behind the scenes, it didn't turn out that bad after all.

## 36: LENNY AND CO.

Now Nosher's back home, and running a pub. The Prince of Wales was right behind Wimbledon dog track, so we picked up a nice bit of custom from the punters. It was a large whitewashed building on a busy roundabout in Garratt Lane, SW19, with a flat above it that went with the tenancy. It wouldn't win any prizes as a jewel in the conservation crown, but it did the business.

When word got around that I was in charge of the shop, a lot of interesting people sprang out of the woodwork. Showbiz, sportsmen, villains, a good mix. It kept us buzzing like blue-arsed flies, but Pauline and I could handle it. Inside two months we'd brought the turnover up from a thousand quid a week to five thousand. Not a bad screw. Add to that the odd bung in cash for a favour, and everything in the garden was rosy.

We had occasional trouble with pikeys, but nothing I couldn't sort. I had my two Dobermanns for back-up, Buster and Leo, if I needed help, and one growl from them was enough to make any nutter shit their pants. Those two beauties would tear your throat out if I gave them the word — the word, incidentally, was "*Attack!*" But the threat was enough to keep the peace.

Sadly, I had to have them both put down because only Pauline and I could control them. Finally they became so savage that we couldn't risk kids being attacked in the car park behind the pub where the kennels were housed, so Buster and Leo had to go.

Meantime, I was the guv'nor of my pub, enjoying life, and able to be generous to my mates. One geezer who used to come into the pub most nights was Big Dave, a good spender who was in the scrap metal business. Whenever Dave came in, it was double vodkas all round, and cheers to the world. He had a good pair of shoulders on him and looked useful in an emergency.

One evening he comes to me and says: "Nosh, I've got the chance of a fucking good deal, but I'm a bit short on the scratch. I need a wad."

Knowing what he was and who he was, I asked: "How much are you short?"

He said: "Two grand."

Without another word I went into the office, opened the safe, and pulled out two grand. In readies. "There you are!"

"Cor — God bless you, Nosher." His eyes were positively watering with gratitude. I didn't even ask for a receipt, because with some people you don't need one.

Then what happened? Big Dave went among the fucking missing! Disappeared clean out of sight. I never did see him for two years. Two whole years! He kept right out of the way. But I was making so much money it didn't bother me, and I forgot all about it. I was that flush.

Then the sky fell in. I was hit by the VAT man, and then by the tax man in a double whammy that put Nosher out for the count. All of a sudden I was in deepest, darkest shit. I had to sell my big American car, my beloved Stingray, and settle for a second-hand Maestro, several years past its sell-by date. Not the best advertisement for a bloke wanting to pass as a man of substance, and I have to admit this was a low ebb in my life.

At one point it even looked like I was going to lose my house as well, though eventually I was able to save the roof over my head.

But one day I was driving around Wandsworth in my battered old heap, and going down Garratt Lane — when I saw him. At first I wasn't sure, because I only saw his back as he pulled up in a brand-new BMW outside a newsagent.

He got out and strolled into the shop — and that's when I realised who it was. Big Dave. I pulled up behind the BMW and I was out of my car and behind the wheel of his car before you could say Mother Goose.

Then I just sat there, waiting.

Dave came out opening a packet of cigarettes, looked up — and saw someone sitting in his car. "What the fuck ...?" he shouted.

Then he saw who it was, and his normally florid face went a funny liver colour. "Oh! Er, hello, Nosh."

I responded with my usual rapier-like speed. "What do you mean Nosh, you c--t? Get in the car. And give me the keys. *Now!*"

Well, he did just that, sliding into the passenger seat with obvious reluctance. Before the door shut I was off like Stirling Moss, down to the end of the street, sharp left at the roundabout, and straight on into the car park of my pub.

"Get out!" I ordered.

He climbed out. "Okay," I said. "Where's my money?"

He started to mumble. "Now, look, Nosher, things have been a bit hard —"

"Hard?" I said. "You bastard! Here am I going around in a beat-up old Maestro, and you're driving a brand-new BMW. Where's the money?" And *whack!* I gave him a big open-handed slap across the face. *Whack* again! Another one made his eyes spin like a top.

That's when he made his second mistake. The first had been to try to screw me.

He came at me head down — and don't forget he was in the scrap business and he was a strong feller. But all the rage and frustration that I'd been through with the VAT man and the tax man came out and I laid into that geezer with both fists. It didn't take long, but I smashed him to fucking pulp. I heard a rib go, and he was pouring blood from his nose and mouth — and in that moment I knew I could have killed him.

It lasted less than a minute, because that's all it takes to finish a fight. At the end that smooth bastard was in a right state, crawling on his hands and knees round the back of his car, moaning and dripping blood on the ground, trying to escape.

I followed him round, still mad as hell, threw him on his back, and pulled his gold necklace off him. Then I took his gold Rolex watch, and finally a three-stone gypsy ring from his finger. Plus £178 in cash that I found in his pocket.

I knelt down beside him on the tarmac, lifted his head, and said: "Now listen, you fucker, I can still carry on if I want to. But instead I'll just tell you this once." I waved his baubles in his battered face. "See this lot here? You've got a week. If I don't get my money, this goes into the pawn shop. I'll get my two grand out of it, and that's all I want. You can forget the cash. I'm keeping it. You know my number. Phone me, or else."

I got up and walked away without looking back.

Three days later he phoned. "All right, I've got your fucking poke." His voice was thick, and he didn't sound happy.

I said: "Right. Do you want to fetch it over?"

He said: "I'll bring it to you in your old pub car park. Tonight."

I said quickly: "No, I'm busy tonight. Tomorrow afternoon, four o'clock."

He said: "Right." And the phone went down.

Now I'm not that stupid, and I could smell a set-up. He's going to have some friends with him, isn't he?

I phoned around.

It took a few calls, but eventually I got hold of the one guy I wanted in my corner, Lenny McLean, located at the Hippodrome where he was minding on the door.

Let me tell you about Lenny. He was probably the most frightening man I ever knew, but we were mates. We go back a long time, Lenny and me. Picture a man as tall as me, but weighing over twenty stone, with a forty-inch waist and a sixty-inch chest. He was *huge*. He was also very dangerous when he got angry, and tended to walk through doors rather than open them. His exploits became the stuff of legend.

I'd met him here and there. But we only got to know each other properly after a grudge match he had with Roy Shaw, another man you treated with the utmost respect.

Roy, who fought under the misnomer "Pretty Boy" Shaw, was reputed to be the only man the Krays were genuinely frightened of, and I can well believe it. He was built like a brick shithouse too, balding and menacing, with close-set eyes that made him look even meaner.

Among other misdeeds, Roy had done time with a fifteen stretch for the armed robbery of a security van. But he was also a professional boxer with an impressive track record. Which gave us something to talk about down at the Thomas À Becket in the Old Kent Road, where we'd both train in the ring up on the first floor above the bar.

Roy and Lenny actually fought each other twice, with a huge crowd each time once the word went out. These two fearsome figures were folklore in South London, and seeing them go head to head was something you'd tell your kids about if they had the stomach to hear it. Blood and teeth everywhere! It was a sell-out each time.

Their first encounter was billed as the King of the Street Fighters Tournament, and was held in Cinatra's Club in Croydon. At the time I was a stunt man on the first *Superman* film, the one where Marlon Brando made headlines by banking three million dollars for a ten-minute appearance as Christopher Reeve's father.

Gene Hackman was the villain, and as the big night approached he overheard me talking about the fight. "Take me along, Nosher," he begged. "I'll pay anything!"

Okay, but against my better judgement. I was able to get him a ringside seat, though I wasn't sure it was a good idea because it was going to be a rough audience.

Sure enough, it was a fucking smash-up. The nut went in, kicking, elbows, crimson everywhere. It lasted four rounds, and in that time Gene was actually drenched in their blood.

I'd helped Roy train for the grudge match, and it was everything the crowd wanted. I refereed a couple of the supporting bouts, but they wouldn't let me take charge of the big one in case I was biased. So I was the official timekeeper, *and* the MC. "Ladies and gentlemen ... will you welcome two street-fighting legends ..." The place was going wild before the opening bell.

Roy won it. The referee stopped it in the fourth. The boys were using gloves because they had to, it was a "legitimate area". But six-ounce gloves on hands the size of turnips are like lace handkerchiefs, as close to bare-knuckle as you can get. Roy got the verdict. But Lenny got his revenge a few months later, leaving Roy spark out inside two minutes. Sadly, they never got together for the final decider.

At the end of their first little get-together, the place was in uproar, as I had expected. Old scores were being settled at the back, and spilling out into the street in what are usually referred to in the tabloids as "scuffles". But these things can get out of hand, and I suddenly had a valuable movie star to protect. Shouldering through the crowd with one hand firmly under his elbow, I got Gene safely out and into his car, and waved him off.

Next morning Hackman turned up at Pinewood dressed exactly as I had left him the night before — in the same bloodstained jacket, shirt and tie. Then he walked around boasting: "Look at the fight I was in last night. You should see the other guy — not a mark on him!" Great guy, Gene, a true gentleman and a droll sense of humour with it.

I found myself bumping into Lenny McLean here and there over the next weeks, as he prepared for his revenge. We'd find ourselves up in the gym above the Thomas À Beckett, pushing the weights or thumping the bag. Afterwards we'd have a drink and a chat, and swap a few yarns. It was during this time that we became mates, largely through mutual respect. You cannot buy respect, you have to earn it. Lenny always showed me the highest respect, and I showed him the same. I always knew I could count on him, just as he could count on me if he ever needed to.

That time came with this geezer Dave and his mates who were going to stitch me up in my own car park.

You'll have gathered by now that Lenny was a useful man to have in your own corner, especially if that corner was a tight one.

He took my call. "'Ello, Nosh, 'ow are yer?" His voice sounded like rusty nails being shaken in a metal tin.

"Fine, Lenny, fine. But I got a problem."

He never said to me "why?" or "what?" He simply said: "Where's the meet, Nosh?"

I told him. "My gaff. The Prince of Wales car park, Garratt Lane."

"What time?"

"Four o'clock tomorrow afternoon," I said.

"I'll be there."

Prompt at four I drove into the car park. Right opposite across the road was a firm dealing in used tyres — and there was Lenny's huge bulk, casually leaning against the fence.

But my immediate concern now was Big Dave, sitting on the bonnet of his shining BMW. Studying his fingernails, cool as a cucumber despite his bruised face. When he saw me coming, he stood up and signalled with one hand. Over on one side I saw an old van, and faces peering out of the windows.

As I walked towards him three big pikeys got out of the van and started towards me.

They joined up with the smoothie, and now there were four of them walking in line just like that scene in *Reservoir Dogs*.

This was it. I knew I'd been right, and I wasn't even tooled up because I only ever used my fists. But that was the moment when another figure came into the equation — Lenny materialised from around the fence, to stroll across to my car and lean against it quietly with his arms folded.

Christ, you should have seen their faces! The first pikey — Eric was his name, a tough local gypsy boy — turned round to Mr Smooth and hissed: "You c--t! You want to get us fucking deaded?" And *whack*! He gave him one across the chops, and Dave went sprawling.

Eric looked past me, at the figure leaning casually against my car. "Sorry, Lenny, sorry! We never knew the SP or we wouldn't be here. If it's about the three grand he's got in his pocket — listen, we're out of here!"

With that the three of them beat a hasty retreat and scrambled back into the van — only to find their way barred by Lenny's huge bulk. He just stood there, with one hand extended.

"What? What is it, Lenny?"

Lenny uttered a single word. "Expenses!"

Staring terrible personal retribution in the face tends to focus the mind like nothing else. Eric pulled out a wad, and threw it at him. "Sure, Lenny. Sorry, sorry ..." And, *whoosh*, they were away like greased lightning.

Meantime, my geezer was getting to his feet. "My money?" I said. He was already pulling out a roll. I counted out two grand, added a further monkey for the inconvenience, threw the remaining five hundred quid at him, and walked off. I never did see that bastard again.

That evening Lenny and I went on to celebrate with a slap-up steak dinner at Jack's Place down by Battersea heliport, a restaurant where a lot of faces used to gather.

He said: "Nosher, you'd have done the same for me."

I told him: "Yeah, course I would. But you deserve a few quid for this night's work." He wound up with six hundred pounds in his pocket, and worth every penny of it.

Over the last brandy, Lenny said: "Any time you've got a problem, Nosh, just phone me." If Lenny's friends had a problem, it became his problem. That's the kind of man he was.

People have asked me if I would ever have taken on Lenny McLean, one to one. The answer is: Yeah, I'll fight Lenny — but only in the ring, and then early on in my career when I was thirty and fighting fit.

As a boxer, he wasn't all that clever. But in the street, that was different. He only had to get his hands on you, and the nut would go in — *BAM*! Elbows, biting — do a Tyson, anything. He used that big domed head as a battering ram to smash people senseless — he was an absolute animal. So the realistic answer now was, *no fucking way!* I'm not that big a mug. Anyway, I was nearly twice his age.

Lenny's favourite saying was: "We'll get it sorted!" He was a big, dangerous bastard, but it's very difficult for me to think of that man being dead. When I heard he'd died of cancer in 1998, I couldn't believe it.

I went to his funeral, took a bunch of flowers, and said a prayer. After all, Lenny never hurt anyone who didn't deserve it.

## 37: ARISE, SIR KNIGHT!

If I wasn't wearing a toga and shouting "Hail Caesar!" it sometimes seemed that I was destined to be a knight in shining armour for the rest of my life, clumping around in chainmail and waving a sword. That was okay with me. I always was a sucker for the King Arthur stuff, and a bit of chivalry never went amiss with the ladies, either.

If you saw me on a big horse I was about ten feet off the ground — six feet (plus four inches) of me, four feet of the horse. That's a good way to look down on the world. And to see the expression on the kids' faces when they gazed up at Nosher on a white Cottage stallion was something to treasure.

One large chunk of my career belonged to jousting. It happened like this. A mate of mine rang from Nottingham to say the county show had been let down by their star act, who had pulled out at the last minute. Flu, or a floozy, he wasn't sure which. I forget the name, but the opening day was a sell-out, and Princess Margaret was due to attend.

Panic in the streets. "Nosher, can you think of anything to put in the main arena?" begged my chum.

Why me? "Someone gave me your name. They say you can fix anything."

With a gauntlet like that thrown down, how could I not pick it up?

Gauntlet. For no earthly reason, a mad idea flashed into my head. "Jousting," I said. "Leave it all to me!"

I formed a team called Tournaments, rang round all my stunt men, and in no time I had a small army of willing would-be jousters. We gave ourselves names. My son Greg became Sir Gregory of Dulwich. Brother Dinny was Viscount Oval. Max Diamond became the Black Knight. Roy Street was the Champion of Essex. I was Sir Frederick of Gaywood, though I'm not sure I'd take that name now. The colours on my shield were the coat-of-arms of Kent with a black raven, the emblem of the Powell family, painted in the middle. Though I say it myself, it was impressive.

We had two weeks to get it together. Luckily, my valiant knights caught the bug, and joined in with enthusiasm. "Got this idea for a lance." Sir Gregory handed me a length of bamboo bound at one end with bandages, with a sponge added for the sharp bit. Good enough. We made shields out of balsawood and cardboard, painted them silver and added garish pseudo-heraldic emblems for effect.

"What do you think?"

"Looks more like McDonald's to me," muttered the Black Knight dourly.

We found our Guinevere in an elderly weaver named Lottie, bless her socks, who agreed to make our costumes, fashioning phoney chainmail out of wool and cotton, then painting it metallic. I just prayed no one would get a run when the trumpets sounded.

Finally I located a metal firm, and ordered twenty swords to be made out of Duralumin, a lightweight metal used in supersonic aircraft, and just about the toughest in the world. The swords had to be right. They weren't like the rapier, where you can be subtle and fast, and lunge. In those days it was all brute strength and hacking.

But the effect was startling. When we emerged from our tent on to the field of battle, we looked as if we owned the place. We greeted each other loudly as "Sir Knight!" with noisy back slaps and much waving of our mailed fists at the crowd. And they loved it.

But I have to admit that from a historical perspective the first show we put on was crap! God knows what HRH thought of it, and since we weren't presented I never got the chance to ask. At least what we lacked in accuracy we more than made up for in enthusiasm, and that seemed to win the day.

When you think of it, two big horses galloping towards each other on either side of that fence, or "tilt", are doing twenty miles an hour apiece, so the collision for the rider is forty miles an hour. And when you get a blunted lance in your chest, or even against your shield, it's like being hit by a fucking bus. Just think of driving your car into a brick wall at forty miles an hour, and you'll get an idea of what we were up against.

But my knights were great guys, and took their battering like heroes. They were under strict instructions. *No one must ever fall unless they are hit.* There was no mocking it. I didn't want them flopping out of the saddle for no good reason.

In a joust, it's also quite easy to miss. If you're going pell-mell down that course, you can spear thin air. On the other hand I've seen it when they've both gone SMACK, with a double-whammy crunch which is truly spectacular, both knights somersaulting backwards out of their saddles like hooked salmon. We had microphones strung along the tilt, so the crash of lance and shield made a noise like the clatter of dustbin lids, only ten times louder.

We didn't want to hurt anyone, but a few broken bones and bruises were unavoidable. I couldn't count the number of ribs I saw — or, rather, heard — cracking over the six years that followed.

The most experienced among us was actually the Black Knight. Max Diamond was an ex-commando and making a nice little earner for himself in the movie business with the largest private army in Great Britain: the Sealed Knot. You might have seen them re-enacting pitched battles for charity and other occasions.

I finally had my own Round Table of twelve knights, with four jousting at any one time. As for the horses, we trained them to joust like the police train their horses in crowd control, except they use thunderflashes and wave flags. We had to get our horses used to noise, so we'd walk round them banging our shields with our swords. Then we'd stand in front with a sword flashing backwards and forwards, always with someone on their back.

We also added a blinker over one eye. If a horse sees a lance coming at him, it stands to reason he'll duck his head and shy away. We cured that by putting a blinker over the left eye, the side nearest to the tilt. I had them made up out of old medieval armour, which worked well and looked like the real thing.

We started to become more adventurous, building the show to ever greater spectacle. One day Viscount Oval approached me. "How about a stirrup drag?" said my brother. "I've got it all worked out."

We kept the horses stabled behind Box Hill in Surrey. In the field where they grazed, Dinny showed me how he'd do it. "The knight comes off his horse, see, but he's got a long wire attached from his foot to the stirrup. When he hits the ground he gets dragged for a dozen yards before he releases the wire and rolls over, playing dead, while the horse gallops off. What do you think?"

Dinny, alias Viscount Oval, volunteered to do the dive himself, so I couldn't say no. It would be the grand finale. I can't remember anybody else fighting to take his place.

The biggest event we had ever attempted was about to take place — at the Tower of London, no less. The governor had allowed us to use the old moat for a week of jousting and spectacle. It cost me thirty thousand quid for the week, but I knew I'd get the money back in three days, and the rest would be profit. "We can change our name to the Jewels in the Crown," the Champion of Essex suggested after a flagon of ale too many.

We set up striped tents in four corners of the arena, with colourful pennants fluttering in the breeze off the Thames. The audience crowded in to occupy seats raised on either side of the tilting ground. It was summer, the sun was out, the school holidays were on, and the place would be packed. A buzz of anticipation filled the air.

The tilt ran down the middle of the moat, with an exit at the far end to the stables. Dinny would be left rolling on the ground while his horse galloped off, with a clear way out and a handful of oats waiting for him in his stall.

"Not a bad crowd!" I stood with my loyal retainers watching the seats fill up. Today I had dispensed with Sir Frederick of Gaywood to become the Norseman, complete with horned helmet, bushy red beard, huge Viking shield, battle-axe, the works. I was riding a big grey Andalucian stallion named Duwendy, sixteen hands high, large enough to take my eighteen stone.

What none of the onlookers knew was that the dried-up moat is actually comprised of thousands of sea shells hidden under the grass — and why should they? As my old mucker Michael Caine would say: "Not a lot of people know that."

A century ago they were looking for something to fill in the moat. Billingsgate fish market was a short cart ride away, actually in Lower Thames Street that runs by the Tower. Over the years, shells from the oysters, clams and winkles had been emptied on to the north bank of Old Father Thames by the market. Eventually there was a pile over a dozen feet high, and they had no idea what to do with them.

Finally someone had a bright idea. They loaded the shells on to carts, trundled them along to the Tower and emptied them into the moat. In the end, they were six feet deep. The result was the most magnificent drainage any gardener could wish for. I found they'd laid a foot of top soil over it, added turf — and when it pissed down with rain, instead of that lawn being soggy, the water went right through.

It was the best surface we knights of old ever rode on. Some of the surfaces we'd had to gallop over had been distinctly dodgy. Nobody wants to throw himself off a horse on to concrete, and packed clay can be just as hard.

On this occasion I'd given myself the week off from being smashed in the chest and somersaulting out of the saddle. My part of the act was to start the show by coaxing my great stallion into a "half-pass", all the way round the arena, facing the audience. His left eye was blinkered with that metal patch, which gave us a dramatic, spooky air.

He was actually walking sideways, with his legs crossing over, a rather tasty piece of horsemanship though I say it myself, and the crowd cheering and the kids screaming their little lungs out was sweet music to my ears.

At the end, the plan was that I would raise my battle-axe, wave it in salute, and charge off through the exit, which was kept clear for all of us.

On this opening day at the Tower, unknown to me, a visitor had asked if he could try one of our horses. This bloke was a mate of one of our team — but he omitted to reveal that he hadn't actually been in a saddle in his life. Somehow he mounted up — and next thing the horse is walking straight across the exit gap just as I come thundering through at full pelt, showing off with both hands in the air. One is waving the axe, the other the shield, and no third hand available for holding the reins to pull up.

Collision imminent. I can still see his stupid face gawping at me as I bore down on him like an express train about to come off the rails. It isn't often that you get a wild, horned figure coming at you like a Viking of old, and I hope the vision still gives that bastard nightmares — if that isn't being too uncharitable.

That day I nearly went to my own Valhalla ahead of time. Duwendy, unsighted with the metallic blinker, galloped on — and cannoned head-on into the other horse with a sound like a butcher's cleaver thwacking a carcass. My stallion did a complete somersault, and I went with it.

Silence. Darkness. I lay on the grass with all the breath and most of the life knocked out of me. Then: a glimmer of light, and frantic hands ripping at my chainmail.

"Nosher! *Nosher!* Can you hear me?" Dinny's voice.

"What happened?" I was semi-conscious, but still felt like I was one dark bruise all over.

"Don't try to talk. We'll take care of it. You'll be okay."

"My horse? Duwendy?"

"He's okay, too. Shaken up, but nothing broken. It was a fucking miracle."

"Thank Christ for that ..." I lapsed into welcoming darkness, drifting away from the bruises and the pain.

But the show must go on, even with the walking wounded. All that night my lads worked to get me on my feet. Every one of us had been trained long ago in massage techniques to rub bruises away. Part of the stunt man's manual.

I had a team of knights, six-handed, working on me for an hour each, which isn't something that happens to everyone in their life. One knight at a time, using an olive-oil liniment we had with us, made up specially for deep bruising. I just lay there, unable to speak or move. When I did try, the pain was so intense I just lay back with a groan. All night long they worked. Even when I drifted off into sleep, they still kept going.

At dawn I was awake, and able to move. "Thanks, lads! I'm grateful. That's one I owe the lot of you."

First thing, I checked Duwendy. Amazingly, he was fine and tucking into his oats. I gave him a pat and had a little word in his ear, just to make sure we were still friends. By noon I was walking stiffly around the yard, taking it nice and easy. By two p.m., I was up in the saddle, aching all over. Even my best friend ached, I tell you. But I did the job, I was still the Norseman.

The show went on.

The other bloke got away with it too. But he never rode again.

We stunt men are a superstitious lot. Why else do I throw up a prayer every time I'm about to jump into space or take a dive off a horse at speed? "*Please, look this way!*"

So on the third day I started to think we might be jinxed when little Mickey Rawlinson, an ex-jump jockey and tough as nails, went up against Roy Street, Champion of Essex. To be historically accurate, the idea was to shatter the lance on the shield to score points, not unhorse the other knight. If he came off, that was a bonus for the crowd.

Our lances were made out of bamboo, which gave a terrific effect when they broke up on a shield. Those first two days at the Tower we smashed so many that I had to find twenty more in a hurry so that we could go through the next day.

All our helmets had a letterbox slit in them for the eyes. In the emergency someone located ten-foot lengths of bamboo, which were thinner than they should have been. You can guess what's about to happen.

We fitted oil funnels round the handles, sprayed them with silver paint — and presto! We had ourselves brand new lances. Add a few pennants, bandage the sharp end and stick a sponge on it, and the boys were away.

Mickey and Roy were both great horsemen, the best. But my knights had been growing increasingly competitive, and a bit of needle had been creeping in. It made the action more dramatic, but on this day they went over the top: they aimed for the helmet instead of the shield. Big mistake. Roy's lance went right through the slit into Mickey's left eye!

Christ, what a mess! Mickey, the original braveheart, rode on — but the lance went with him, sticking out of his eye with blood spurting from under his helmet. The cheers died away suddenly. Then someone screamed.

The ambulance took Mickey to Moorfields Eye Hospital, and the show went on, though in a somewhat muted atmosphere. As soon as it finished I raced over to the hospital, and collared the doctor. He explained what had happened.

"When the lance went in, it hit the eyeball, pushed it to one side and slid round the side. The lance had been trapped beteween the eyeball and the socket."

Ouch! But, believe it not, that guy was jousting two days later with a patch over his eye. It always amazes me how resilient the human body can be.

We learned our lesson. After that we thickened up the bamboo with more bandages, so there was no way it could happen again.

I also had special saddles made with a high square pommel so the lances couldn't go through and spear your stomach. We took other precautions. The armour was lightweight fibreglass, made to measure. The spurs were rubber, because if you came off and had a real spur up your arse, you'd know all about it. But there were some things we couldn't control, and we still broke a few bones and dislocated other parts of ourselves.

The day after the accident I called the Round Table together for a meeting in one of the tents, and read the Riot Act. I don't suppose King Arthur spoke like this, but the message got through. "Now listen, you mugs," I told them, "all we're doing is earning a living and putting on a great show. What do you want to fucking kill one another for? From now on we take it in turns. We'll all have the same number of wins, and the same number of losses."

After that there was less needle — and less carnage on the field of battle.

The portcullis slammed down on our enterprise when I signed a deal to take my jousting team to Spain as part of a fairground show. I trusted the wrong bloke, and he ran out of money. That's the nutshell of it. I had to sell all my horses and equipment to pay off the boys and fly them home.

Basically I ended up skint. But what great years they'd been!

## 38: FIRST KNIGHT

When you're dealing with our four-legged friends, things can get out of hand. Sometimes I think W. C. Fields was right about not working with children and animals. Witness *First Knight*, and what happened to me on a moonlit plain in Hampshire.

Sean Connery and Richard Gere were the stars of this stirring tale of derring-do, filmed on the Stratfield Saye estate of the Duke of Wellington. My son Greg was horse-master and in charge of the second unit.

The crucial action scene was about to be filmed. I was doubling for Sean, leading a horseback charge that would be the climax of the film. Two hundred knights would be strung out behind me, pelting hell-for-leather over the plain in full armour. There was one slight worry: they'd decided to film it at night. "Jerry wants to get the full effect of moonlight shining off helmets and shields," Greg explained, referring to the director Jerry Zucker. "Add to that the chink of spurs and then the thunder of hoofs, and the visual effect will be stunning."

Stunning? It was surreal. Yellow arc-lights shone down on us from sixty-foot cranes. Horses pawed the grass, growing increasingly restless as the night wore on and we got ourselves hyped up for action.

I looked around for my trusty steed, as we hadn't been formally introduced. "Which is mine?" No one seemed to know.

Greg came up, a slight frown creasing his forehead. "Listen," he said. "Connery's horse is a bastard, but I can't do anything about it. We've hired every horse in the county, and now they've run out. You'll have to ride it — but be careful."

"All right, son," I said. "Don't you worry about me. You've got enough on your plate with this lot."

Someone approached, leading a big horse by the reins. In the light from the arcs, I took a closer look at him — and I wasn't too happy with what I saw.

Any mug can ride a good horse, one that responds to the reins and to your authority. But it takes a good rider to ride a bad horse. This one was a bad horse, a big, high-stepping bay with a nasty attitude. His ears pricked up as I examined him, and we eyed each other with mutual suspicion.

"Okay," I said finally. "I'm ready."

Did I say big? They gave me a fruit box to stand on, but heaving myself into the saddle was like climbing up the side of Everest. Immediately I felt the strength of the beast, and the resentment with it. But I kept the reins tight, and I thought I'd survive without falling off.

Tension grew. They always say that waiting is the worst part, and with a big scene like this one coming up, everyone was getting the jitters.

More pawing and snorting. Greg was directing the charge himself, and he called up instructions through cupped hands as I sat tall in the saddle, trying to keep the fractious grey under control and my dignity as leading knight intact.

"I'll be out front ahead of you in the camera car. We're lining you all up in an arrowhead, and you're the tip of it, leading the whole thing. Okay, Dad?"

"Okay, son."

The charge would run close to a mile, starting at a slow trot, then a canter, finally breaking into a full gallop, swords waving. I've been here before, I thought, with memories of *Henry V* coming back to me like a ghost from the past.

The plain ended in a large dry moat around a castle, with a bridge across it that led to the stables half a mile further on up the road. Greg gave me one final word. "Watch out for the other riders. We've got some cowboys with us tonight."

What he meant was that there were a few madmen among us, stable lads who owned their own horses and had given the film company an ultimatum: "You want my horse, I come with it."

They probably picked up fifty quid for the night. They also knew the countryside blindfold, which is more than the rest of us did, so they had a distinct advantage. Cameras set along both sides of the plain would be churning away, recording the whole thing from different angles.

A voice through a loud-hailer. "Stand by. Ready everyone? Good luck!"

A whistle blew. *"Action!"*

I dug in my heels, snapped the reins, and the big bay started off obediently, high stepping like a circus trouper with the rest following in a great arrowhead. The plain stretched ahead pale yellow into darkness. It was a magnificent spectacle, and I felt the old thrill down my spine as the adrenalin started churning.

I snapped the reins again, and the big grey broke obediently into a trot. Snap again, canter. I drew my sword, and waved it above my head ferociously. Snap once more for the charge — and that was when the visor of my helmet clanged down over my eyes, completely obliterating my view, as the giant bay surged into a full gallop.

So here I am, and I can't see a fucking thing. I'm cannoning into a horse on one side, then veering away to bounce off another like a billiard ball. The stable lads, little bastards, are swerving in and out, whooping and hollering like the Sioux Indians at Custer's Last Stand and having the time of their lives.

Somewhere ahead is that twenty-foot ditch, getting closer all the time. All I can hear is the thunder of hoofs, the shouts and the yells, and the hollow asthmatic sound of my own breathing inside the helmet. Did I say blindfold?

But what the fuck can I do? I can't adjust my visor. What would people think if they spotted the leading knight struggling with his helmet? The only thing was to hang on and pray. I kept the sword pointed ahead in the "Charge" position, and hoped I was looking good.

If someone shouted, "Cut", I never heard it. The maniac of a horse showed no sign of stopping, but suddenly there was a resounding clatter of hoofs on wood, and more galloping — and then I couldn't hear anyone else. Finally the horse came to a halt.

Silence. Nothing moving. No sound. Gingerly I pull up my visor. And there I am, back in the warmth of the stable, lovely smell of hay, sitting there all alone like a lemon.

Where is everybody?

At that moment a roar from outside heralds the arrival of Greg on a three-wheel motor-bike.

"What the fucking hell are you doing?" he inquires, with all the respect of a dutiful son to his father.

I turn my sweating face down to him under the helmet. "I couldn't fucking do nothing," I said. "My visor jammed."

"Well, fucking unjam it," my son the boss shouted unfeelingly. And roared off without a backward glance.

Next day both Sean and Richard Gere made a point of shaking my hand. "We heard all about it, Nosher," said Gere. "You're the talk of the county. I haven't stopped laughing." He was a strange guy, Gere. He was always spouting Buddhism and peace, and he'd hobnobbed with the Dalai Lama. But he still earned his living kicking shit out of anyone who annoyed him. Personally, I found him a complete gent.

But, then, I never annoyed him.

Looking back, I've often wondered if any local yokel, making his way home from the pub after closing time, glimpsed a lone knight galloping across the fields like a lost horseman of the Apocalypse. If so, he probably gave up drink on the spot.

## 39: EAT THE RICH!

Can you see me as the Home Secretary? Be honest, now.

But someone could. One day I got a telegram from Peter Richardson, a director who was casting a film with the oddball title *Eat the Rich*. It read: PLEASE COME TO MY OFFICE AND SEE ME.

Why not? I'd been doing bits and pieces with Robbie Coltrane and Jennifer Saunders in *The Comic Strip*, putting on the usual scowl and growl, and Peter had seen a couple of my fleeting appearances. In his office he threw a script on the desk. "I've got a film here, Nosher, and I want you to read for me. Imagine someone like Arthur Mullard ... as the Prime Minister!"

I'd known Arthur of old. His voice had shifted more gravel than mine. "What, me?"

Unfazed by my reaction Peter went on: "Yes. I'm looking for a rough and ready guy who calls a spade a spade, and a c--t a c--t!"

Well, that sounded like me all right.

"We want you to speak the way you do, and we're even going to use your name: Nosher Powell, Home Secretary. How does that sound?"

"I thought you said Prime Minister —"

"Don't get ambitious!" Peter snapped. So I settled for Home Secretary. Sandra Dorne was my wife, a bubbly blonde actress I remembered from the fifties, now as fat as a juicy pork chop, but still with that *oomph* going for her!

Peter expanded the plot. "It's got terrorists, and Jools Holland running a restaurant for the ultra-rich. There's a mincer in the kitchen. You see a human leg being pushed into it. There are a few fights. You don't take any crap from anyone."

What kind of film *was* this? "One high spot," continued the director, radiating enthusiasm, "is where you're in a car with Fiona Richmond, having a plate in the back with her." He saw my eyes widen, and carried on: "You've got your trousers open, and we see her head bobbing up and down, okay? Excuse me for being graphic."

"Please carry on," I said faintly. I mean, if it's inevitable, I'll lie back and enjoy it. Fiona used to be one of Paul Raymond's Revue Bar girls, and she was a little darling. "Is that all?"

"Not quite. One of the terrorists is a man who always dresses as a woman. You'll like him. The climax is when you're chasing him across the fields in open countryside. We'll want you to hang from a helicopter."

This film was starting to sound as mad as *Alice in Wonderland*. The trouble was, I seemed to be cast as the March Hare. But what the heck? I signed for it.

A muddy field in Kent, two months later. Hop country. Green hills, hedgerows and oast houses, picture-postcard stuff.

And Nosher, dressed in a virulent green silk suit — the gear every self-respecting Home Secretary wears, right? — plus white socks and flashy tie, hanging by a strap from a helicopter over a ploughed field.

We came down from eight hundred feet, straight at the cameras. "That hanging bit looks great!" shouted a voice through a loud hailer. "But we can see the belt, and we want you to drop from the chopper to the ground."

"How high do you want me to drop?" I shouted back. The whole county could hear our conversation.

The director riposted: "How high *can* you drop?"

"Twenty feet?" Don't forget I'm a heavy guy, seventeen stone now, with a swollen knee that hadn't fully healed from an earlier stunt.

He shook his head from below. "That doesn't sound very high to me, Nosh!"

To the pilot I said: "Land her right here!" I beckoned the director over, and Peter squelched through the mud to the chopper. "Come with me." And I gripped his arm, and hoisted him on to the runner. Then I strapped the harness on him.

"Right," I said to the pilot. "Take her up twenty feet!"

Up she went. "Now look down," I said.

"Cor," he said. "I see what you mean."

In the end I jumped from around eighteen feet. But I knew I was pressing it. Dropping into a ploughed field is a gamble. You can hit one of those ridges and your ankle's gone. We did it in two takes, and it went sweet as a nut. I rolled over and was up on my feet as if I was chasing someone, then charged out of picture. And all this to catch a transvestite!

To my eternal astonishment, that film made me a cult figure. The fan mail came in by the bucketload. Suddenly Nosher Powell was flavour of the month.

I went to the première at the Prince Charles Cinema off Leicester Square, and I took Lenny McLean with me as my guest. Soon enough, he'd make his mark on celluloid too, with the marvellous gangster movie *Lock, Stock and Two Smoking Barrels*. We sat in the back row, and at the end the whole audience stood and turned round and applauded me.

Out of the side of my mouth, I said: "Tell you what, Lenny. A few years back and I could have said: '*A star is born!*'"

"Nosher," he rejoined, "it's never too late."

One of the rewards of being flavour of the month is the amount of invites you get to functions, charity dinners, sporting occasions, premières and the rest. Ever one for the social scene, I accepted them all with alacrity.

One that got me unexpected headlines was a centenary dinner held at a brewery in the City of London. A good few celebrities turned up, and I found myself sitting next to Jimmy Tarbuck and my old wrestling friend Jackie Pallo.

Everything was going smoothly when a large figure in a rumpled dinner jacket loomed up and stumbled past. We recognised the unmistakable figure of Oliver Reed, with a glazed look in his eyes, a bemused smile on his lips, and a glass in his hand.

"Oh-oh!" I said. "Look out for trouble!"

Tarbie looked up, and groaned. "Christ," he said. "Who let him in?"

Now I always had a soft spot for Ollie. He could get a bit tiresome with a drink inside him, but you've got to admit he certainly livened up a few TV shows — even if he couldn't remember much about it afterwards. Right now he was about to be extremely tiresome.

He plonked himself down at the next table, which happened to have Patrick Mower sitting opposite, and right away picked up his plate of pasta and ham, and turned it upside down on his head. Then he started on the verbals. I could hear him, and so could most of the room.

"What are you doing sitting at my table?" he demanded. Patrick tried to defuse the situation by responding with a friendly grin and raising his glass in a mock toast.

But Ollie wasn't satisfied. He got up, and lumbered unsteadily round the table to grab Patrick by his lapels and yank him to his feet. A string of obscenities followed.

Jimmy Tarbuck hissed across the table. "Nosher, can't you do something?"

"It's nothing to do with me," I said. I was here for a nice night out, not to revert to old habits.

But it was getting noisier and more embarrassing by the minute. So finally I got to my feet, walked round to Ollie who was still grappling with Patrick, and grabbed him by the arm, putting a pressure grip on his wrist. It's a good grip, and you don't get out of it easily — especially when you've had a few.

Ollie turned. "Oh, it's you, Nosher." And then he tried to nut me.

I slapped his face away with my other hand, hard. "Okay, Ollie — out! You try that again and you'll end up the other side of the room. You're going home, sunshine!"

I marched him to the door, and out into the street — to be greeted by dazzling flashes of light as a dozen cameras popped away in gratitude at a picture that would be in all the next day's papers. Somehow I bundled Ollie into his car, banged on the roof and watched it speed off into the night. Then I went back to enjoy the rest of my dinner.

Next day a large Bentley pulled up outside my house in South London. A chauffeur got out, and rang the bell. He handed me a package and a white envelope. Inside the package was a bottle of El Paradiso brandy, and inside the envelope was a hundred pounds in readies. From the sponsors. with thanks.

Two weeks later I bumped into Ollie at Pinewood. He didn't remember a thing about that night. "But I saw the photos, so I suppose it must have happened," he said.

"That's okay, Ollie," I told him. "Next time you're going to make a fucking ass of yourself let me know, and we'll split the hundred quid!"

I was saddened, but not surprised, when Ollie raised his glass for the last time in Malta while filming *The Gladiator* for Steven Spielberg. Drinking, as I would have expected, at a local waterfront bar and not at some glitzy five-star hotel. He loved people, he lapped up the local atmosphere along with the wine, and he loved to talk. Ollie was a one-off, and we will not see his like again.

## 40: THIS IS YOUR LIFE!

I never suspected. It was a broiling hot summer's day, and I was in my chainmail doing a full dress rehearsal for a jousting tournament near Windsor Castle. I was trying to control a high-spirited grey Andalucian mare, and she was really one big fucking handful.

A camera crew had turned up, and were hanging around looking as if they were waiting for something to happen. A phone call had come through earlier to say they'd be there filming for some programme called *Look at Life*.

I should have guessed.

Finally I slid down from the saddle and approached the man in charge. "What are you waiting for? Do you want us to put on a show, or what?" I asked.

He shifted his feet. "We're waiting for Tom Bloggs, he's the interviewer."

Tom Bloggs?

"He's the interviewer. Ah." He looked past me. "Here he comes now."

Across the field came an armour-clad figure in full regalia, complete with plumed helmet, striding purposefully towards us. The visor was down over his face. Still I didn't get it.

He walked right up to me. "Nosher Powell?" Where had I heard that Irish brogue before?

"Yeah, that's me."

"Nosher Powell — *this is your life!*" And Eamonn Andrews pushed back the visor to reveal his grinning face, and brought out a large red book from behind his back.

I responded as one does in such a situation. "Bollocks! You're having me on!"

But he wasn't. "No. This *is* your life!"

Oh, shit. I'd said "bollocks," straight into the camera. But they got me into a car, and on the way to the studios. Alone in the back, I said to the driver: "I'm dreaming. This has got to be a joke."

"No, you're not, Mr Powell," the chauffeur assured me.

Half-way along the M4, I developed a raging thirst. Also, my bladder was sending urgent messages. I'd been out in the sun for hours without a drink, and dehydration was setting in. "We've got to stop. I need a drink and I need a slash."

With some reluctance, the driver turned off the motorway and found a pub. I rattled the door handle. "It's locked," said the chauffeur. "We always do that. If I let you out, will you promise you won't do a runner?"

I was in full chainmail armour. "You've got my word," I said. "For Christ's sake, let me out!"

I clanked into the public bar, did my best to ignore the stares and pretend there was nothing out of the ordinary, and ordered a pint. Then I went to the gents. Cor, was I relieved! "Give me an empty bottle to take with me," I told the barman. "And please don't say anything we might both regret."

At Teddington Studios I clumped through the foyer into a dressing room, and got out of my gear. In a wardrobe one of my suits was hanging up, with a clean shirt — which meant that Pauline had been in on it. I'd have a word with her later.

But once we got going — what a great night! I have to admit it was marvellous, tear-jerking stuff. My whole past came up and swam before me like a mirage. Somehow they'd found two little girls who had been evacuated with me in the war.

Then the celebrity list began, and it was like a roll-call of my life. Henry Cooper, Gerald Harper, Sammy Davis Jnr, Charlie Drake, Tommy Steele, Diana Rigg. What was it she said? "I had to do a fight scene with Nosher in *The Avengers*, and knock him over a piano. Believe me, when I hit him, I hurt my own arm!" Lovely girl, that Di!

And I learned one thing that night. Tom Bloggs is the name that

Eamonn and now Michael Aspel used as a cover. So, if it ever happens to you, don't say I didn't warn you!

In the end it was a night to treasure. But, you know, that was only the half of it. Because if you've read this, as I hope you have, you'll realise one thing.

*This* was my life.

Publicity poster for the film that made me a cult hero.

# Nosher Powell: Professional Credits

*Henry V*, 1944, stunts
*Caesar and Cleopatra*, 1945, stunts
*Bonnie Prince Charlie*, 1948, stunts
*Oliver Twist*, 1948, role
*Passport to Pimlico*, 1949, stunts
*There is Another Sun*, 1951, role
*Emergency Call*, 1952, role
*Cosh Boy*, 1953, role
*The Robe*, 1953, stunts
*The Master of Ballantrae*, 1953, stunts
*Hell below Zero*, 1953, stunts
*Lilacs in the Spring*, 1954, stunts
*Beau Brummel*, 1954, stunts
*The Quatermass Experiment* (TV), 1955, stunts
*King's Rhapsody*, 1955, role
*The Dark Avenger*, 1955, role
*Doctor at Sea*, 1955, stunts
*The Bridge on the River Kwai*, 1957, stunts
*The Adventures of Robin Hood* (TV), 1957, stunts
*Dunkirk*, 1958, stunts
*Dracula*, 1958, stunts
*A Night to Remember*, 1958, stunts
*Captain Moonlight* (TV), 1957, stunts
*The Mouse That Roared*, 1959, stunts
*Ben Hur*, 1959, stunts
*Exodus*, 1960, stunts
*The Guns of Navarone*, 1961, stunts
*Richard the Lionheart*, (TV), 1961 stunts
*The Longest Day*, 1962, stunts
*Lawrence of Arabia*, 1962, stunts
*Road to Hong Kong*, 1962, role and stunts
*Cleopatra*, 1962, stunts
*Danger Man* (TV), 1962, role and stunts
*Call Me Bwana*, 1963, role and stunts
*The Day of the Triffids*, 1963, stunts

*From Russia With Love*, 1963, stunts
*The Pink Panther*, 1963, stunts
*Zulu*, 1964, stunts
*For a Few Dollars More*, 1964, double and stunts
*Goldfinger*, 1964, role
*A Shot in the Dark*, 1964, role
*The Saint* (TV), 1964, role and stunts
*Lord Jim*, 1965, stunts
*For a Few Dollars More*, 1965, stunts
*Thunderball*, 1965, stunts
*The Hill*, 1965, stunts
*Battle of the Bulge*, 1965, stunts
*Those Magnificent Men in Their Flying Machines*, 1965, double and stunts
*Allah is Not Always With You*, 1965, role
*The Crooked Ring*, 1965, role
*A Man for All Seasons*, 1966, stunts
*Khartoum*, 1966, stunts
*Circus of Fear*, 1966, role and stunts
*The Sandwich Man*, 1966, role
*Epitaph for a Hero* (TV), 1966, role and stunts
*The Dirty Dozen*, 1967, stunts
*Half a Sixpence*, 1967, stunts
*Casino Royale*, 1967, stunts
*You Only Live Twice*, 1967, stunts
*Great Catherine*, 1967, stunts
*The Persistent Patriots*, 1967, role and stunts
*Mission Highly Improbable*, 1967, stunts
*Charge of the Light Brigade*, 1968, stunts
*Where Eagles Dare*, 1968, stunts
*Salt and Pepper*, 1968, stunts
*Oliver!*, 1968, role and stunts
*On Her Majesty's Secret Service*, 1969, stunts
*The Italian Job*, 1969, double and stunts
*Crossplot*, 1969, role and stunts
*The Battle of Britain*, 1969, stunts
*The Assassination Bureau*, 1969
*School for Sex*, 1969, role
*Department S* (TV), 1969, stunt and role
*The Magic Christian*, 1970, stunt co-ordinator
*The Last Valley*, 1970, stunts

*Carry On Henry*, 1970, stunts
*Waterloo*, 1970, stunts
*Cromwell*, 1970, stunts
*One More Time*, 1970, role
*You Can't Win 'Em All*, 1971, role and stunts
*Diamonds Are Forever*, 1971, stunts
*On the Buses* (TV), 1971, role and stunts
*The Alf Garnett Saga* (TV), 1972, role
*Venom* (TV), 1972, role and stunts
*Pope Joan*, 1972, stunts
*The Mackintosh Man*, 1972, role and stunts
*Nearest and Dearest* (TV), 1973, role and stunts
*Live and Let Die*, 1973, stunts
*Love Thy Neighbour* (TV), 1974, role
*The Man with the Golden Gun*, 1974, stunts
*Brannigan*, 1975, role and stunts
*The Sweeney* (TV), 1977, role and stunts
*The Spy Who Loved Me*, 1977, stunts
*Are You Being Served?* (TV), 1977  role
*Superman*, 1978, stunts
*The Stick-up*, 1978, role
*Moonraker*, 1979, stunts
*Flash Gordon*, 1980, stunts
*For Your Eyes Only*, 1981, stunts
*Victor/Victoria*, 1982, role and stunts
*Krull*, 1982, role and stunts
*Octopussy*, 1983, stunts
*Ellis Island*, 1984, role and stunts
*The Zany Adventures of Robin Hood*, 1984, role and stunts
*A View to a Kill*, 1985, stunts
*Eat the Rich*, 1986, starring role and stunts
*The Comic Strip* (TV), 1987, starring role and stunts
*Willow*, 1988, role and stunts
*Jasper Carrott* (TV), 1989, role
*The Secret Life of Ian Fleming* (TV), 1990, stunts
*Teed Off* (TV), 1993, role
*First Knight*, 1995, stunts
*Legionnaire*, 1997, role and technical adviser